QUESTIONS OF
THE DAY

QUESTIONS OF THE DAY

By

JOHN A. RYAN
D.D., LL.D., Litt.D

Professor of Moral Theology and Industrial Ethics
at the Catholic University of America; Professor
of Political Science at Trinity College; Professor
of Social Ethics, National Catholic School of Social
Service; Director of Department of Social Action,
National Catholic Welfare Conference; author of
"Distributive Justice," "Social Reconstruction,"
"Declining Liberty," etc., etc.

Essay Index Reprint Series

BOOKS FOR LIBRARIES PRESS, INC
FREEPORT, NEW YORK

First Published 1931
Reprinted 1967

LIBRARY OF CONGRESS CATALOG CARD NUMBER: 67-26779

PRINTED IN THE UNITED STATES OF AMERICA

1422083

NIHIL OBSTAT

January 12, 1931
HUMPHREY MOYNIHAN
Censor Deputatus

IMPRIMATUR

January 13, 1931
JAMES C. BYRNE
*Administrator, Archdiocese
of St. Paul*

Acknowledgment

Grateful acknowledgement of permission to include in this volume productions that had originally appeared in their pages is due to the following periodicals and organizations: *The American Ecclesiastical Review, The Catholic Charities Review, The Catholic World, The Commonweal, Current History, Harvard Business Review, The Nation, National Catholic Welfare Conference, The National Popular Government League, The New Republic, Public Ownership, Public Utilities Fortnightly,* and *Studies*.

JOHN A. RYAN.

Washington, D. C.
March 1, 1931.

Contents

PART I

PHASES OF PROHIBITION

PART II

CATHOLICS AND POLITICS

PART III

ECONOMIC QUESTIONS

CONTENTS

Part I
PHASES OF PROHIBITION

1. Prohibition and Civic Loyalty[1]

THE press of the country was almost unanimous in the judgment that the President's declarations on law enforcement and law observance constitute the most prominent and most definite part of his inaugural address. With most of what he said on these subjects the large majority of citizens would be disposed to agree. The prevalence of crime, the disregard of law, the need for drastic improvements in the federal machinery of justice, are all pretty obvious. But when President Hoover turns from these topics to that of popular responsibility, he lays down two or three propositions which are extremely questionable.

"The worst evil of disregard for some law," he says, "is that it destroys respect for all law." This is a very considerable exaggeration. That persistent and wide-spread disobedience of a particular law has some influence in weakening respect for law in general, is undoubtedly true. That it "destroys" respect for law in general is an assertion that lacks the support of experience. To take only one example, there are the so-called Blue Laws which have been generally disregarded for decades in several of our states without producing any notable lack of reverence for law in general. While it is probable that wide-spread violation of the prohibition laws has dulled to some extent the perception of the binding force of other federal legislation, this result probably affects only a small proportion of those who feel at liberty to disobey the Volstead Act and the Eighteenth Amendment. Probably the great majority of those who purchase and possess intoxicating liquor make a clear distinction between the validity of the prohibition laws and that of other federal enactments.

"If citizens do not like the law, their duty as honest

[1]Reprinted from the *Commonweal*, April 3, 1929.

3

men and women is to discourage its violation; their right is openly to work for its repeal," declares the President. In other words, "honest men and women" are obliged not only to refrain from violating a law which they do not like, but also to discourage its violation by others. The only relief morally lawful to them is through repeal. If the President had in mind legal duty, his statement was obviously erroneous, for no such duty is expressed in any civil statute. If he meant moral duty, his statement implied functional usurpation. Among the prerogatives of the President of the United States, there is not included that of supreme interpreter of the moral law.

In his speech on the Jones Bill, Senator Borah expressed this opinion in even stronger terms. The enforcement of the prohibition laws, he declared, involves "the existence of our government." The distinguished Senator from Idaho, who is always eloquent but not always either logical or profound, denied the right of the individual to disregard a law which he believes to be wrong, and went on to say: "what is contained in the Amendment is right under our form of government until the people revise their judgment," and "the highest evidence of morality is to obey the law which the people have written." In view of the long-continued disregard by Congress of that part of the Fourteenth Amendment which requires the congressional representation of a state to be reduced proportionately whenever the right to vote is denied to any of its adult male citizens, and in view of the equally long-continued disregard of the Fifteenth Amendment by several southern states, the Senator's fearful assertion that "the existence of the government" is dependent upon the enforcement of the Eighteenth Amendment sounds a trifle reckless. President Hoover's milder language expressing the same thought is equally unconvincing. The ethical propositions laid down by Senator Borah to the effect that it is never right to violate a civil law, that a constitutional amendment is always morally right and morally binding until it is re-

4

pealed, are false propositions. President Hoover subscribes to them, at least by implication.

That the citizens are obliged to obey civil laws, even those that they do not like, is true in general, but not necessarily true in every case. Although the presumption is always in favor of the moral binding force of a duly enacted law, whether organic or statutory, there are exceptions. Suppose that the law imposes grave hardship upon a considerable minority or even a majority of the citizens; suppose that it cannot be repealed for many years; suppose further that the net effect of the law is injurious rather than beneficial to the community as a whole. In these circumstances is it reasonable to impose upon the citizens the moral obligation of obedience? This appears to have been the situation with regard to the Blue Laws. When the forces of fanaticism made formal repeal impossible, the mass of the citizens annulled these obnoxious statutes by indirection, that is, by persistently disobeying them. Thus they created a custom contrary to the law, and customary law of this sort is quite as valid as formally enacted statutes. So, at least, we are informed by the canonists and the moral theologians. The Congress of the United States and the people of the Southern states have been unwilling or unable to repeal the provisions, respectively, of the Fourteenth and Fifteenth Amendments referred to above; nevertheless they have not felt obliged to maintain these portions of the Constitution. They have simply disobeyed them. Is it not just possible that in a similar situation, disregard of the Volstead Act and the Eighteenth Amendment will be at least equally reasonable and equally free from moral blame?

The nature of constitutional prohibition clearly deprives it of all claims to respect by liberty-loving citizens and believers in the democratic principle. The forces that drove through the Eighteenth Amendment were not content with an enabling act. They insisted upon putting into the Constitution a statute. It is practically the only provision in

5

the Constitution which is addressed to individuals, which restricts individual liberty, and it is absolutely the only one which confers police power upon the national government. To be sure, none of these objections is necessarily fatal. In the development of the nation's life and experience, conditions might arise which would justify changing the Constitution in all these respects from its scope as contemplated by the men who sat in the Constitutional Convention. The unforgivable offense committed by the Eighteenth Amendment is the fact that it is a legislative statute rather than an enabling act. National prohibition could have been brought about by an amendment empowering Congress to legislate the liquor traffic out of existence. Had this course been taken, the amendment would undoubtedly have been adopted and Congress would undoubtedly have enacted such legislation. This procedure would have been democratic, even though unwise. The unwisdom could have been corrected through subsequent repeal of the law by a majority of the two houses in Congress. In that event, the President's demand that the people observe the prohibition law until they could muster a majority for its repeal would have had a considerable appearance of reasonableness.

The organized advocates of the Eighteenth Amendment were unwilling to give the citizens this option and this opportunity. They were unwilling to entrust the fate of prohibition to future Congresses. They insisted upon trampling underfoot the principle of majority rule. They indulged the fond and futile hope that if repeal could be made impossible for two or three generations, the majority of the people would forget all about the appetite for liquor. In other words, they felt that they had to protect the people against the people's own folly. They believed that they knew what the people needed better than the people themselves could judge, and that, as persons of superior wisdom and superior moral principles, they had a right to impose their will upon the majority. This has always been

6

the attitude of the tory mind, and it deserves as little consideration from free and self-respecting men in the present instance as any other kind of toryism has ever deserved anywhere. In a word, the Eighteenth Amendment is in direct and flagrant contradiction to the principles of democracy.

A very disturbing manifestation of the tory spirit that animates prohibition is seen in the economic arguments by which it is frequently defended. The working classes have been or could be, greatly benefited by prohibition. Therefore, they ought to accept it loyally and not agitate themselves about personal freedom. In other words, they should be treated as children, as incapable of assuming responsibility for their own lives. This attitude of the superior classes is aggravated when they violate the prohibition law themselves and assume that it was made only for the lower classes—a point of view which seems to be pretty general. Another form of the economic argument contends that the machinery of production has so increased in speed that access to intoxicating liquor can no longer be safely permitted. This means that individual liberty is to be sacrificed to accelerated production. The life of the wage earner is to be subordinated to the instruments with which he works. He is to be treated as a part of this vast, dizzily revolving economic machine. His human dignity is to be ignored.

Until the prohibitionists are willing to take statutory prohibition out of the Constitution, until they are willing to convert the Eighteenth Amendment into a mere enabling act, they stand convicted of toryism and contempt for democracy. Until they do this, their invocation of "the will of the people" and similar slogans on behalf of the prohibition laws will remain a kind of blasphemy and a very real hypocrisy. They themselves will continue to deserve the contempt of all genuine believers in democracy and the Eighteenth Amendment will continue to be

7

"A fixed figure for the hand of scorn
To point his slow, unmoving finger at."

Suppose that a very considerable majority of the people of the United States should clearly manifest a desire for the repeal of the Eighteenth Amendment. Would President Hoover still contend that they were obliged to "discourage its violation" and work for and wait for its repeal at some time in the indefinite future? Suppose that only a minority of the people, but a very considerable minority, are at the present time opposed to prohibition, upon what ground can President Hoover or anyone else contend that they are under such obligation? Neither the Eighteenth Amendment nor the Volstead Act forbids the *purchase* of intoxicating liquors. There is, therefore, no definite *legal* obligation upon the citizens to refrain from such purchases. Of course, the President is well aware of this legal situation. What he seeks to do is to convey the impression that "honest men and women" are under some vague and general constraint of civic decency to refrain from purchasing or consuming intoxicating liquors. In view of the origin and nature of the Eighteenth Amendment as described above, one is justified in refusing to accept this assumed obligation of civic decency. If someone objects that thirsty citizens are under *moral* obligation to refrain from co-operating with those who illegally sell liquor, the sufficient reply is that the law does not impose upon them even the legal obligation of such self-denial, and it is a maxim of both the canon and the civil law that burdensome and penal provisions are to be interpreted narrowly and strictly. If the makers of the prohibition legislation wanted to penalize the purchaser as well as the seller, they should have framed the laws accordingly. This very proposal was offered in Congress as an amendment to the Jones Bill, but it was rejected by a very large majority, even of the prohibition membership.

What course is open to the millions of "honest men and women" who detest the tyranny and toryism of national

8

prohibition? Are they utterly powerless to remove or mitigate the abomination? By no means. They can continue to denounce the anti-democratic character of the Eighteenth Amendment and the enormous evils that it has inflicted upon American society. They can continue to demand referendums on modification and repeal. If they buy liquor they can feel assured that they are violating no civil law, nor any moral obligation arising directly out of the prohibition enactments. When they manufacture, transport or possess liquor for their own use they can rely upon the settled policy of the prohibition administration to discontinue all attempts at enforcing these portions of the Volstead Act. Of course, these provisions never had a shadow of validity in morals. "Honest men and women" can lawfully agitate for such modification of the Volstead iniquity as will permit the manufacture and sale of beer with an alcoholic content of 3 or 4 per cent. The states can lawfully repeal their enforcement acts and thus concentrate popular attention upon the impossibility of national prohibition. Congress could lawfully repeal the Volstead Act. Either the House of Representatives or the Senate, or both together, could by a simple majority vote lawfully refuse to appropriate money for enforcement. In that event those states that desired prohibition would have to enact and enforce it themselves, while those that did not want it could make their own definitions of intoxicating liquor, including whatever beverages they wished to include and adopting one of the systems now operating in Canada.

All these changes are legally and morally possible without repealing the Eighteenth Amendment. If a stubborn and fanatical minority persisted in blocking repeal, through control of the legislatures in thirteen or more thinly populated states, the Supreme Court could be relied upon to find reasons for refusing to interfere with the extraordinary definitions of intoxicants adopted by the populous states. Possibly it might decide that the prohibitory provisions

9

of the Eighteenth Amendment apply only to private persons and corporations, not to state or federal governments. In that critical situation the Supreme Court would hardly stand in the way of majority rule and public welfare. It would follow public sentiment rather than legal precedents, just as it did when it first upheld a state prohibition law, in the case of *Mugler* vs. *Kansas*.

Despite the President's admonition and censure, the law-abiding opponents of prohibition may possess their souls in patience. They can derive consolation and courage from the reflection that they are battling for fundamental democracy, for majority rule, for the vanquishment of fanaticism, intolerance and toryism, for security against prohibition of tobacco, against the Puritan Sabbath, against compulsory birth control for the poor, against sterilization for "social inadequates," and against all the other tyrannies that the self-righteous and superior sections of our population would impose upon their "inferior" fellow-citizens. Every one of these outrageous proposals is due fundamentally to the same attitude of mind and the same disposition of will that produced the Eighteenth Amendment. In a word, the "honest men and women" who actively oppose prohibition in all lawful ways can rightfully feel that they are engaged in a great crusade for fundamental liberties, for liberties that are not a whit less sacred and precious than those which were fought for by the men who made the American Revolution.

APPENDIX

A REJOINDER TO PRESIDENT HOOVER

The following paragraph is taken from the address which President Hoover delivered at the meeting of the Associated Press in New York City, April 22, 1929:

No individual has the right to determine what law shall be obeyed and what law shall not be enforced.

PROHIBITION AND CIVIC LOYALTY

If a law is wrong, its rigid enforcement is the surest guaranty of its repeal. If it is right, its enforcement is the quickest method of compelling respect for it. I have seen statements published within a few days encouraging citizens to defy a law because that particular journal did not approve of the law itself. I leave comment on such an attitude to any citizen with a sense of responsibility to his country.

The following comments of mine appeared in the New York *Herald Tribune*, April 23, 1929, in response to a request by that journal.

There are two propositions in the President's speech which must fill every thoughtful citizen with alarm and astonishment. The first is ethical, the second political. "No individual," he says, "has the right to determine what law shall be obeyed and what law shall not be enforced." What about the right of the individual conscience? Must a man obey a civil law which he believes to be wrong? Apparently the President would not only deny the moral supremacy of conscience but cast opprobrium upon those honored names of men and women who in every country and in every age have dared to put their conceptions of right above their fear of political penalties. President Hoover aligns himself in effect with those who hold that the State can do no wrong. He bids us bow our knees before the Omnipotent State. This is neither good ethics nor good Americanism.

His other astonishing proposition is: "If a law is wrong its rigid enforcement is the surest guaranty of its repeal." Neither the superficial plausibility nor the hackneyed character of this assertion is a guaranty that it is in accord with the facts of life and experience. Our Blue Laws—to take only one illustration —show that the people can sometimes get rid of tyrannical laws by other methods than formal repeal; that repeal may be impossible and general disobedience may be the only remedy. Long after the great

11

majority of the people of the United States shall have declared for repeal of the Eighteenth Amendment thirteen thinly populated states could thwart the will of the majority, regardless of the extent to which the Amendment had been enforced. Would the President have the majority submit eternally to a fanatical minority in deference to an exploded theory of political policy?

2. Prohibition and Social Legislation

ALL laws are social since they apply to society or to a social group. Usage, however, restricts the term "social legislation" to ordinances for physical, mental or moral welfare, particularly in the case of the poorer and weaker classes. In this paper, I intend to consider two kinds of social legislation which notably diminish human freedom.

Examples of the first kind are: laws establishing a minimum wage, an eight hour day, compensation for accidents and compulsory insurance against unemployment. This kind of social legislation prevents men from oppressing their fellows under the guise of free contract. It enforces justice between two important social classes. Like all other preceptive legislation, it diminishes freedom. Unlike most other social legislation, it restricts the liberty of a small group in the just interest of a much larger group.

The other kind of social legislation to be considered in this paper does not seek to enforce justice between classes, nor to curtail the excessive liberty of one group in favor of another group. It aims to restrain persons in general from actions which are detrimental to themselves. Of this nature are the laws which prohibit public gambling-houses, the traffic in narcotics and the sale and use of alcoholic liquor.

Unfortunately, many social workers, as well as many other groups, neglect this obvious distinction. Regarding both kinds of social legislation merely as beneficial to the economically or morally weak, they overlook the difference between the restrictions upon liberty involved, for example, in a minimum wage law and those involved in a national prohibition law. They do not ask themselves whether the statute produces its beneficial effects by preventing injustice or by diminishing general liberty and gen-

13

eral responsibility. They ignore the difference between a law which forbids one man to injure another and a law which forbids men to do something which may harm themselves.

Yet the difference is fundamental. The evils prevented by social legislation of the first kind are inflicted upon men without their consent. Low wages, long hours, insecurity of employment, inadequate protection against accidents, are all unwillingly accepted by their victims. They are caused by other men through unjust economic pressure. On the other hand, the man who loses his money at a gaming-table, or acquires the cocaine habit, or gets drunk, is himself the voluntary cause of his evil condition. He was not compelled to harm himself through an extortionate contract, nor was he compelled to enter a gambling-house, nor to buy cocaine or strong drink. But the laborer is frequently compelled to enter an unjust employment contract. To be sure, the latter has the alternative of starvation, just as the former has the alternative of denying to himself the pleasure of gambling, or drugs or drink; but no reasonable person puts these alternatives on the same level of importance, or holds that the men facing them, respectively, suffer the same injury to their liberty.

We may, indeed, lump together the unregulated labor contract, the gambling-hall, the liquor shop and the traffic in narcotics, calling them all bad *social institutions,* condemning them equally to suppression by law, but this method of classification and evaluation is lacking both in logic and in wisdom. To abolish a social institution which compels a man to choose between insufficient wages and no wages at all, is one thing; to abolish a social institution which merely attracts, induces, lures a man into doing something which may harm him, is a vastly different thing, and the difference must be held fundamental by anyone who fully appreciates the significance of human liberty, responsibility and self-development.

Obviously this difference does not justify the inference

14

that those social institutions which merely attract men to evil, leaving them free to yield or to resist, should never be legally suppressed. Public facilities for gambling, drinking and the purchase of narcotics are not necessary for human welfare. Access to them is not a natural right of the same importance as the right to a living wage or to freedom of movement. Hence these institutions and opportunities may reasonably be abolished for the sake of a larger good.

The "larger good" will have to be definite and of great importance, however, in order to justify interferences with human liberty. Without freedom a person can neither satisfy his present needs nor develop his personality. Adequate freedom supposes the power to abuse freedom. Responsibility cannot be developed without the opportunity of making mistakes. A person who is prevented by law from abusing his liberty remains essentially a child, a dependent creature, not a self-reliant master of his own fortunes.

The question of legally prohibiting a social institution which injures merely through its attractiveness, is always a question of comparative evil. Would the curtailment of liberty be less harmful to human welfare than the conduct of which the offending institution is the alluring occasion? The cases of public gambling and public traffic in habit-forming drugs seem to demand an affirmative answer. The opportunity to play games of chance in a public resort is of slight benefit to anyone at any time, while the number of persons who gravely abuse it is so great as to make the evil far outweigh the good, whether measured by actual satisfactions or by the promotion of self-control and self-restraint. For legal suppression of the public traffic in narcotics the case is even clearer.

Alcoholic beverages present certain features which are absent from the practices that we have just been considering. The vast majority of those who regularly or occasionally consume these beverages are able to do so without notable harm to themselves or anyone else. At least, this has always been true of peoples who refrained from enacting

15

total prohibition. The drunkards of the world have never been conspicuous by their numbers. The drinkers who have notably lowered their efficiency or spent excessive amounts of money for liquor have not exceeded a small minority. Even if we think that alcoholic liquor has done some injury to the health or efficiency of the majority of those using it, we must concede that, in most cases, the injury was not great as compared with the other evil experiences and follies of mankind. Let us not lose our sense of proportion. The money spent for drink might, indeed, have been wisely laid out for food, clothing, shelter, intellectual improvement, charity and religion, but so might the expenditures for theatres and "movies," banquets and elaborate social functions, unnecessary amusements and travel, tobacco, tea and coffee, to say nothing of jazz music, chewing-gum, soda fountain products, wasteful changes of fashion and a hundred other relatively irrational objects.

"Excessive expenditures" for alcoholic liquor should be measured not only by comparison with other unnecessary expenditures, but also in relation to the amount of innocent satisfaction obtained by the drinkers. One of the most surprising features of the controversy on this subject is the obstinate refusal of extremists to admit that men have always and everywhere got comfort out of alcoholic drink, and that, for the great majority, that comfort has been as real, as effective and as rational as that obtained from any equal outlay of money for things which are not strict necessities.

While I believe that the foregoing is a conservative statement of the relatively small injury caused by liquor to the great majority of its consumers, I have a lively realization of the evil that it has always brought to a minority. The traffic ought to be so regulated as to reduce the evil to the lowest dimensions consistent with reasonable human liberty. It is so regulated in the greater part of Canada, particularly in the Province of Quebec. Alcoholic liquors are sold by the government under such conditions as make

16

them not unduly easy to obtain. With this system of strict regulation is combined total prohibition in those towns and other local areas where that arrangement is approved by an effective majority. For two reasons this is a rational and feasible kind of prohibition: first, because it is desired by a sufficient proportion of the people to make it enforcible; second, because it does not prevent the more eager drink-lovers from lawfully obtaining liquor in some distant selling-place. The Quebec plan offers the best solution of the liquor problem that has yet been devised. It puts the maximum practicable restriction upon the number and the facilities of the liquor shops, and it creates all the difficulty for the drinker that is compatible with public approval and reasonable liberty.

The word "liberty" has been used with great frequency throughout this discussion. It has not been over-emphasized. The greater part of the opposition to national prohibition is based not so much upon human thirst as upon human resentment. The average man regards prohibition as an unnecessary and unjustified assault upon personal freedom and natural rights. He sees clear through the sophistry which represents prohibition as merely the suppression of a harmful social institution and which puts the use of liquor on the same moral plane as the use of narcotics. The average man thinks that a much fairer comparison could be drawn between liquor and automobiles. He believes that almost as good a case could be made out for the total prohibition of the latter as of the former. I am inclined to think he is right.

Second only to the blindness of prohibition advocates with regard to the average man's passion for freedom is their failure to see the harm done to character-development when legislation is unwisely substituted for self-control. Few movements in history are more impressive than the growth of total abstinence in the United States. Within my own lifetime this gospel and practice have effected an enormous improvement, not only in the habits of millions

17

of individuals but in the public attitude toward alcoholic liquor. Steadily, and in many places rapidly, the traffic was coming under such social control that within half a century its evils would have been reduced to negligible dimensions. The organized champions of prohibition were not satisfied with this sound and steady progress. In an evil hour they decided to abandon the methods of self-control and local control in favor of compulsion by national enactment.

Well, the method of national compulsion is doing more harm than good, and the movement for voluntary abstention has been destroyed. When a more rational system of legislative control has finally been substituted for the present anarchical condition, the great task of educating to total abstinence will have to be undertaken all over again. Such is the penalty of attempting a fundamentally wrong kind of social legislation, of not realizing the limits of compulsion.

Throughout this paper I have considered social legislation in its relations to individual human beings. I have studiously avoided the word "community." Apart from its component individuals, the community is a mere abstraction. It is the usual recourse of extremists when they seek to justify an invasion of liberty. They speak pompously of curtailing individual freedom in the interest of the community, when the real effect of their proposals is either to benefit a small minority or to coerce the majority into refraining from conduct which in their opinion is bad for the majority. Social legislation which cannot be justified in terms of individual welfare is incapable of justification.

3. Three Controversal Letters

M Y DEAR DR.——: Your long letter is greatly appreciated even though it shows that I have not yet succeeded in making clear what I meant in my *Commonweal* article by the phrase "compulsory birth control for the poor." As I have already informed you, those words were not used with reference to proposals for legalizing birth-control information nor in relation to any prominent advocate of artificial birth restriction. Now I wish to assure you that they were not intended to be synonymous with "sterilization of the unfit," as I made the latter phrase cover an entirely different category of persons. "Compulsory birth control for the poor" was meant to describe just what the words expressed: namely, legal prohibition of more than a certain number of children per family. In my former letter I called attention to a certain California professor who not long ago advocated precisely that kind of law to be applied to the less desirable classes of the population, for example, Mexicans and Negroes. The name of this professor is S. J. Holmes, author of *Studies in Evolution and Eugenics,* and he teaches at the University of California. He is by no means alone in desiring this sort of legislation. I have heard of more than one social worker who would like to see such a law enacted and I have no doubt that most of the professional advocates of birth control cherish the same desire. You seem to think that project utterly ridiculous and fantastic, but you will recall that many sober-minded persons thought in the same way about national prohibition twenty years ago.

You distinguish between sane prohibitionists and fanatics. I admit that the distinction is valid, that there are thousands of believers in national prohibition to whom my severe words do not apply. However, these constitute the

19

inactive, inconspicuous and unofficial elements of the movement. The active, official and public exponents and representatives of prohibition are the Anti-Saloon League, the Methodist Board of Temperance, Prohibition and Public Morals, the Southern prohibition organization of the same church, and individuals such as Bishop Cannon, Dr. Clarence True Wilson, Dr. F. S. McBride, and Dr. Ernest Cherrington. While national prohibition could never have been brought about without the support of the former elements, it is the latter groups and the latter kind of persons that have carried on the campaigns of publicity and politics that were indispensable. It is these that have determined, and they are still determining, the character of the movement. They represent its peculiar and persistent mentality. In this mentality are included such enormities as the applause with which Congress greeted the description of the killing by a policeman of a boy in Washington who happened to be driving an automobile which contained liquor; the Jones Act; the attempted usurpation of the function of moral law-giver by President Hoover in his Inaugural and Associated Press Convention addresses; the shameless arousing of religious intolerance during the recent presidential campaign by men like Bishop Cannon as a means which was apparently regarded as justifying the end, namely, the defeat of an anti-prohibitionist; the hypocrisy of communities in several states that want both liquor and prohibition; the anti-democratic attitude of the well-to-do, particularly in the business world, who are willing to have the prohibition law violated on their own behalf, but think that it is a good thing for the working classes; finally, the distrust of democracy manifested in making the Eighteenth Amendment a legislative statute instead of an enabling act.

I agree with you that "the rights and liberties of the people who do not wish to drink are quite as sacred as the rights and liberties of those who do wish to drink," but they are not more sacred. My complaint against the official and vocal prohibitionists is that they deny to the drinkers

20

and the would-be drinkers any rights whatever in that relation. They regard the consumption of intoxicating liquor as not only unnecessary but more or less abnormal, and consequently hold that the desire to drink deserves no consideration. They forget that the majority of persons in the Western World have for centuries drunk liquor and that the majority of those who have done any drinking have not seriously harmed themselves or anyone else. On the other hand, the opponents of prohibition have never denied the right of any person to refrain from drinking.

It seems to me that your statements about the "rights and liberties of those who do not wish to drink intoxicants," about "a social nuisance" and "the social curse," et cetera, are not free from some confusion of thought. "A social nuisance" does not necessarily violate human rights. It may be merely a temptation, an allurement to foolish conduct or sinful conduct. Undoubtedly, the saloon was of that character. Undoubtedly any kind of facility for obtaining liquor easily can be regarded as that kind of "social nuisance." But such an institution violates no individual rights, whether of life, liberty or property. When the prohibitionist claims the right to be protected against such a source of temptation, he is asking that the law give him protection against his own appetite. He is demanding that the law should do for him what he ought to do for himself through the exercise of his will power. This is an unreasonable attitude, for millions of his fellow citizens desire the presence of this kind of "social nuisance" and are able to patronize it without serious injury to themselves or anyone else. It is precisely here that prohibitionists "are careless of the personal rights and liberties of other people."

Undoubtedly the abuse of intoxicants does often result in a real violation of rights. It leads to murder, assault and disregard of property. Your description of these results is so general and contains so much exaggeration that it is strongly reminiscent of the highly emotional and reckless temperance speeches which I frequently heard as a boy.

21

Automobiles and "high powered machinery" have not increased in any important degree the hazards to life and property which would be present if the liquor traffic were legalized.

The violation of personal rights and of property rights which formerly occurred as a result of the abuse of intoxicating liquor were a small proportion of the entire number and quantity of such crimes. If the liquor traffic were to be legally reinstated tomorrow, the law would afford the protection that it has always afforded against these injuries. To assume that further protection is needed in the form of prevention of the liquor traffic, is essentially no more reasonable than to demand the legal suppression of automobiles on the ground that they are responsible for the same sort of crimes. The difference is only of degree, and possibly not a very great degree. This morning's papers report ten violent deaths yesterday caused by automobiles. Apparently all the drivers were sober. What the average prohibitionist, it seems to me, needs above everything else is to cultivate the habit of investigating and analyzing facts as they are, of seeing facts in their proper proportion and of distrusting emotionalism and easy generalizations.

In the foregoing paragraphs I have argued as though legal prohibition was identical with actual prohibition. Of course, that is not the situation. While adequate knowledge is not available and probably cannot be obtained, I am willing to risk the "easy generalization" that the balance of evil—taking all sorts of evil into account—is on the side of our prohibition conditions; that, on the whole, things are worse now than they were before 1917. Moreover, such a comparison is misleading and unduly favorable to prohibition. For the saloon as we know it, ought not to return. The Canadian system is vastly better than either the open saloon or prohibition, and it probably represents the sanest and most effective method of dealing with the liquor problem that has yet been devised.

22

You deplore the fact, as it appears to you, that I am "using my influence to lead the American people astray." Permit me to say that between 1920 and 1925 I was somewhat sympathetic with national prohibition, although somewhat skeptical about its ultimate success. Since the latter date, I have come to realize the futility, the unnaturalness, the manifold dangers to liberty, the enormous amount of hypocrisy and self-deception which are involved in national prohibition. Instead of "leading the American people astray," I firmly believe that I am, in my small way, striving to do them service. You refer to my "sociological enthusiasm," meaning, I take it, the efforts with which I have long been associated toward better economic conditions for the masses of the American people. Well, I regard the enterprise of striving to discredit prohibition as even more beneficial than the activities to which I have just referred. It is more fundamental because it has to do with personal liberty and, after all, it is better to be free than well-fed.

I join most heartily with you in the statement that "it is not for either of us in any ultimate way to sit in judgment on the other." Each of us must in his own way pursue the right "as God gives him to see the right."

SIR: In the *New Republic,* August 21, 1929, Alice Warren objects to George Young's statement: "The success of prohibition in America is explained by the Puritan origin of its society, just as the resistance to it is exemplified in the Roman Catholic reaction." Her objection calls to mind the words of the Divine Master to James and John: "You know not of what spirit you are." As a matter of fact, Mr. Young's formula is substantially correct. If Mrs. Warren will turn to the chapter on Prohibition in André Siegfried's penetrating and illuminating study, *America Comes of Age,* she will find convincing evidence that prohibition originated in, was foisted upon us by, and receives its main support from Puritanism. The spirit of prohibition is the

23

authentic spirit of Puritanism; that is, satisfaction with oneself and a restless urge "to purify the life of the community and uplift the state"; the spirit which puffs a man up, as Mr. Siegfried says on page thirty-four of the same book, with "the idea that his duty toward his neighbor is to convert, purify and raise him to his own [that is, the Puritan's] moral heights."

Directly opposed to all this is the spirit of Catholicism. The latter cherishes individual liberty in all things which are not forbidden, explicitly or implicitly, by the revealed law of Christ or the moral law of nature. Since Catholic ethics does not accept the shallow doctrine that the consumption of intoxicating liquor is *per se* wrong, the Catholic spirit is averse to that fundamental interference with liberty which is inseparable from national prohibition. On the other hand, it favors temperance always and total abstinence whenever that is the only adequate safeguard against abuse of intoxicants. But it wishes the abstinence to be accepted by the free act of the individual, not imposed upon him by the state. The difference between the spirit of Puritanism and the spirit of Catholicism is concretely illustrated in the methods and personalities of Bishop Cannon and Father Mathew. The former would compel men to be even as he, would make them sober by force for their own good; the latter sought to persuade men that they ought to abstain as a free act of self-denial.

Not only the Catholic spirit, but the Catholic heritage predisposes the average member of the Church unfavorably toward national prohibition. Very many Catholics have supported "local option," and even state prohibition when it was demanded by a considerable majority, when it was not opposed by any considerable and compact minority and when the laws did not aim at making it utterly impossible for those men who wanted liquor badly to obtain it. Before the Eighteenth Amendment most American prohibition regulations were of this general character. In many

24

lands and for many centuries the Church has been in a position to observe the working of coercive civil ordinances, particularly those of a sumptuary nature. During this long period she has obtained a pretty accurate notion of the possibilities and the limitations of this kind of legislation. And her practical judgments and conclusions never originate in naïve desire or fond emotion. Sharing in this precious heritage of experience and of sanity, the average Catholic is inclined to regard the "noble experiment" with a healthy skepticism. Moreover, his habit of realistic thinking and his belief in the intrinsic worth of every human individual, protect him against being fooled by the attempts, whether made by Puritans or by industrialists, to identify national prohibition with social welfare.

There is no "large society of Catholics favoring prohibition." The Secretary of the association to which Mrs. Warren refers testified before a Senate Committee a few years ago that its total membership was considerably less than five hundred in the entire United States. If the number has since increased, the fact has not been revealed. At any rate, the organization functions mainly on the official stationery used by its Secretary.

Nothing that I have said in the preceding paragraphs should be construed as implying that a good Catholic cannot be a sincere believer in the Eighteenth Amendment. Here, again, the Catholic spirit is the spirit of individual liberty. No Catholic who thinks that national prohibition is morally right and socially beneficial need fear the disfavor of his Church. On the other hand, there are some Catholics who acquiesce in national prohibition because they think it unwise to antagonize what they conceive to be dominant public opinion. Even these may possess their souls in peace; they will not be rebuked by the authorities of the Church. They might well ask themselves, however, whether the cause of human liberty and human rights is not of more enduring importance than conformity with temporary and misguided public, or pseudo-public sentiment, and whether the inevitable failure of prohibition might not be achieved with less agony if all who realize its falsity and its enormity would permit their views to become articulate. In the long run genuine expediency is identical with right and truth.

SIR: In your issue of December 11, Thomas Addis Tone has a letter in which he upholds the thesis that the legal prohibition of intoxicating liquor is a Catholic, rather than a Protestant, principle, because it is in the Catholic Church that "so many other prohibitory and restrictive laws still find a natural home." This is plausible, but superficial. It fails to distinguish between kinds of prohibitions or between kinds of Protestantism, and it confuses total prohibitions with partial prohibitions, that is, with mere regulations and restrictions. The differences which Mr. Tone overlooks are more important than the resemblances which he emphasizes.

The first difference between the legal prohibition of liquor and the various prohibitions which are laid down for the faithful by the Catholic Church is that the former is imposed upon all citizens by the power of the state, whereas the latter are imposed only upon those persons who freely accept them because they accept the Catholic Church. No non-Catholic citizen of the United States, nor even any Catholic citizen who disregards these Church prohibitions, will fall under the penalties of a Volstead Act, or a Jones Act, or any similar instrument of legal coercion. This difference is of considerable practical importance to the Catholic, as well as to the non-Catholic.

The second difference which Mr. Tone fails to note is that the Church prohibitions which he recounts are either partial, as in the case of the use of meat on Fridays and fast days and the Lenten regulations generally, or prohibit actions which are forbidden by Christ or by the moral law. The most nearly exact parallel between any of the Church prohibitions mentioned by Mr. Tone and legal prohibition is provided by the law requiring abstinence from meat. Conceivably, the Church might have prohibited the use of meat entirely, just as the American State prohibits completely the manufacture and sale of intoxicating liquor. As a matter of fact, the Church has confined the meat prohibition to certain days, just as the American State formerly prohibited the liquor traffic on certain days and hours. To the Catholic, the difference between legal prohibition and the law of abstinence from meat is very great, indeed. The Catholic also finds a very considerable difference between Church prohibitions of actions which are forbidden by Christ or by the moral law and a prohibition which is aimed at an entirely lawful action, namely, the consumption of intoxicating liquor.

The third difference neglected by Mr. Tone is that which is found among different branches of Protestantism. By their origin and traditions, the Lutherans and the Anglicans, or Episcopalians, should naturally be opposed to such a restriction upon individual liberty as legal prohibition. Possibly the majority of them exemplify faithfulness to those traditions in their attitude toward the Eighteenth Amendment and the Volstead Act. But the Protestant churches which carry on, or have adopted, the Calvinistic and the Puritan traditions are in an entirely different category. Religious denominations which are capable of regarding as essentially evil dancing, card playing and betting, do not have far to go in order to take the same attitude toward intoxicating liquor. In other words, the minute regulations and prohibitions of personal conduct which are found in what may be called the Puritan churches make them "the natural home" of the prohibition dogma. Among these churches, the principal are Methodists, Congregationalists, Presbyterians, Baptists and Disciples of Christ. Taken together, they are sufficiently powerful and sufficiently vocal to suggest that American Protestantism has committed itself to legal prohibition.

27

Moreover, the inheritor of the Puritan tradition quite naturally calls upon the state to adopt and enforce his views of conduct and of moral discipline. He is not moved by theories of individual freedom or personal rights against state tyranny; for he assumes that he has the duty of reforming and uplifting his neighbor, regardless of any childish notions which the latter may entertain under the head of personal freedom.

4. The Evolution of an Anti-Prohibitionist

SINCE the appearance of my article in the *Common-weal*, "Who Shall Obey the Law?" not a few persons have commented on my supposed change of attitude toward prohibition. To be sure, it is not necessarily irrational to change one's mind on a contentious subject. Such a change may exemplify mental progress and wider knowledge. On the other hand, a change of opinion sometimes calls for justification by positive reasons. Again, the supposed change may not be as deep or as thorough as is assumed by those who are kind enough to be interested. Inasmuch as the history of my own opinions on prohibition is probably typical of the changes and the progress that thousands of other Americans have made in their thinking on this subject, a summary presentation of that history may be of some interest.

So far as I can recall, the first statement of mine on prohibition that ever got into print was published in the *Fortnightly Review*, April 1, 1916. A note at the top of this very short contribution informs the reader that it was written at the request of the editor. The following extracts from the article constitute the only part of it that is pertinent to the present discussion:

I am in favor of prohibition wherever it can be reasonably enforced. If the amount of liquor consumption is reduced by three-fourths, I should call that condition one of "reasonable enforcement." The state of Kansas exemplifies, I think, that situation. To be sure, there is a considerable difference between rural and urban observance of the law. A state may so enforce the law that only quite exceptional persons get liquor in the country and the small towns, the great majority of the young growing up without any knowledge or thought of intoxicating drink, while a considerable proportion of the city dwellers get it, either from outside the state or through illegal sellers within the city. Even then, I think the law may be on the whole desirable and beneficial. . . .

Assuming that the law is enforced to the extent indicated, I cannot see that anyone's moral rights are violated . . . Rights are necessary and valid in proportion to the importance to human welfare of the spheres of action which they cover; they are not, with the exception of the right to life, ends in themselves. Now I do not believe that drink is so important to the welfare of men in general, or of any man in particular, that the assumed right thereto may not disappear in the face of the great social good that may be effected by the abolition of the opportunity to drink. . . .

Of course, the motives, the viewpoint, the undemocratic spirit, and the false philosophy of the professional prohibitionists and the Anti-Saloon Leaguers, are quite another matter. For these features of the prohibition movement I have nothing but detestation and contempt.

Evidently the foregoing paragraphs referred to state, not federal prohibition. In the years 1918 and 1919 I published under the following titles three editorials in the *Catholic Charities Review:* "Undemocratic Prohibitionists" (April, 1918) ; "Intolerant Prohibitionists" (June, 1918) ; and "Prohibitionist Tyranny" (February, 1919). Shortly before the first of these productions was written, the Eighteenth Amendment had passed Congress and been submitted to the states for ratification. Here is the most significant paragraph in the first editorial:

The prohibitionists show a disregard for individual liberty in their attempt to establish national prohibition. There seems to be no sound reason why the people of each state should not be permitted to decide this question for themselves. There is no national exigency demanding uniformity of legislation on this

30

subject. . . . The states that prefer to have liquor can enjoy that condition without hindering the desire of other states to have prohibition. The latter already have the power to protect themselves against the contaminating influence of the former by excluding liquor shipments entirely. Yet their representatives in Congress have sought to impose prohibition on the liquor states by means of an amendment to the federal Constitution. They wish to confer and impose the benefit of prohibition upon those benighted states that have not sense enough to adopt the measure themselves. This is essentially the same attitude of undemocratic paternalism and superior tyranny that, as we noted above, is taken by the professional prohibitionists toward individual drinkers.

In the second editorial, I reaffirmed this position and quoted a letter from an angry subscriber which contained this delectable effusion:

None but the unthinking will be deceived by the oft-refuted booze rot in your April number, but it is a pity you saw fit to publish such illogical stuff. It sounds very much like the inexhaustible shallow prattle of one of those beer-foam philosophers of Baltimore, but no matter where it came from I could smell the beer on it quite distinctly, and read the same stuff in the brewers' journal and other liquor organs, time and again. When my subscription expires, please stop sending me the magazine. If I want pro-booze arguments, I can get all I want of them, and get them first-hand, and put up in better style, from the booze press, and they have the additional merit of being what they profess, booze organs.

The last of the three editorials was written after the ratification of the Eighteenth Amendment and a few months before the enactment of the Volstead bill. In the opening paragraph I said that the wisdom and the justification of national prohibition were not at the moment practical questions, that we should have to "wait and see"

31

whether it would prove efficacious. The question that was still within the realm of actuality, I said, was whether the Anti-Saloon League would succeed in its efforts to get into the enforcement act (the Volstead bill) a clause forbidding the manufacture and possession of liquor for personal use. This extreme proposal I denounced as an unjustifiable exercise of legislative authority.

My next production on the subject was a short article in the *American Ecclesiastical Review*, April, 1924, under the heading, "Are Our Prohibition Laws Purely Penal?" This was a reply to a solution of a "case of conscience" which had previously appeared in that magazine. The greater part of the reply consisted of a technical argument in refutation of the preposterous proposition that all civil laws are "purely penal." At the end of the article I drew the conclusion that the Eighteenth Amendment was not "purely penal" and that it had "the same validity as any other civil law." As to the Volstead Act, I said that those provisions of it which forbid a person to manufacture, possess or transport liquor for his use or to give it to his friends "are tyrannical and unjust interferences with the liberties and rights of the citizen." I then added this paragraph:

> Therefore, the person who day after day carries on the business of bootlegging is guilty of a grave violation of an important, morally binding law. It is difficult to see how he can be absolved in the tribunal of penance unless he promises to discontinue his illicit occupation. Does the person who purchases liquor from him likewise sin gravely? Probably he does not, unless his patronage be more or less continuous. If it is given only on rare occasions, the co-operation can probably be regarded as lacking the degree of importance necessary to constitute a mortal sin.

An article which I published in the *Catholic World*, May, 1925, set forth at considerably greater length the conclusions just summarized. Here are its most important conclusions:

> The Eighteenth Amendment and those provisions of the Volstead Act which forbid the sale of intoxicating liquor and which prohibit acts involved in or immediately connected with the sale of intoxicating liquor are binding in conscience. . . . On the other hand, the non-commercial and private manufacture, possession and transportation of liquor for consumption by oneself or one's friends, remain lawful in the field of conscience and morality. . . . Inasmuch as the law which they [bootleggers and saloon-keepers] violate has to do with a grave matter, it is difficult to see how they can carry on their traffic without committing a sin which is grave. . . . The person who buys liquor only occasionally and for his own use cannot be held to co-operate so gravely in the evil traffic that each purchase renders him guilty of grave sin. On the other hand, it is difficult to see how these acts can be regarded as entirely free from moral guilt.

These conclusions were based upon the assumption that federal prohibition of the liquor traffic was not an unjust interference with individual liberty; for it had approved itself to the public authorities as the best method of abolishing or reducing grave social evils. I admitted that if the legislators were mistaken in this judgment the prohibition laws were unjustified, but I contended that they and the laws were entitled to the benefit of a legal and moral presumption that no such mistake had been made. If this presumption is to be overthrown, I said, "a vastly greater amount of evidence will have to be brought forward than has thus far appeared." Nevertheless, I gave it as my own opinion that state prohibition or the Canadian system, or a combination of both, "would in the long run have proved more effective."

In the latter part of the year 1926 I revised the *Catholic World* article for my book, *Declining Liberty and Other Papers*, which appeared in April, 1927. The revision in-

33

cluded the first and most fundamental change that has occurred in my opinions on prohibition. I have consistently held that national prohibition involved such a grave restriction upon individual liberty and individual rights that it could be morally justified only when it was not only an effective, but the most effective, kind of liquor legislation. Previous to 1926 I had held that the federal prohibition laws enjoyed the presumption of conforming with this condition. By 1926 that presumption seemed to me to have been negatived by the consequences of the legislation. Hence I put the following paragraph into the book cited above:

> Six years of experience with the legislation have changed its moral aspect. There is now grave reason to doubt that the conditions necessary to justify this degree of interference with individual rights really existed. The degree of success which attended state and local prohibition prior to the national legislation, the degree of success achieved by the Quebec system, and the degree of failure which has characterized the attempt to enforce national prohibition, constitute sufficient evidence to warrant a reasonable and prudent man in holding that the Eighteenth Amendment was an unnecessary, unwise and unjust enactment.

Two questions which had been discussed in the *Ecclesiastical Review* and the *Catholic World* articles received no mention in the book: namely, the moral status of the liquor merchant and of his customers. Had I dealt with these questions I undoubtedly would have drawn the obvious inference from the paragraph just quoted, that, so far as the law itself is concerned, both seller and buyer are free from moral guilt or blame if they feel morally certain that the law is devoid of ethical validity. The morality of conducting and patronizing a business which involves violence, corruption of officials and other serious risks and dangers, I have never discussed anywhere. This is a much

34

more complex question than that of merely violating the law as such. 1422083

My article in the *Commonweal*, April 3, 1929, presented only one change of opinion from previous printed statements. This was the judgment that no person is under moral obligation to refrain from purchasing liquor, by reason of the law itself, even if the law were considered binding in conscience. The basis of this judgment I found in the deliberate refusal of Congress to prohibit purchases. This refusal clearly indicated that the lawmakers did not intend to impose even a civil obligation or penalty upon those who desire to buy liquor. Consequently, no foundation existed upon which to erect a moral obligation. This phase of the situation I failed to consider when I was writing the articles for the *Ecclesiastical Review* and the *Catholic World*. The other, and the more important, of the two main propositions defended in my *Commonweal* article, was that there exists no universal moral obligation to obey *every* civil law, and to continue to observe *every* such statute until it is repealed. Of course, I have never subscribed to the contrary doctrine, at once tyrannical and shallow.

Incidental to the question of the purchaser is an amazing assertion recently made by Dr. S. E. Nicholson, associate superintendent of the Anti-Saloon League. "The real purpose of the Eighteenth Amendment and its enforcing statutes was the prohibition of the traffic in beverage intoxicants, including manufacture, sale, transportation and exportation." The critics of prohibition have committed, he declares, "the fatal error of assuming that the primary purpose of the law is the inhibition of the personal use of liquor." One is moved to inquire how the lawmakers expected liquor to be available for use if the law were enforced. "Inhibition of personal use" may not have been the "primary" purpose of the Eighteenth Amendment, but it was certainly the ultimate object of the Volstead Act. The third section of the latter ends thus: "and all the provisions of this Act shall be liberally construed to the end that the use of intoxicating liquor as a beverage may be prevented." Dr. Nicholson either does not know his Volstead Act or he has become ashamed or afraid of this tyrannical and futile avowal of its final purpose.

Following is a summary comparison of my present and past attitudes. Concerning the unwisdom of national prohibition and the menace to individual liberty which it involves, and concerning the immorality of including in such legislation the manufacture and possession of liquor for personal use, my opinions have never changed except in the direction of greater intensity. Concerning those provisions which forbid the sale of liquor and its manufacture and transportation for sale, I still hold, as I did from 1920 until 1926, that they enjoyed during those years a presumption of social utility and ethical validity. Cumulative experience, however, has definitely destroyed the presumption that favored the "noble experiment" during the early years of experimentation. The manifold evil consequences of national prohibition have shown, to all who have eyes to see, that it is not only not the best but probably the very worst method of dealing with the liquor problem. Therefore, I do not think that the national prohibition laws are any longer directly binding in conscience. The question of their indirect obligation, on account of the social disorder which their violation entails, is one that I am not now called upon to discuss.

5. The Anti-Saloon League[1]

OBERLIN COLLEGE, Oberlin, Ohio, deserves to be called the birthplace of the Anti-Saloon League. At a meeting held there March 20, 1874, an organization was formed under the name of the Oberlin Temperance Alliance. Its founders did not intend merely to add one more to the long list of associations whose members pledged themselves to refrain, partly or entirely, from the consumption of intoxicating liquors. They devoted the new organization to the complete suppression of the traffic in and use of intoxicating liquors; in other words, they committed it to prohibition. It is of interest to note that the same year saw the founding of the Women's Christian Temperance Union and that one year later this society made a declaration in favor of prohibition as essential to the full triumph of temperance. The liquor traffic was pronounced "not only a crime against God, but subversive of every interest of society."

Within a few years, the Oberlin organization established similar societies in other college towns of Ohio, with the result that in 1882 a local option law applying to such towns was enacted by the state legislature. Five years later the Alliance began to advocate a local option law for all townships in the state. To promote this object the Local Option League was organized and within a short time was successful in getting its efforts translated into law. Up to this time, the movement was mainly local in character and did not aim at more than local prohibition.

In 1893 the executive committee of the Oberlin Temperance Alliance met in the Oberlin College Library to form a state-wide organization. To it was given the name, the Anti-Saloon League. Its main objects were declared to

---

[1]Peter H. Odegard, *Pressure Politics: The Story of the Anti-Saloon League* (New York: Columbia University Press).

be: the development and unification of a temperance public sentiment; the enforcement of laws already on the statute book, and "the enactment of further legislation as public sentiment may warrant in order that our people may be saved from the evils of the drink habit, and delivered from the debauching curse of the drink traffic." It will be observed that this declaration includes no endorsement or advocacy of prohibition except in so far as this purpose may be implicit in the rhetorical characterization of the liquor traffic. It is also to be noted that the meeting at which was adopted the platform of the new organization was held in the First Congregational Church.

So rapidly did the Anti-Saloon League spread and develop in its native state that its sponsors began to consider the formation of a national organization along the same lines. Before the Ohio group were able to get out their invitations for a national convention, the Anti-Saloon League of the District of Columbia invited them and others to assemble for the same purpose. Accordingly, the convention was held at the Calvary Baptist Church in Washington, December 18, 1895, with one hundred and sixty-one delegates present. At the second national convention, the following year, five hundred and fifty-seven persons were in attendance, representing thirty-six states and territories.

A brief digression must be made here in order to notice a reference made by Mr. Odegard to Archbishop Ireland in connection with the founding of the national organization. That the first national convention was held in Washington rather than somewhere in Ohio is said to be "the result of conversations between Archbishop Ireland of the Roman Catholic Church, the Rev. Luther B. Wilson, president of the District of Columbia Anti-Saloon League, and Dr. A. J. Kynett, chairman of the Permanent Committee on Temperance and Prohibition of the Methodist Episcopal Church." If this statement is historically true it indicates that the great Archbishop of St. Paul was in favor of a

national organization such as that contemplated by the
Anti-Saloon League of the District of Columbia and Ohio.
It would, however, be a grievous wrong to the Archbishop's memory to infer that he favored national prohibition. I was born in his diocese, received my college
and seminary training there, and taught in the St. Paul
Seminary for thirteen years, leaving there only three years
before the Archbishop died. I heard him make many
addresses on temperance and many denunciations of the
saloon, but never either in public or in private, did I hear
him avow himself in favor of prohibition. He supported
local option, indeed, but so did Cardinal Gibbons. I have
reason to doubt that he had any considerable sympathy
with state-wide prohibition and my best judgment is that
he regarded national prohibition without any sympathy
whatever. Nevertheless, he could quite consistently look
sympathetically upon the Anti-Saloon League program as
it had been formulated in the year 1895. As already noted,
that program included local option and other restraints
upon the power and influence of the saloon but it did not
clearly nor honestly advocate complete prohibition. As late
as the year 1908, William Allen White declared that the
movement promoted by the Anti-Saloon League was "not
a prohibition wave but an anti-saloon wave, a protest
against the conduct of the liquor business as it has developed in this country." About a month later the *American
Issue*, the organ of the Anti-Saloon League, severely criticized an article by Arthur Brisbane which had represented
the liquor question as "between prohibition and license."
The real issue, said this official organ, is between "the saloon and social order." Of course, we all know now that
protests and distinctions of this sort were quite disingenuous, not to say dishonest, for the leaders of the Anti-Saloon
League undoubtedly aimed at national prohibition from
the day when the organization was founded. That they
did not openly avow this object in the beginning was
clearly due to considerations of expediency. As Mr. Odegard

39

interprets this policy of concealment: "Moderate drinkers and total abstainers, who balked at the idea of absolute prohibition, were willing to admit that the American saloon had become a noisome thing."[2] Archbishop Ireland was not the only one holding this view who gave some support to the Anti-Saloon League in ignorance of the ultimate aim in the minds of its leaders.

The Oberlin Temperance Alliance, which developed into the Anti-Saloon League, was an organization of Methodists. The meeting which adopted the League's first platform was held in a Congregational church. The first national convention of the League assembled in a Baptist church. As it was in its beginnings, so it has continued without interruption or wavering, to be an organization of Protestant churches. That is to say, its membership, support and officers have been drawn, with inconsiderable exceptions, from Protestant ecclesiastical bodies. The Board of Directors of the national organization is chosen by State Boards, which are in turn made up of representatives from the various co-operating churches. By far the greater part of the funds have been collected in or through the churches. However, not all the Protestant bodies have participated. The Episcopalians and the Lutherans seem to have kept almost entirely aloof. Apparently the great majority of the League members belong to four denominations, namely, Methodist, Baptist, Presbyterian and Congregationalist. Even these churches have generally failed to extend to the League official and formal support and endorsement. Nor is it certain that a majority of their members have actively identified themselves with either the state or national organizations. The number of Catholics in the League has always been negligible.

Pretty consistently the League seems to have been supported and dominated by the more emotional elements in the participating churches. "The League," says Mr. Odegard, "set itself the task of creating through the instru-

_____
[2]*Op. cit.*, p. 38.

mentality of a powerful propaganda an emotional abhor-
rence of the saloon and the liquor traffic." The Reverend
H. H. Russell, often called the "father" of the League,
uttered these gems at a convention of the organization in
Columbus, 1913:

> The Anti-Saloon League movement was begun by
> Almighty God. . . . He molded my life and even
> used untoward events in such a way as to make it His
> errand for me to set this League in motion. . . .
> During my ministry in those cities whenever I passed
> a saloon I sent up a prayer, "O God, stop this!" At
> length God plainly said to me, "you know how to do
> it; go and help answer your own prayers!" . . . At
> a Conneaut, Ohio, church in the winter of 1893, a
> pastor, introducing me to his congregation, said:
> "There was a man sent from God whose name was
> John; it is equally true there was a man sent from
> God whose name was Russell!" In the awed silence
> of my heart I was compelled to believe the statement
> was true.

The prominence of the emotional elements in the
Anti-Saloon League naturally made a great part of its
propaganda violent and exaggerated in language and in
statement. Here is a typical example:

> The saloon is the storm center of crime; the devil's
> headquarters on earth; the schoolmaster of a broken
> decalogue; the defiler of youth; the enemy of the home;
> the foe of peace; the deceiver of nations; the beast
> of sensuality; the past master of intrigue; the vaga-
> bond of poverty; the social vulture; the rendezvous
> of demagogues; the enlisting office of sin; the serpent
> of Eden; a ponderous second edition of hell, revised,
> enlarged and illuminated.[3]

Among other typical exaggerations in the League "literature" may be mentioned the assertion that 10 per cent of
the annual deaths in the United States are due to alcohol;

---

[3] *American Issue*, Kentucky Edition, April, 1912.

41

that from 60 to 100 per cent of the divorces are due to liquor; that the saloon produces 80 per cent of the criminals; that from the faucet of the liquor business has flowed the deluge of paupers, blind, epileptics, criminals, etc. Many of the statistical statements and inferences therefrom in the League propaganda suggest either emotion run wild or deliberate misrepresentation. In general, the addresses and printed matter tended to persuade sympathetic hearers and readers that there could be no such thing as a decent saloon and even that to take a drink of intoxicating liquor was morally wrong. The League propaganda was calculated "to create a fear-psychology which in the name of civic and moral righteousness would rise and destroy [the saloon]."

These characteristics of the organization were accentuated by the fact that its constituency is overwhelmingly rural and that this is true even with regard to the urban congregations. "The Protestant Church in American cities is largely the property and product of rural immigrants." Mr. Odegard quotes this sentence from *The World Survey of the Inter-Church Movement*. He continues:

The rural church, particularly the Protestant church, is ideally adapted to crusading. It is more than a place of worship; it is a meeting house, a forum. The rural Protestant seems to be a natural-born reformer. To him the city is a place of vice and corruption, a fleshpot to be feared. It is the home of the "foreign element" which he abhors. In the city, on the other hand, strange persons, strange ideas, and strange customs meet and mingle. A live-and-let-live philosophy prevails; there is less demand for conformity. The inter-stimulation of a variety of sects and creeds works for tolerance bordering on indifference. Any other attitude would make city life unendurable. Villagers and the inhabitants of Main Street live in glass houses; every man is his brother's keeper. The village dweller, his own life drab and uneventful, is an ideal soldier for a moral crusade. He takes

42

literally the admonition of St. Paul, "It is good neither to eat flesh, nor drink wine, nor anything whereby thy brother stumbleth, or is offended, or is made weak." Reformist movements in cities emphasize the social and economic rather than the moral; prohibition has been essentially a moral movement. Its leaders used economic and political arguments, but to the rank and file it was at bottom a moral problem. Drink was not only the cause of disease, destitution and depravity; it was above all "the Great Destroyer of the Temple of the Soul," the inciter of base passions and the arch enemy of Christian virtue.

Emotionalism, fanaticism, narrow sectarian zeal and all the other irrational and unlovely features of the League movement would have been inadequate and comparatively futile without effective organization. To this factor must be attributed by far the greater part of its success. Mr. Odegard represents the League as resting upon four pillars; paid professional officers and workers giving it their entire time; monthly supporting subscriptions; political agitation for the defeat of wet and the election of dry candidates, and complete concentration upon the liquor question. In its structure the League is highly centralized and capable of making quick and definite decisions. The Board of Directors and the Executive Committee have substantially supreme power in the national organization, just as have the State Boards of Trustees in the several commonwealths. While national conventions are held biennially, the delegates have no power to determine the policy of the organization or indeed to cast effective votes on any subject. To be sure, even the National Board of Directors could be removed by the members of the underlying church bodies, acting through the State Boards of Trustees, but this method is roundabout and not practically available except when the great majority of the supporting churches are in a state of active insurgency.

The lack of democracy in the League organization is

further illustrated by the provision that no single state may have more than five representatives on the Board of Directors. The obvious purpose of this restriction is to prevent control by the populous urban states. While it has always pleaded for the right of communities to vote out saloons, it has never admitted that dry communities have a right to vote the saloons back. In its early years the League confined its efforts to local option, that is, to bringing about prohibition in townships, towns and cities. As soon as it became sufficiently powerful, it worked for county option; then for state prohibition, and finally for the abolition of the liquor traffic throughout the nation. Of course this meant a progressive disregard of the wishes of large minorities and the subordination of urban groups to the rural and small-town groups. For the latter the League claimed not only the right to have prohibition within their own territories but to impose it upon the city inhabitants. In view of the pronounced differences between the urban and the rural groups it would seem fair and reasonable that each should be allowed to determine for itself the question of wetness or dryness. The Anti-Saloon League has never admitted this principle. To the urban communities it has permitted only one choice, that of being dry.

From the foregoing strictures it must not be inferred that the Anti-Saloon League has exhibited a greater contempt for democracy than the organizations which opposed its efforts. Associations of saloon-keepers, of distillers, of brewers and of other groups interested in the maintenance of the liquor traffic invariably showed themselves quite as averse to representative government and popular choice. Indeed there are very few organizations of any sort that are willing to give up any benefits which they derive from existing political processes and institutions. Devotion to the principles of pure democracy rarely impels any organized group to forego whatever advantage it can find in existing arrangements.

The Anti-Saloon League

The efficiency, effectiveness, and success of the Anti-Saloon League are clearly and interestingly narrated in chapters III-VI of Mr. Odegard's book. At the beginning of chapter III, he enumerates the outstanding features of its methods as follows: "Centralization of authority; singleness of purpose; political utilization of the power of the Protestant churches; avoidance of entry into politics as a separate political party." With rare exceptions the men who led and directed the League campaigns were not only earnest, aggressive and untiring but competent, clever and adroit. This statement applies particularly to their activities as lobbyists before state legislatures and Congress, and as manipulators of political pressure. Mr. Odegard describes many instances of these tactics, varying from gentle persuasion to crude bulldozing.

The first notable success of the League in the field of national legislation occurred in February, 1913, when Congress passed the Webb-Kenyon bill, which considerably restricted the freedom of liquor shipments from wet to dry states. President Taft vetoed it on constitutional grounds, but both the Senate and the House repassed it by considerably greater majorities than the required two-thirds. Anyone who is surprised at this outcome should reflect that in the year 1913 nine states had complete and thirty-six partial prohibition. Upwards of fifty million Americans were living in territories from which the saloon had been excluded by law. A substantial majority of the members of Congress came from these dry areas.

The same year saw the initiation of the League's campaign for national prohibition. Present in the national convention were representatives from every state in the Union, including "ministers, judges, social workers, scientists, senators, congressmen, governors and the League's own leaders trained in pulpit and politics, all dedicating themselves to a final assault on the bulwarks of evil." Typical of the spirit which permeated the convention were these words uttered by Bishop Wilson: "As Moses approached with unsandled feet that bush of flame and taught the word of God, so come we to this hour and in its solemn hush we read and recognize the divine hour for a new advance—Prohibition for all our land." In view of the mass of threatening evidence the *National Liquor Dealers' Journal* confessed:

To us there is the handwriting on the wall and its interpretation spells doom. The liquor business is to blame. It seems incapable of learning any lesson of advancement or any motive but profit.

The resolution submitting to the states the constitutional amendment for national prohibition was introduced in both houses of Congress, December 10, 1913. "Congress was all but buried in an avalanche of communications from the people back home. The wires were hot with messages. The local leagues spurred on the church folks and it seemed that the flood of public opinion had broken on an unsuspecting Congress. A partial list of endorsed petitions contained the names of 9,296 organizations with a total membership of 3,358,586."[4] Apparently the resolution did not come to a vote in the Senate, but it passed the House by a majority of seven. In the course of the debate Representative Mann of Illinois proposed that the resolutions should be ratified by conventions chosen for that purpose instead of by the legislatures in the several states. Congressional spokesmen for the League objected to this proposal on the ground that the same people who chose the legislatures would also choose the delegates to the suggested conventions. As a matter of fact, fifteen of the state legislatures which ultimately ratified the amendment had been chosen before it was adopted by Congress. In any case the members of a convention selected for the one purpose of passing upon a prohibition amendment might well differ greatly in personnel and in attitude towards this question from the members of a state legislature elected at the end of a cam-

---

[4] *Pressure Politics*, p. 153.

46

paign which involved many other issues. Of course the real reason of the League's unwillingness to accept the convention proposal was its distrust of a popular vote in many states on this specific issue. Its spokesmen were well aware from experience that they could deal more success-fully with a small body of legislators than with an entire state electorate in an open campaign.

By the fall of 1916 twenty-three states were dry and a sufficient number of dry representatives had been elected to both houses of Congress to justify the hope that the pro-hibition amendment would soon be submitted to the state legislatures. Before the hope could be realized Congress declared war against the Central Powers, and the advocates of the amendment were compelled to be content with a provision in the Food Control bill which made illegal the use of food stuffs in the manufacture of spirituous liquors. They had contended strongly for the inclusion of beer and wine and desisted in their efforts only after President Wilson had written a letter to Bishop Cannon, requesting him and his fellow-prohibition leaders not to endanger the enactment of the bill by insisting upon this demand. The humiliation thus accepted by the President of the United States is at least as discreditable as that imposed upon Congress in connection with the Adamson Eight Hour bill. Much ink has been spilled in deploring the latter but little or nothing has been said in the condemna-tion of the former. Of course the prohibition provisions in the Food Control bill represent sheer hypocrisy, inasmuch as the amount of food materials that would have been consumed in making whiskey was not vital to the war operations, while the gain thereby effected was only a partial compensation for the ensuing loss in government revenue.

In December, 1917, the resolution for a prohibition amendment was introduced in both houses of Congress. Wayne Wheeler, the chief lobbyist for the League, insisted that the resolution be passed in the current session lest the

matter be delayed until after 1920, when a reapportion-
ment was to be expected and "forty new wet Congressmen
will come from the great wet centers with their rapidly
increasing population." Here is Mr. Odegard's comment:
"So much was the Anti-Saloon League concerned with the
will of the majority." Yea, verily. Only one day was
allotted to debate in the House, at the close of which the
resolution was adopted by a vote of two hundred and
eighty-two to one hundred and twenty-eight. That was
on December 17th. The following day the Senate con-
curred, forty-seven ayes to eight nays. Thus the resolution
obtained considerably more than the required two-thirds
majority in both houses. Accordingly it was submitted
to the state legislatures and within fourteen months was
ratified by the required number. One year later, January
16, 1920, it became a part of the Federal Constitution.
Before that date all the other states had approved it except
New Jersey, Connecticut and Rhode Island. The first
named of these ratified the amendment in 1922; the other
two enjoy the distinction of having failed to do so.

In the seventh and eighth chapters, Mr. Odegard presents in considerable detail the record of the League in the
matters of contributions, expenditures and corruption.
With regard to the first two his conclusion is that the
record contains little that is discreditable. The amount of
corrupt conduct by representatives of the League is likewise
found to have been not unusual nor extraordinary. The
author summarizes his judgment on this point in a quotation from an article by Frank Kent in the Baltimore *Sun:*

> I recognize that to conceive that the Anti-Saloon
> League is anything but a bunch of crooks will cause
> a good many wets around here severe pain. . . .
> What I have said about the character of these men is
> a fundamental fact which it seems to me ought to be
> understood. They are not only honest but the real
> leaders are amazingly astute, incredibly efficient, prac-
> tical to a point and with an ability to see ahead about
> eight times as far as the average political party leader.

THE ANTI-SALOON LEAGUE

The last chapter is entitled "High Politics," and sketches the propaganda and the political performances of the liquor interests. Needless to say their record in these fields is at least as black as that of the Anti-Saloon League.

The assertion has often been made that the favorable vote in Congress and the votes in many if not most of the state legislatures were brought about through enormous deception; that, in the language of the day, national prohibition was "put over upon the people while they were not looking." This view seems to be without adequate supporting evidence. The Congress which by more than a two-thirds majority of both houses submitted the amendment to the legislatures was not elected under the influence of war feeling, for the great majority were chosen five months before America entered the conflict and two-thirds of the Senate had been members of that body for still longer periods. The League representatives claimed, apparently without contradiction, that they had a sufficient majority in Congress the day after the election, November, 1916. To be sure, the distorted views and emotions produced by the war might have exercised some influence upon many members of Congress when they voted on the proposal, but these factors do not seem to have been decisive. As regards the process of ratification, it must be kept in mind that twenty-seven states already had prohibition laws on their statute books or in their constitutions.

Again, it is asserted that both the members of Congress and those of the ratifying state legislatures were subjected to overwhelming intimidation and pressure by the Anti-Saloon League, that if they could have voted on the measure in secret, the required majority would not have been forthcoming. The latter contention is, of course, impossible of proof or disproof. As to political pressure, the only difference between the kind used by the Anti-Saloon League and that employed by many other organizations seems to have been a difference in the degree of efficiency. The intimidation that the League practiced was likewise not unusual, for it consisted essentially in threatening hesitating legislators with defeat by their constituents at the next election.

What then is the explanation of this revolutionary victory by the Anti-Saloon League? Its constituency never included more than a small proportion of the country's electorate. As a tentative answer, one might hazard the statement that the League was successful in its efforts partly because of its effective organization and propaganda, partly because it took full advantage of the emotional condition under which Congress and the majority of the people labored in the war time and partly because millions of persons having no affiliation or sympathy with the Anti-Saloon League were strongly opposed to the saloon and carelessly assumed that national prohibition would be feasible and desirable, even as state and local prohibition had seemed feasible and desirable. This general attitude was based upon many considerations, among which economic factors were probably stronger than those of a moral character.

Some of the methods and purposes of the League are clearly subject to just condemnation. Its refusal to permit a popular referendum through state conventions chosen precisely and solely on the question of ratification of the amendment was undemocratic and incapable of rational defense. Equally to be condemned is its insistence upon a prohibition statute instead of an enabling act in the Federal Constitution. The Eighteenth Amendment is the only provision of its kind in our organic law and it is undoubtedly at variance with all the elements of that instrument. Previous to the insertion of the Eighteenth Amendment the Federal Constitution comprised three kinds of provisions: those describing the framework of the federal government; those enumerating the powers conferred upon Congress and those restricting the powers of Congress in favor of individual rights. The Eighteenth Amendment is the only part of the Constitution which

50

regulates and restricts the conduct of the people. While the Nineteenth Amendment does affect directly a large class of citizens, it is not a restriction, but a grant of power; it enables women to vote. Had the Anti-Saloon League been devoted to the principles of democracy and to the genius of the Federal Constitution, it would have been satisfied with an enabling act, that is, an amendment authorizing Congress to enact national prohibition. It insisted upon a statute instead of an enabling act because it did not trust future Congresses. One of the latter might have repealed the prohibition statute which the Congress chosen in 1916 or in 1918 undoubtedly would have enacted.

Even more flagrant was the League's disregard of individual liberty. Always it attacked the saloon as a social institution, ignoring the fact that no social institution is maintained except by the desires and support of the citizens. The wishes of those who like to consume intoxicating liquor were never given consideration by the Anti-Saloon League. Indeed, a large proportion of the organization seemed to have regarded the consumption of intoxicating liquors as intrinsically immoral. Certainly the majority of its members regarded government licensing of drink shops as morally wrong. Leaders of the League were willing to and did impose these ethical notions upon a very large minority, if not indeed a majority, of their fellow citizens. While conditions are conceivable in which national prohibition would be a justifiable restriction of individual liberty, those conditions did not exist in America in the second decade of the twentieth century. Nor do they exist today.

The political activity of the Protestant churches on behalf of prohibition has been severely criticized and stoutly defended. Mr. Odegard takes the latter view, contending in effect that the Church may with as much propriety use political influence in favor of measures that it advocates as a labor union or a manufacturers' association. In pure theory and in conditions which present a moral

51

or religious crisis, this doctrine is sound. In American practice and in the vast majority of situations, the doctrine is unsound. The traditional theory of separation of Church and State in our country includes the condemnation, or at least the discouragement, of political activity by the churches as organizations unless their own interests are vitally threatened. Our traditional practice does not sanction church appeals for votes, whether at the ballot box or in the legislatures, on behalf of so-called moral issues to which a large proportion of the electorate denies that character.

A rather disingenuous distinction has been drawn by several Protestant leaders in this matter of political activity by the churches. Churchmen may properly use their pulpits for political discussion when a "moral" issue is involved, provided that they are exercising mere "influence" but not "authority." Obviously, this distinction was invented in order to justify Protestant churchmen while condemning Catholic churchmen for the same sort of activity. So far as the effects are concerned, the difference between "influence" and "authority" is merely one of degree. The exertion of "influence" by those who possess that power might easily constitute a greater danger to public welfare than the exercise of "authority."

Some of the principal sources of strength in the Anti-Saloon League are in the long run factors of weakness. They account for much of its success but they also are and will continue to be responsible for its inevitable failure. Emotionalism, fanaticism, lack of balanced judgment, disregard of democracy and of individual rights, excessive political pressure, improper activity of the churches, have all made a large contribution to the adoption of the Eighteenth Amendment. On the other hand, the essential falsehood and injustice of these things will prove no inconsiderable part of the reasons for the ultimate failure of national prohibition. No such revolutionary change in

52

human habits and institutions can endure on the basis of a lie.

Mr. Odegard has produced an extremely useful book. It reflects an enormous amount of painstaking investigation and a high degree of impartiality. Both as a record of the League's activities and as an explanation of the Eighteenth Amendment it will probably continue for a long time to be the most satisfactory and reliable publication available to the American people.

Part II

CATHOLICS AND POLITICS

6. Church, State and Constitution

IN the April, 1927, number of the *Atlantic Monthly*, Mr. Charles C. Marshall called for a statement to clear away all doubt concerning the reconcilability with constitutional principles of the status and claims of the Catholic Church. The following paragraphs attempt to answer, one after another, all the questions and difficulties that he raised.

First (page 541, column two) : Mr. Marshall quotes Pope Leo XIII to the effect that no religious society other than the Catholic Church possesses divine sanction and that none of the other churches has a natural right to function on the same basis.

This is the Catholic position but it does not conflict with the Constitution, for the simple reason that the Constitution has nothing to say about this doctrine. The Constitution defines legal rights, not natural rights.

Second (page 541, column two) : Mr. Marshall cites a statement from the *Catholic Encyclopedia* concerning "dogmatic intolerance" as the right and duty of the Catholic Church.

This is merely another way of asserting the claim described above. Obviously it has nothing to do with the Constitution.

Third (page 542, column one) : Mr. Marshall quotes Pope Leo XIII as saying that the Church "does not condemn those rulers" who for sufficient reasons allow each kind of religion to have a place in the state. Then he translates "does not condemn" into "will allow," which is a bit invidious.

There is nothing in the Constitution which forbids the Catholic Church or any other church to take this attitude. Mr. Marshall's indignant question, "whether such favors

57

can be accepted in place of rights by those owning the name of free men?" is irrelevant and gratuitous. Since the claim which he is criticizing is not forbidden by the Constitution or the laws of the land, it does not concern him as an American citizen. Of course, he has the legal right to resent the claim, as a member of the Anglican Church.

Fourth (page 542, column two) : Mr. Marshall points out that the Catholic Church claims the right to determine the line which separates its jurisdiction from that of the state in those "mixed matters" in which both have an interest. According to Mr. Marshall, "the Constitution of the United States clearly ordains that the state shall determine the question." What he seems to mean is that this principle is implicit in the Constitution, inasmuch as the Supreme Court has declared that "practices inconsistent with the peace and safety of the state shall not be justified." In other words, the American state constitutionally claims the right to determine for itself what practices are inconsistent with its peace and safety.

Obviously it does, and must, within the limits fixed by the Constitution. However, the Supreme Court has not left the matter quite so vague as it appears in the words which Mr. Marshall quotes from *Watson* vs. *Jones*. In another sentence of that decision, the Court declared that Americans have the right "to practice any religious doctrine which does not violate the laws of morality and property and which does not infringe personal rights." In *Mormon Church* vs. *United States*, the same Court decided that "the state has a perfect right to prohibit polygamy." The Catholic Church likewise condemns all these practices. On the other hand, the Supreme Court has never construed as unconstitutional any practice of the Catholic Church. Hence, there is no conflict in the realm of actuality. If any had existed in the realm of possibility it would have been converted into reality long before now.

Fifth (page 543, column two) : Mr. Marshall adduces the words of Pope Leo XIII to the effect that it is not lawful for the state "to hold in equal favor different kinds of religions," and then cites these words of the Constitution: "Congress shall make no law respecting an establishment of religion or prohibiting the free exercise thereof."

At last we seem to be confronted with a genuine conflict. The Pope seems to declare unlawful an arrangement which the Constitution requires Congress to maintain. But the Pope is speaking of normal or ideal conditions, that is, those which should obtain in what is technically known as a "Catholic state." He is not referring to such a state as ours. In his encyclical letter on Catholicity in the United States, the same Pope implicitly approved the relations between Church and State existing in this country. The distinction between a "Catholic state" in which the normal arrangement is a union between the ecclesiastical and civil powers, and a country containing several religious societies already established, is well known in Catholic doctrine. Why does Mr. Marshall ignore it? Why does he not recall here the statement which he cites from Pope Leo earlier in his article, namely, that the Church does not condemn such religious equality as we have in the United States? If he desired to be completely accurate and fair, he would have quoted the declaration of a distinguished German theologian, Father Pohle, that it is very doubtful whether a single "Catholic state" exists today. When we examine the whole situation we find that the apparent contradiction vanishes into thin air.

Sixth (page 543, column two): Mr. Marshall quotes Pope Leo as saying that the Catholic Church deems it unlawful to place all other religions on the same footing as the true religion, whereas, the Supreme Court, in *Watson* vs. *Jones*, declared that our law "knows no heresy and is committed to the support of no dogma, the establishment of no sect."

Here again Pope Leo is discussing the normal and ideal situation, not conditions such as obtain in the United States. Even so, his statement is not formally contradicted by the words of the Supreme Court. The Court does not say that all religions are equally good or true. It was not considering that question. It used the words quoted above in order to emphasize the difference between the attitude of American courts and that of British courts toward the validity of ecclesiastical statutes. Whether one religion is as good as another or whether the Catholic religion is the only true one, are questions upon which the Constitution is silent and to which the Supreme Court will in no conceivable circumstances presume to return an answer.

Seventh (page 544, column one): Mr. Marshall cites Pope Leo's rejection of the opinion "that it would be universally lawful or expedient for State and Church to be, as in America, dissevered and divorced." This statement, he finds, is somehow in conflict with our constitutional separation of Church and State.

Of course, there is no such conflict. Mr. Marshall thinks that separation of Church and State is the best arrangement for the United States. Practically all American Catholics hold the same opinion. Mr. Marshall thinks that is the best plan, not only for our country, but for all countries everywhere, and he intimates that this abstract opinion is imbedded in the Constitution. This is absurd. In providing for separation of Church and State the Constitution no more implies that this order ought to obtain everywhere than that a republic is the best form of government for all peoples.

Eighth (page 544, column one): Mr. Marshall asks Governor Smith whether he believes that the Catholic Church or the Supreme Court should prevail when they differ upon a question of jurisdiction.

For the reasons given above, especially under Fourth, Governor Smith or any other Catholic can logically deny the possibility of actual conflict.

Ninth (page 544, column two): Had the pleadings on behalf of the Oregon Anti-Private School Law, says Mr. Marshall, included the assertion that the parochial schools

60

"gave instruction inconsistent with the peace and safety of the state," the Supreme Court would necessarily have pronounced the law valid.

If this interpretation of the mind of the Court is correct, counsel for the State of Oregon were negligent or unfortunate or both in having failed to associate Mr. Marshall with the defense of the law.

Tenth (page 545, column one): Mr. Marshall goes on to specify the Catholic teachings which he regards as "inconsistent with the peace and safety of the state," and which he says would so appear to the Supreme Court. Here they are: it is not universally lawful for the state and the Catholic Church to be separated; the non-Catholic religions have no natural right to state protection; dogmatic intolerance is the right and duty of the Catholic Church; when laws conflict that of the Church should prevail.

As we have already seen, the first three of these declarations are abstract propositions upon which the Constitution has nothing to say, for it is not concerned with general doctrines of this sort, but with practical policies. The principle that the law of the Church should prevail over that of the state in case of conflict would scarcely be noted by the Supreme Court, so long as no evidence was presented to show that Catholic schools or the Catholic pulpit taught disobedience to the state. Here as in many other paragraphs, Mr. Marshall fails to distinguish between the application of practical doctrines to "Catholic states" and their adaptation to states which recognize no particular form of religion.

Eleventh (page 545, column one): The Catholic Church, says Mr. Marshall, claims the right to fix the conditions for the validity of all marriages of baptized persons. Hence, the Roman authorities declared invalid the marriage of the Marlboroughs on the ground that it lacked one of the required conditions. This act constituted an "utter disregard of the sovereignty" of New York State and of Great Britain.

61

The State of New York considers invalid the divorces which many other states grant for "incompatibility of temper" and subsequent marriages contracted by the parties to these divorces. Does this show "utter disregard of the sovereignty" of the sister states? The State of South Carolina does not recognize divorce for any cause. Several states do not recognize marriages between white persons and Negroes. Do these restrictions imply "utter disregard of the sovereignty" of the other states of the Union? The church of which Mr. Marshall is a distinguished member will not remarry persons who obtain civil divorces for any cause except marital unfaithfulness. Does his church thereby show "utter disregard of the sovereignty" of those commonwealths which grant divorce for other reasons? Here are several "conflicts" on the subject of marriage. They differ only in degree, not at all in kind, from the difference which obtains between our civil regulations concerning marriage and the law of the Catholic Church. Of course, the Church would prefer that all the other states prohibited divorce as does South Carolina. Of course, the Church holds that the states do wrong in granting divorce. Here is a genuine conflict between the theory practiced by our states and the doctrine held by the Church. Nevertheless, I have never heard of a Catholic priest being arrested for violating the marriage laws of the state in which he resided.

Moreover, Mr. Marshall's entire discussion about education and marriage is irrelevant and impertinent in a letter addressed to a possible candidate for President of the United States. The federal government has no control over either of these fields. Consequently the President is never called upon to take any official attitude thereupon, and in no circumstances could he change the civil laws governing either education or marriage. As Governor of New York State, Mr. Smith does enjoy some power of these sorts, but I have never heard it charged that he exerted it contrary to the Constitution or the laws of New York.

Twelfth (page 545, column two): Mr. Marshall drags

in the Mexican situation, but his only pertinent contention is that Mr. William D. Guthrie was speaking "officially" for the Catholic Church when he declared that armed intervention by the United States would be justified by "many historical precedents."

As a matter of fact, Mr. Guthrie's statement had no official character or value whatever and he would be the last person to make any such claim. Why does Mr. Marshall ignore the pastoral letter of the American hierarchy on Mexico which is the only official pronouncement that we have and which explicitly disclaims any desire for armed intervention by the United States?

Thirteenth (page 548, column two): Mr. Marshall assures us that he will be satisfied if Catholics "will but concede" that the claims which he has been discussing will, unless modified, "precipitate an inevitable conflict between the Roman Catholic Church and the American state, irreconcilable with domestic peace."

Well, we will not concede anything of the sort, for we know the teaching and spirit of our Church better than does Mr. Marshall, and we think we understand the provisions and implications of the Constitution. We even indulge the supposition that we have a better acquaintance than he with the rules of logic.

Fourteenth (page 549, column two): Mr. Marshall reaches across the ocean to England and to Rome in order to exploit his grievance against Pope Leo XIII for having declared the invalidity of Anglican Orders. Surely this is mere trifling. The Papal action which he criticizes was a matter of internal administration of the Catholic Church. It denied admission into the Catholic priesthood of Anglican clergy without reordination. What has this to do with politics? And what possible basis does it set for a conflict between the American state and the Catholic Church? Here again Mr. Marshall seems to be speaking, not as an American citizen, but as a member of the Anglican Church who resents the Pope's attitude toward his denomination.

63

Fifteenth (page 549, column two) : Finally, Mr. Marshall goes back three and a half centuries to tell us about John Felton, who was hanged during the reign of Queen Elizabeth for treason but who was beatified in 1886 by Pope Leo XIII.

The burden of his complaint in this case seems to be that the Pope does not always approve every action performed by a political government. Does Mr. Marshall ask us to hold that every state is morally omnipotent? If he will read Professor Laski's *Studies in the Problem of Sovereignty* he will find an interesting record of other churches that refused to obey some of the laws passed by the British Parliament. He asks whether "the record of the Roman Catholic Church in England is consistent with the peace and safety of the state." As addressed to Governor Smith this question is irrelevant and impertinent. The only political group properly interested are the people of England, and they seem to have been far less excited about these episodes than Mr. Marshall.

Governor Smith is to be congratulated on the publication of Mr. Marshall's questions. They are professedly located on a lofty plane and they are propounded by a distinguished lawyer. Yet the last five pages of the article have no relation to the office of President of the United States. Education and marriage are the exclusive concern of the several states, the opinions of Mr. Guthrie on the Mexican situation have no official authority, while Anglican Orders and the beatification of John Felton are beyond the control of any American citizen. The "conflicts" between the Catholic Church and the Constitution of the United States which Mr. Marshall strives to show in the first four pages of his article, fade out of the picture when we recall that the Catholic doctrine of union between Church and State applies practically only to "Catholic states"; that Pope Leo XIII implicitly approved the separation which exists in the United States, and that the Constitution neither defines the natural rights of religious societies, nor enunciates any abstract doctrine about their equality, nor pronounces upon the value of the American system as a universal arrangement, nor asserts any claim of religious or moral jurisdiction which could bring the American state into actual conflict with the Catholic Church.

7. Union of Church and State[1]

THE closing paragraph of Governor Smith's reply to Charles C. Marshall included "a fervent prayer that never again in this land will any public servant be challenged because of the faith in which he has tried to walk humbly with his God." This prayer has not been answered everywhere. The Rev. Charles Hillman Fountain has repeated the challenge and reasserted Mr. Marshall's contention that "the public teaching of the Governor's Church is out of harmony with our Constitution." Inasmuch as Governor Smith's reply to this charge was almost universally approved by intelligent and fair-minded Americans, any restatement of the charge is somewhat extraordinary. It raises the presumption that the author must have something to say which Mr. Marshall overlooked. Is this presumption verified in the article contributed by Mr. Fountain?

His paper contains many more words than Mr. Marshall employed, and it includes much new matter, especially in the form of quotations from Catholic printed productions; but it presents no new facts which are relevant, and it includes all the mistakes of commission and omission which weakened so greatly Mr. Marshall's argument. In comparison with the latter, Mr. Fountain's production exhibits a considerably greater capacity to confuse concepts which are really distinct. For example, at the end of the second paragraph Mr. Fountain asserts that "the Catholic Church is opposed to the principles of democracy." The general definition of democracy is that political régime in which the people determine the Constitution and the officials who carry on the government. Later in his article Mr. Fountain

---

[1] Reprinted by special permission of the *Current History Magazine*, the monthly periodical of the New York Times Company. See issue for March, 1928.

concedes that the Church does not oppose democracy in this sense. What he means in the words just quoted is that the Catholic Church opposes certain principles which Mr. Fountain chooses to regard as a part of the democratic theory. Other examples of this confused thinking will be noticed later.

The greater part of the matter which is new in Mr. Fountain's paper consists of quotations from and discussion of the Encyclical Letter of Pope Pius X, *Pascendi Gregis,* condemning Modernism. These paragraphs occupy more than one-fourth of the entire article. In substance they assert that this document condemns the separation of Church and State, and that it is regarded by Catholics as an infallible pronouncement. But this particular condemnation had been uttered many years previously on several occasions; for example, in the *Syllabus* of Pius IX, and in the Encyclical on the *Christian Constitution of States* of Pope Leo XIII; and the proscribed theory figured largely in Mr. Marshall's letter to Governor Smith. Why does Mr. Fountain take the trouble to dig out of *Pascendi* a topic which had already been discussed by Mr. Marshall and Governor Smith? Apparently because he thinks that the condemnation in this encyclical is held to be infallible, whereas it may not have this character in either the *Syllabus* or the *Christian Constitution of States.* Nevertheless, the whole discussion of *Pascendi* is a waste of time and space. In the first place, the condemnations of the separation doctrine issued by Pius IX and Leo XIII are entirely binding upon the consciences of Catholics; therefore, that contained in *Pascendi,* even though it be infallible, merely increases the degree of obligation. In the second place, the elaborate argument of Mr. Fountain to show that the latter is an infallible document must be set down as so much wasted energy, in the light of the statement made by the Rev. A. Vermeersch, S.J., that Catholic authorities disagree on this question *(Catholic Encyclopedia,* Volume X, page 421). As Mr. Fountain points out in a subsequent paragraph, it is a well-recognized principle that if canonists and moralists disagree about the infallibility of any Papal pronouncement, the individual Catholic is free to regard it as not infallible.

UNION OF CHURCH AND STATE NOT DESIRED

In the first paragraph following the heading, "Papal Teaching Alone Authoritative," Mr. Fountain declares that those Catholics whom Governor Smith quoted as favoring the separation of Church and State in America are in conflict with the Encyclical, *Pascendi*, and if they spoke thus subsequently to the oath which Catholic priests were obliged to take in support of that encyclical, they were in "open defiance of the Apostolic authority of the Holy See." Well, one of the quotations made by Governor Smith in this connection was taken from something that I wrote myself. It is to be found in *The State and the Church*, pp. 37, 38, by Ryan and Millar, which was published in 1922, therefore several years after the anti-Modernist oath became binding. As a teacher in Catholic educational institutions, I have taken that oath every year since 1910, but I have never assumed that it forbade me to believe in the separation of Church and State in our country. My ecclesiastical superiors have never intimated the existence of any such conflict as Mr. Fountain asserts. Apparently they are not so strict as he in their interpretation of canon law and ecclesiastical obligation.

Just when and where Archbishop Ireland made the statement quoted in Governor Smith's reply and alluded to by Mr. Fountain I cannot say, but since I taught in his ecclesiastical seminary for thirteen years and knew him intimately, I am quite certain that the statement is an authentic expression of his views. Here is another utterance of his on the same subject. It was spoken at Milwaukee, August 11, 1913 (note the date), and may be found in *The State and the Church*, p. 287: "Would we alter, if we could, the Constitution in regard to its treatment of religion, the principles of Americanism in regard to religious freedom? I answer with an emphatic No." In a statement issued in his episcopal city, April 6, 1927, the Right Rev. John F. Noll, Bishop of Fort Wayne, quoted with approval the statement attributed to Cardinal Gibbons, that he had "advocated in the City of Rome itself, before the Pope himself, the sort of arrangement between Church and State that we have here." The Right Rev. John J. Dunn, Auxiliary Bishop of New York, expressed in a radio address, November 24, 1926 (note the date), his conviction that, even though the Church "is not a partner of the state here, as in some countries, she has here a freedom, an opportunity to work, that is not surpassed anywhere." Evidently he is not longing for a union of Church and State in America. Yet the Pope has not admonished Bishop Dunn that these sentiments are "in open disregard of the oath and in open defiance of the Apostolic authority of the Holy See."

The following six paragraphs in Mr. Fountain's article contain nothing noteworthy except his comment on Governor Smith's question: "And by what right do you ask me to assume responsibility for every statement that may be made in any encyclical letter?" He thinks that these words imply an unorthodox attitude on the part of the Governor, because he assumes that "every statement" in an encyclical is held by good Catholics to be infallible. This is not true, even of encyclicals that are certainly endowed with that attribute. Only those portions are infallible which express formal decrees and propositions concerning faith or morals: the reasoning by which these are supported and the contextual discussion generally are neither infallible nor necessarily obligatory. Of course they are to be received with respect, and not rejected except upon weighty grounds. Therefore, Governor Smith, or any other Catholic, could with entire propriety repudiate the assumption that "every statement" in even an infallible encyclical is binding upon his conscience.

The paragraphs under the heading "Religious Freedom

69

Condemned" merely restate the Catholic doctrine on the union of Church and State, as set forth in the *Syllabus* of Pius IX and Pope Leo's Encyclical on the *Christian Constitution of States*. As I have already noted, these objections were urged by Marshall and answered by Smith. I shall deal with them in later paragraphs.

Under "Status of Church in America Not Ideal," Mr. Fountain cites the statement of Pope Leo XIII that the Church "would bring forth more abundant fruits if, in addition to liberty, she enjoyed the favors of the laws and the patronage of the public authority." On the other hand, Cardinal Gibbons, as quoted by Governor Smith, declared that he could "conceive no combination of circumstances likely to arise which would make a union desirable to either Church or State." Both are right. The difference in their statements is due to the fact that the Pope is speaking hypothetically, the Cardinal with an eye to practical probabilities. Undoubtedly the Church, as any other public institution, would reap advantage from the express favor of the state, provided that the latter refrained from interfering in the province of the former. Inasmuch as this condition would be utterly improbable of fulfillment in the United States, Cardinal Gibbons and every other intelligent American Catholic would honestly say that he could "conceive no combination of circumstances likely to arise" which would make a union of Church and State desirable in our country.

MISINTERPRETING THE *SYLLABUS*

Mr. Fountain cites eight of the propositions condemned by Pius IX in the *Syllabus*, and then sets forth what he conceives to be the positive teaching of the Church on each of these subjects. Only one of his eight formulations is correct without qualification. All the others are either wholly wrong or partly wrong or gravely misleading.

His failure is due either to ignorance of or disregard of the correct principles of interpretation. Under this head he

70

exhibits three mistakes. First, he ignores the context of the erroneous propositions. More than fifty years ago Cardinal Newman, in his *Letter to the Duke of Norfolk,* replying to the *Expostulation* by the Honorable William Ewart Gladstone, pointed out that the *Syllabus* of Pius IX is, under one aspect, an index to proscribed doctrines which are found in their proper context in various encyclicals, allocutions, Apostolic letters and other Papal pronouncements. In passing, it should be observed that this production of the great English Cardinal anticipated by more than half a century all the objections urged by Mr. Marshall in his letter to Governor Smith, and indeed all the plausible objections that ever can be urged against the loyalty of Catholic citizens. It remains and probably will always remain the best written and most effective refutation of this unjust charge. As Cardinal Newman observes, and as anyone who takes the trouble to consult the propositions of the *Syllabus* in an official Latin publication will see, each of them is immediately followed by a reference to the Papal pronouncement in which they were originally noted and condemned. Mr. Fountain made no such investigation. Instead of having done, as he says, "full justice to the context," he gives no context at all, and apparently has never seen any. The evil effect of failing to consult the sources is exemplified in his treatment of the first and second propositions. He does not realize the importance or the meaning of the phrase "guided by the light of reason" in the first, nor of the word "force" in the second.

In the paragraphs immediately following his statements of Catholic teaching, he quotes from the article in the *Catholic Encyclopedia* on the *Syllabus* to show the binding power of that document. Why did he not take note of another paragraph in the same article which shows that the first in his list of condemned propositions means that every one is free to choose his religion on the basis of reason alone and to disregard divine revelation; in other words, to disregard the voice of God? This is the sense in which the proposition is condemned. It professes absolute rationalism. Therefore, he simply caricatures the Catholic doctrine on this subject when he states it in this form, "all men are not free to embrace the religion they believe in." Had he taken note of this paragraph in the *Encyclopedia,* he could not have written down such nonsense. The word "force" in the second condemned proposition in his list he evidently interprets in the sense of physical coercion against the will of the person upon whom it is exerted. Had he been able to consult the book in which this proposition originally appeared, or the *Apostolic Letter* of August 22, 1851, in which it was originally condemned, he would have found that the word "force" has a much wider meaning. Having failed to make this investigation of the context, he misrepresented the Catholic doctrine.

The second, and the least excusable, mistake of interpretation which he commits is his substitution of an abbreviated and inadequate form of words for the exact language in the condemned proposition. This is illustrated in the first and the fifth of his statements of Catholic doctrine. In the former he leaves out the vital qualification already mentioned, namely, "guided by the light of reason," while in the latter he omits the very important phrase "a Christian state." As a consequence, his description of the Catholic doctrine on this point implies Church control of the public schools in a country such as the United States. The proposition which the Pope condemned expressly declared that the Church should have no control over the public schools of a *Christian* state, even of a Catholic state.

His third error is one of which he has no monopoly. It has been perpetrated by almost every person who considers Papal condemnations of erroneous doctrine from an unfriendly point of view. It consists of the assumption that the true doctrine on the subject affected by the condemnation is ascertained by formulating the *contrary* of the proposition condemned. In fact, the correct doctrine is expressed by the *contradictory* proposition. That this is the

72

correct rule of construction Mr. Fountain could easily have ascertained by noting in the article of the *Catholic Encyclopedia* from which he quotes, namely, *Syllabus,* the following sentences: "The view held by the Church in opposition to each thesis is contained in the contradictory proposition of each of the condemned theses. This opposition is formulated in accordance with the rules of dialectics by prefixing to each proposition the words 'it is not true that . . .' " This construction must appear to Mr. Fountain the only one possible as soon as he has accompanied me on a little excursion into the field of elementary logic. He has assumed that the denial of a universal affirmative proposition implies the assertion of the universal contrary, whereas the opposing proposition is merely a particular negative. Suppose you assert that every Negro is named Johnson. When I denounce this as false, I do not by implication assert the contrary universal, that *no* Negro is named Johnson. All that my denial commits me to is the proposition that *not all* Negroes bear that cognomen. This elementary rule of dialectics is violated by Mr. Fountain when he assumes that the condemnation of Nos. IV and VIII is equivalent to the affirmation of the corresponding propositions in his second list. In extenuation he may plead ignorance of dialectics, but what excuse can he give for ignoring the plain words of the article, *Syllabus,* in the *Catholic Encyclopedia?* This article informs us that condemnation of the proposition which he has labeled IV does not mean that "in every conceivable case of conflicting laws the greater right is with the state"; and, referring to VIII, that, "if the modern claim of general separation between Church and State is rejected, it does not follow that separation is not permissible in any case." In other words, the condemnation of these two propositions implies no greater assertion of positive doctrine than that the state should not *always* prevail in a conflict between its laws and those of the Church, and that the Church should not *always* be separated from the state. Mr. Fountain was acquainted with this article in the *Catholic Encyclopedia;* yet he tells us that the Catholic doctrine requires Church and State to be always united. He had also read the Encyclical on *Catholicity in the United States,* in which Pope Leo declared by clear implication that in this country separation of Church and State is lawful. "We ought not," said the Pope, "draw the conclusion that . . . it would be universally lawful or expedient for State and Church to be, as in America, dissevered and divorced." Exactly. The fact that the separation doctrine is condemned implies no more than that separation is not always and everywhere the best arrangement.

I have taken up a great deal of space in refuting Mr. Fountain's extraordinary assumptions and assertions concerning these propositions in the *Syllabus* of Pius IX because no other Papal document has been in our time so much misunderstood and misrepresented. I have done so, not with any expectation that Mr. Fountain will not have imitators to repeat the old mistakes and perversions, but in the hope that men of good-will and average intelligence will hesitate before expressing themselves dogmatically on the subject. After all, the interpretation of canon law, like that of civil law, is a science. It has its own rules and its own methods, a comprehension of which is not acquired by intuition, let the intellect be ever so brilliant and capacious. If this caution is kept in mind by the well-disposed and the competent, we can bear with the dishonesties of the malevolent and the futilities of amateur canonists.

THE UNITED STATES

At the end of this section of his paper Mr. Fountain refers to the questions and answers on Church and State contained in the *Manual of Christian Doctrine,* to which Mr. Marshall devoted so much space in his rejoinder to Governor Smith's reply. A brief comment on this portion of that volume may not be out of place here. It might take this form: The *Manual* states the traditional doctrine on the union of Church and State in an extreme and indeed repellent form and without adequate qualification as regards other than Catholic states; the book was written in France; while it is rather widely used in Catholic secondary schools, there is no evidence that the section on the relations of Church and State has been taken seriously by the average teacher or that any pupil has gotten from it the notion that we ought to have a union between the Catholic Church and the American state; finally, the translator of the book might well have omitted this section, as not adapted to conditions in America.

He goes on to quote from the *Catholic Encyclopedia* this statement: "The ideal relation between Church and State is to be found not in the separation of the two but in their harmonious co-operation." Well, what of it? Our industrial system is not ideal either, but most of us are not seeking its overthrow. And there is nothing in the Constitution of the United States which declares that the policy of separation is an ideal arrangement, or which forbids any American citizen to hold that it is not ideal.

In *The State and the Church,* by Ryan and Millar, I said that the doctrine of union between Church and State has full application only to the completely Catholic state. This means a political community that is either exclusively or almost exclusively made up of Catholics. In the opinion of Father Pohle, "there is good reason to doubt if there still exists a purely Catholic state in the world." The propositions of Pope Pius IX condemning the toleration of non-Catholic sects do not now, says Father Pohle, "apply even to Spain or the South American republics, to say nothing of countries possessing a greatly mixed population." He lays down the following general rule: "When several religions have firmly established themselves and taken root in the same territory, nothing else remains for the state than either to exercise tolerance toward them all, or, as condi-

75

tions exist today, to make complete religious liberty for individuals and religious bodies a principle of government."[2]

Mr. Fountain quotes an equivalent statement of mine which occurs in the same chapter to the effect that when the Pope teaches the union of Church and State he is not referring to such a state as ours. "This argument," says Mr. Fountain, "cannot be maintained." Why? Mr. Fountain does not contend that Pope Leo or any other Pope has ever commanded American Catholics to oppose the separation of Church and State, or to strive for a union of the two. Implicitly Mr. Fountain admits that Catholics are under no degree of ecclesiastical obligation to seek a change in the present arrangement. Inferentially he concedes that Governor Smith was right in his contention that Catholics can conscientiously approve the separation of Church and State in America, and that nothing in the Papal teaching on this subject furnishes ground for accusing Catholics of disloyalty or for refusing to support the candidacy of a Catholic for President of the United States. Therefore, all Mr. Fountain's arguments up to this point were superfluous and represented a waste of his own time and that of his readers.

Why, then, does he say that "this argument cannot be maintained"? Because Pope Leo has said that it is the duty of all Catholics to endeavor to bring back all civil society to the pattern and form of Christianity which is found in the Catholic Church. But this "pattern and form" implies the union of Church and State in all civil society, including, necessarily, the United States. In other words, Catholics are not bound explicitly and now to seek a union of Church and State in this country, but they are committed to that program implicitly, inasmuch as they are obliged to try to make America Catholic in the indefinite future.

[2] *Catholic Encyclopedia*, article "Tolerance."

UNION OF CHURCH AND STATE

THE REAL "DANGER"

This is the one and only contribution which Mr. Fountain's paper makes to the discussion. Of course other men have made the same point, but it has not been stressed heretofore in the controversy that has been occasioned by the possible candidacy of Governor Smith for the office of President of the United States. Mr. Fountain might with advantage have restricted his paper to this single topic. This, then, is the real danger which he foresees, and against which he would warn his countrymen: Five hundred or five thousand or fifty thousand years hence the majority of Americans may be Catholics, and they may change the Constitution so as to bring about a union of Church and State.

Digressing from this topic, Mr. Fountain quotes Pope Leo XIII in condemnation of such a thing as a national Catholic Church in America, or anywhere else. To be sure, a national Catholic Church is undesirable and impossible. The true Church must be one in doctrine everywhere, and one in obedience to the Vicar of Christ. A national Catholic Church is about as rational as a national multiplication table. Mr. Fountain would like to see the Church in America "imbued with the American spirit." In a sense it has that character, just as in other countries it reflects something of the national spirit. The Church in our country is sufficiently American in spirit to be of peculiar service to our social and national well-being. More than that is unnecessary.

In Mr. Fountain's opinion, the "fine political creed" with which Governor Smith closes his letter "is wholly contrary to the age-long and universal teaching of the Catholic Church." Mr. Fountain's authority as an interpreter of the "universal teaching of the venerable Church" has already been sufficiently discredited. I prefer to accept the authority of Governor Smith's ecclesiastical superiors, Cardinal Hayes and Pope Pius XI. So far as I know, neither of them has admonished Governor Smith that his "fine political creed" is out of harmony with Catholic principles.

At this point Mr. Fountain returns to the consideration of the "future and the ominous possibilities it may contain. . . ." "If the time should come," he says, "when Catholics are in the majority in this country and wield great political power, the Bishops might seek to bring about a union of Church and State." Mr. Fountain assumes too much. There are several countries, both on this hemisphere and in Europe, whose populations are today Catholic by great majorities, yet the Pope has not ordered their rulers to establish a union of Church and State. Of course Mr. Fountain is aware of this, but he is not willing to take any chances. Hence, he opposes a Roman Catholic's becoming President of these United States because it would be the first step toward giving his Church "prestige that it could and would use as a vantage ground, and more power and more influence with which to impress upon our people its political conception of the Christian Church, with the consequent subjection of the state thereto. . . . Hence, not only should no Catholic be made President, but no Catholic should be elected to any political office."

Why does he confine his opposition to the field of politics? The "prestige" of the Church is increased in consequence of the high position occupied by Catholics in industry, in the professions, in science, in education, in social service and in activities of every kind. Why not inaugurate a general Protestant boycott against Catholic merchants, manufacturers, bankers, lawyers, doctors, engineers and, in fact, against Catholics who hold high-salaried positions in any department of American life? Why not try to keep them all from rising above the level of unskilled laborers? The "prestige" of the Church in America has been enhanced by the sacrifices of the thousands upon thousands of American Catholics who have risked and lost their lives in the service of their country. Why not guard against

78

this sort of thing by forbidding members of the Catholic Church to enlist in the army or the navy?

If Mr. Fountain will pardon a personal reference, I would remark that for more than a quarter of a century I have been active in the fight for wider social justice. In this work I have, both in my native state and in the city of Washington, been closely associated with scores of my non-Catholic fellow-countrymen, including not a few clergymen. More than one of them have been kind enough to characterize my work in terms which imply that it has had a not unfavorable effect upon the "prestige" of my Church. By the logic of Mr. Fountain's argument these good Protestant men and women should forthwith withdraw from me their association and co-operation. The Federal Council of Churches should order my good friends, the Revs. F. E. Johnson, Worth M. Tippy and Charles S. Macfarland, to cease their indirect contributions to the "prestige" of the Catholic Church.

"A HIDEOUS PREJUDICE"

The sum of the matter is that Mr. Fountain would, from fear of a remote and hypothetical danger, sentence the Catholic people of America to be treated by their non-Catholic fellow-citizens as veritable Pariahs.

The following is not an unfair summary of his paper as a whole. The first two-sevenths are superfluous and useless; the greater part of the next four-sevenths is a reassertion of charges that have been thoroughly exploded in Governor Smith's reply and elsewhere; the last few paragraphs conjure up a contingency so hypothetical and so remote that it does not justify a moment's worry in a well-balanced mind, and they propose an ostracism of American Catholics as atrocious as any that has ever been suggested by the A. P. A. or the Ku Klux Klan.

It is all profoundly discouraging, not only to Catholics but to all lovers of justice and haters of intolerance. His repetition of the calumny that the Catholics of America are required by their religious authorities to desire and seek a union of Church and State in our country, after that charge had been repeatedly refuted, indicates one of two things: that he is either insincere or a victim of, to quote the words of the New York *Times*, "a hideous prejudice." I am sure that it is upon the latter horn of the dilemma that he is impaled. And I refrain from giving the term "prejudice" any meaning more unfavorable than it bears in the definition of the Century Dictionary: "An opinion or decision formed without due examination of the facts or arguments which are necessary to a just or impartial determination; a prejudgment; also a state of mind which forms or induces prejudgment. . . ."

As I began this paper, so I close it, with a reference to the concluding paragraph of Governor Smith's reply to Marshall, but my prayer is not so ambitious as that offered by the Governor. I do not think that we have a right to expect such a large-scale miracle. My prayer goes no further than this, that Almighty God may grant Mr. Fountain the grace to become, at a not too distant date, thoroughly ashamed of his performance.

8. Catholic Officials and Catholic Voters

To a Fearful Patriot

MY DEAR MR. ——: . . . You understand Catholic teaching to mean "that the Roman Catholic official is guilty of sin if he enacts laws which protect" you in the exercise of that freedom of speech which is guaranteed by the Constitution. In this respect your "understanding of Roman Catholic teaching" is ridiculously and hopelessly wrong. Starting from the false premise that your inferences about Catholic teaching are correct you easily pass to the astonishing conclusion: "It is possible and probable that the Roman Catholic public official will find himself unable to support hundreds of our statutes." I should be interested to hear of even one statute of this sort. Your assertion that Catholic officials "probably have dispensations to ignore certain Church laws" is gratuitous and unworthy of anyone who pretends to reason logically or to judge fairly.

Your interpretations not only of Catholic doctrine, but of constitutional law and obligation, are loose and faulty. For example, you seem to think that because Governor Smith criticized the Eighteenth Amendment and helped to bring about a repeal of the New York State Enforcement Act he was violating his oath to support the Constitution. If you will read the very able address delivered by Governor Ritchie at the Institute of Public Affairs held at the University of Virginia, August, 1929, or the book by Professor McBain of Columbia University Law School, entitled *Prohibition, Legal and Illegal,* you will find that the oath taken by the governors of the several states does not include or imply any such obligation. . . .

You "emphatically" deny that I have said that a Catholic may take a true oath to defend the Constitution of the

81

United States. Now, I had thought I had said that very thing in my characterization of certain statements of yours as "wrong and erroneous." However, I will try to be more specific, since your demands under this head are so meticulous. Hence, I assert without qualification that "a true Catholic may take a true oath to maintain, defend and preserve the Constitution of the United States." I wish to add that I have never heard any bishop or priest disagree with this proposition, nor have I ever read of a dissent from it uttered by priest, bishop or Pope. . . .

I have no intention of entering upon a discussion with you concerning the meaning of any of the condemned propositions which appear in the *Syllabus* of Pope Pius IX, further than to remind you that interpretation of them is a highly technical matter and that no interpretation is correct which leaves out of account the context in the original documents from which they were taken. If you want to go into this matter further, I suggest that you read the article on the *Syllabus* of Pius IX in the *Catholic Encyclopedia* and also the discussion between the Rev. Mr. Fountain and myself in *Current History*, March, 1928.[1] Meantime, I "emphatically" assert that there is nothing in the *Syllabus* which prevents a Catholic official from taking an honest and conscientious oath to support the Constitution. As I told you in my last letter, the whole trouble with you is that you think you are interpreting correctly certain statements of doctrine and discipline and applying them correctly to conditions in the United States, whereas you are giving a wrong interpretation and a wrong application. The suggestion which I made in my last letter that you take an attitude of diffidence in your own capacity to interpret Catholic teaching still remains pertinent.

Ex-Governor Smith and Mayor Walker have *not* "been compelled to violate the teachings and laws of the Church" in the discharge of their public duties. When you assert the

---

[1] No. 7 of the papers in this volume.

82

contrary you are giving expression to your own inference from Catholic teaching, not to a fact.

You may have "refrained from using any but authoritative and approved sources," but you have not refrained from misusing and misinterpreting these documents. Of course, it is always physically possible for you to hold you know more about interpreting these sources than do the Catholic Bishops. . . .

You say that you are still "of the opinion that the passage at issue [Proposition XLV of the *Syllabus of Errors* condemned by Pope Pius IX] was intended to apply to the United States" and that you "believe the majority of canonists and learned laymen are in favor of [that] opinion." You think that your interpretation of authoritative Catholic documents is more correct than that of the Catholic authorities themselves, and you make assertions concerning the opinions held by "canonists and learned laymen" when you have no adequate evidence to support these assertions.

You say that I deny that there is anything in the *Syllabus* of Pius IX "which prevents a Catholic official from taking an honest and conscientious oath to support the Constitution." That is correct. You go on to charge me with "admitting that the Constitution requires the upholding of errors condemned in the *Syllabus*." This statement of yours is uncalled for and false, for in my letter of October 3, which was before you, I explicitly repudiated such an admission.

What you mean is that if I were logical I ought to admit that the Constitution requires officials to uphold some of the errors condemned by Pope Pius IX. While you may honestly hold this opinion about my defective logic, you are not thereby justified in saying that I have actually drawn the conclusion which you think I ought to have drawn. This is dishonest polemics on your part.

Let me make my position entirely clear, if I am capable of doing so. Not a single proposition in the *Syllabus* is condemned either explicitly or implicitly in the Constitu-

83

tion of the United States or in any of the state constitutions, nor are the actions or principles which are condemned in these propositions of the *Syllabus* imposed by either the federal or state constitutions upon any federal or state official. You think that the federal or the state constitutions do affirm and require some things which Pope Pius IX condemned in the *Syllabus of Errors.* You are mistaken because you have not interpreted these propositions correctly. As I informed you in an earlier letter, I am not going to discuss with you all the propositions of the *Syllabus* which you think you have presented. However, I am willing to call your attention to certain flagrant mistakes that you have made. Some of these mistakes you will find noted in my reply to Rev. Mr. Fountain.[2] You make the general mistake of confusing statements of political policy with statements of ethical principle. For example, Proposition XV in the *Syllabus* expresses a moral right in the field of freedom of religion. Pius IX rejected such a moral right. You think that the Constitution in the First Amendment asserts freedom of religion as a moral right, whereas it does nothing of the sort. It merely prohibits Congress from making any law interfering with freedom of religion. This is a matter of political policy. The men who wrote this amendment into the Constitution were concerned with practical policies of government, not with ethical principles about freedom of religion or freedom of speech.

On the other hand, you attribute to our federal or state constitutions powers which they do not confer upon Congress and the state legislatures respectively; powers, which as a matter of fact, they deny to the law-making bodies. For example, Propositions XIX, XX and XLVIII of the *Syllabus* declare that civil governments have the right to limit arbitrarily and even to abolish the opportunity of the Church to exercise its functions and also to prevent the Church from setting up matrimonial impediments for its own subjects. As a matter of fact, our political constitu-

---

[2] No. 7 of the papers in this volume.

tions forbid our governments to interfere in this way with the Church, inasmuch as they guarantee freedom of religion. Finally, you assert that ex-Governor Smith and Mayor Walker have disobeyed papal authority inasmuch as they have upheld freedom of conscience and freedom of speech, whereas these were condemned by Gregory XVI. Here again, you are confusing ethical principle and political policy. Gregory XVI declared that the doctrines of complete freedom of conscience and of speech were morally wrong. The Constitution of the State of New York makes no pronouncements on this ethical question. It merely guarantees a reasonable amount of freedom of speech as a matter of practical political policy. In passing, I might remark that the unlimited freedom of conscience and of speech which Gregory XVI condemned are not guaranteed even as a matter of policy by any of our political constitutions.

There are certain forms of words in some of the propositions of the *Syllabus* which are explicit or implicit in our political constitutions. In every case, however, the sense of these words in the condemned propositions is different from the sense which they bear in our constitutional provisions and implications. No partial statement of a proposition in the *Syllabus* can be fairly interpreted without the remainder. Moreover, no entire proposition of the *Syllabus* can be rightly understood until it is examined in the original document from which it was taken. The sense which the proposition has in the original document is the sense in which it is condemned in the *Syllabus*. Now, I venture to say that you have not seen this wider context of a single one of the propositions of the *Syllabus* which you quote or mutilate. Again, I would suggest that an attitude of diffidence is a reasonable one for you to take when you are tempted to think that you know just what the propositions of the *Syllabus* express and what they imply.

You ask whether I and my fellow instructors in the Catholic University teach doctrine in conformity with my answer to the Rev. Mr. Fountain. The answer without qualification is in the affirmative. And I venture to say that the same doctrine is taught in every Catholic college, seminary and university in the United States, and, in all probability in every such institution throughout the world.

You say that you "have argued from the standpoint of the majority of the canonists." Pardon my directness, but I must assure you that you have done nothing of the sort when you have argued that a Catholic official cannot honestly take his oath of office to support the Constitution of the United States. You will not be able to find a single canonist, or bishop, or Pope, who interprets either the encyclicals of Leo XIII or the *Syllabus* of Pius IX as in any way forbidding a Catholic to take such an oath. Your demand that I prove that my interpretation is right and yours wrong by "references to papal utterances or the laws of the Church" is preposterous. It is the kind of thing which I told you in my first letter makes me weary. Catholic officials have been taking the oaths which you say they cannot conscientiously take for upwards of a century and a half. In all that time, neither priest, bishop nor Pope has told any of them that such an oath was inconsistent with Catholic teaching. This evidence ought to be sufficient to satisfy any reasonable person concerning the lawfulness of such oaths and the interpretations put upon the oaths on the one hand and Catholic teaching on the other by the Catholic authorities. In the face of this evidence, the demand that the Church authorities should "stand and deliver" a formal interpretation of Catholic teaching against the unfriendly interpretations put upon it by incompetent outsiders is little short of impudent.

A SUGGESTION TO CHARLES C. MARSHALL

Mr. Marshall maintains that if the Catholics were sufficiently numerous in this country they would under the leadership of the Pope, "change the Constitution, make the Roman Catholic religion the state religion and the Roman

Catholic doctrine the foundation and crown of public education." This is a rash and gratuitous incursion into the field of prophecy. Approximately two-thirds of the population, properly distributed throughout the states, would probably be able to amend the Constitution in the way Mr. Marshall fears. What right has he to predict that such a Catholic proportion would "do just what the Roman Catholic majority and the Pope have done in Italy"? The chances are easily one hundred to one that they would do nothing of the sort. In following this course, they would not be violating "Roman Catholic doctrine," for it nowhere requires a Catholic majority to put into effect the Catholic principles of the ideal relations between Church and State as soon as they possess the requisite political power. The situation would not be quite so simple.

For the sake of argument, however, we will assume the correctness of Mr. Marshall's prediction. The dread events which he foresees are either so near and so probable as to constitute a present danger which good citizens are obliged to counteract now, or they are not of that character. In the latter hypothesis, all that Mr. Marshall has written on the relations between Church and State, beginning with his letter to Governor Smith, was uncalled for, impertinent and unworthy of any man who professes to be a realist. On the other hand, if he really believes that these dreaded future contingencies should even now be considered and prevented, he ought, as a good citizen, to do everything within his power to curtail the political and civil rights of Catholics.

Towards the end of his letter, he declares that he will "do nothing so foolish" as to petition the courts and legislature to deprive Catholics of their constitutional rights. Obviously that course would be foolish, in view of the constitutional limitations upon legislative and judicial authority. There is, however, a way open to him that would be at once constitutional and tremendously effective. He could advocate and agitate for such changes in the Constitution and statutes of the states as would deprive Catholic citizens of the right to vote, the right to practice and propagate their religion and the rights of free speech, free press, and free assemblage. These changes would undoubtedly make the contingency of a union between the Catholic Church and the American state much more improbable and remote than it now seems to Mr. Marshall. To have initiated the campaign for their accomplishment should be a great comfort to him as a vigilant citizen and patriot.

"The right of Roman Catholics to vote and hold office in this country is as effectually guaranteed by the present Federal Constitution as the right to life itself," says Mr. Marshall. This is an astonishing assertion to come from a lawyer. The right to life is secured against Congress and the states in the Fifth and Fourteenth Amendments, respectively. The right to hold office is quite as comprehensively guaranteed in the last clause of the Sixth Article of the Constitution. The right to vote, however, is protected only against Congressional interference. All the other rights specified above are in the same position. Neither the First, nor the Fourteenth, nor the Fifteenth Amendments to the Constitution would, or could, prevent the states from depriving Catholics of these rights.

For Mr. Marshall's edification, I would call attention to just a few of the many decisions of the Supreme Court which establish the proposition that I have just laid down: on the right to vote, *United States* vs. *Reese,* 92 U. S. 214, and eight other decisions; on religious liberty, *Permoli* vs. *First Municipality,* 3 How. 609, and a dozen other decisions; on the other liberties, *United States* vs. *Cruickshank,* 92 U. S. 552; on the effect of the Fourteenth Amendment, *Maxwell* vs. *Dow,* 176, U. S. 581. Judged by their vote in the last presidential election, there are several states in which Mr. Marshall might obtain a wide and sympathetic hearing in the campaign I have suggested.

This course ought to approve itself to Mr. Marshall as peculiarly urgent, in view of a more immediate danger to

88

which he has in many places called the attention of the American public. In a letter to the *Forum* magazine, published in July or August, 1928, written in reply to my review of his book, *The Roman Catholic Church in the Modern State,* which had appeared in the same magazine the preceding June, Mr. Marshall said that "the obedience and subordination of the citizen, irrespective of his free conscience, in all matters belonging to morals, to the sovereignty of the Pope as a sovereignty imposed on all Christian citizens by the act of God, under the penalty of damnation, obstructs the exercise, in matters of relating morals, of that free conscience on which the civic order or system of the modern state depends." Referring to discrepancies between the canonical and the civil status governing marriage and education, he questions "whether a Roman Catholic can properly discharge a political trusteeship over matters so affected by the differences and disagreements between the laws of his Church and the State without the risk of doing violence to one allegiance or the other. Different minds will resolve the question differently, but the grave difficulties between the Roman Catholic Church and the American states, to the existence of which Dr. Ryan gives expression as pointed out above, cannot be ignored, however the citizen may decide to cast his vote." In the New York *World,* August 20, 1928, he stressed again the control of the Pope over the consciences of Catholic citizens and declared: "A situation so anomalous cannot be left to silence in a political campaign in which a highly respected Roman Catholic is a candidate for the presidency."

While Mr. Marshall has carefully refrained from saying that good citizens ought to vote against a Catholic candidate for office, the net effect of his ubiquitous criticisms is to encourage all prejudiced persons to cast their ballots in that way. On account of his high professional standing, and on account of the lofty academic plane from which he insinuates this alleged danger to the American Republic, the doubts which he expresses do more harm than the more

89

positive assertions of cheap politicians and notorious bigots. If he were an unprejudiced realist, he would recognize that he had completely failed in his book, *The Roman Catholic Church in the Modern State,* to show that the danger lurking in possible and hypothetical conflicts between the Catholic Church and the American states had been translated from possibility into actuality at any time or in any state since the foundation of our government.

Since he is not an unprejudiced realist, he ought at least to be sufficiently courageous and consistent to draw from his argument the conclusions which many others have drawn, and which necessarily follows from the emphasis which he has, in so many places, put upon this alleged danger. He should not only urge his fellow citizens to vote against Catholic candidates for office, but seek to have Catholics deprived of those political, civil and religious rights which are at the disposal of the several states. To the field of activity which I have suggested above, I might well add the State of Rhode Island, where Catholics are approximately half the population, and where, in the inevitably near event of their becoming a majority, they might take steps to deprive all non-Catholics of those same political, civil and religious rights.

Again, I confront Mr. Marshall with the dilemma stated above: Either the dangers which he stresses are sufficiently near and urgent to require cognizance and counteracting measures now, or they are not. If they are, Mr. Marshall, as a good citizen, should advocate the practical measures that I have suggested. If the dangers are not of this definiteness and magnitude, he stands convicted of arousing animosity against and inflicting grave inconvenience and injuries upon millions of his fellow citizens. He may impale himself upon whichever horn he chooses, but he cannot find room between them.

90

9. Religion in the Presidential Election of 1928[1]

T HIS paper represents an attempt to estimate the part played by religious antagonism in the defeat of Governor Smith. Attention will be centered upon those states which Governor Smith expected to carry but did not, and which would have assured his electoral success. The views expressed are those of the writer alone.

Probably the majority of participants in a Presidential election make their final choice of candidates on the basis of more than one issue. Their vote is determined by more than one motive. Hence the dominant motive cannot easily be identified. Indeed, the word "dominant" itself is susceptible of at least three meanings. It may indicate that consideration which is merely the most weighty of several in the voter's mind, without being alone sufficient to determine his choice; or that reason which would of itself move him to vote in a certain way, even if all the supplementary factors were absent; or that motive without which the voter would make a different choice from the one that he actually makes. In other words, the dominant motive in this sense not only is more important than all the others combined, but it impels the voter to cast his ballot for the opponent of the one for whom it would have been cast if this motive had not been present. This is the meaning which I shall attach to the phrase "dominant motive" in relation to the religious factor.

The well-known political journalist, Frederick William Wile, thinks that Governor Smith was defeated mainly through "the three P's" — Prohibition, Prejudice and Prosperity. "Prohibition, Prosperity and Protestantism"

[1]Reprinted by special permission of the *Current History Magazine*, the monthly periodical of the New York Times Company. See issue of December, 1928.

91

was the phrase used by Lady Astor. To these we might add a fourth "P," standing for Party. Probably the majority of the voters made their choices between the two candidates mainly, if not exclusively, on the basis of their habitual political affiliations. The existing prosperity, apparent, partial or alleged, undoubtedly was the main determinant in the support given to Hoover by thousands upon thousands who otherwise would have voted for Smith. Prohibition was likewise a considerable factor in the votes cast for Mr. Hoover. But of itself, it probably would not account for more than a relatively small number of these ballots.

Prejudice, the second of Mr. Wile's trinity, and which he declares was probably the most potent, is wider than religious animosity. In the recent election it included snobbishness and a combination of cultural and racial intolerance. Snobbishness, in its highest (or lowest) degree, was exemplified in the case of those persons who voted against Governor Smith because they did not want to see as mistress of the White House a woman who at one time did her own housework. It is estimated that many thousands among the women voters were moved by this species of snobbishness. In a less contemptible form it determined the vote of persons who could not bear to support a candidate who is not a college graduate. Cultural and racial prejudice appeared in those speeches and publications which stressed the connection of Governor Smith with Tammany. Very few of these represented any real fear that Tammany would exert an unfavorable influence upon Governor Smith in the White House, any more than in the Executive Mansion in Albany. To a great majority of those who used or were affected by this factor, Tammany was a symbol of the rising power of an alien, non-Nordic element in our population. Governor Smith in the Presidential chair would vividly express the challenge of this element to the Nordic and Puritan ascendancy. This sort of preju-

92

dice was latent, if not conscious, in the addresses of such men as William Allen White.

The Religious Factor

Finally, we come to that prejudice which is based upon religious affiliation, religious feeling and religious opposition. This is what we are seeking to identify, to isolate and to evaluate among the factors responsible for the defeat of Governor Smith. Writing four days before the election, Mr. Charles Michelson, one of the most intelligent and most reliable of newspaper writers on politics, declared that if Smith were defeated it would be on account of his religion, and that were he a Protestant there would be no doubt of his election. Mr. Michelson asserted, moreover, that this judgment was shared by substantially all the political reporters who had been covering the campaign. A large proportion of the leading newspapers have expressed the same opinion since the election.

Of course, these are fallible human judgments. Are there any specific facts which present an appearance of objective evidence on behalf of the assumption that the religious factor exercised a determining influence? I think there are. Consider the vote in the following states: Connecticut, Missouri, New York, North Carolina, Tennessee, Texas, Virginia and Wisconsin. Had 10 per cent of those who voted for Mr. Hoover in these states cast their ballots for Governor Smith, they would have put these states in the Democratic column. Their combined vote in the Electoral College is one hundred and thirty-nine. Consider now the states of Florida, Illinois and Maryland. If 15 per cent of those who supported Mr. Hoover in these states had given their votes to Governor Smith, he would have had forty-three additional electors. Combining the votes of these two groups of states with the eighty-seven Governor Smith received, we get a total of two hundred and sixty-nine, or three more than were necessary and sufficient. No one who is acquainted with the extent of religious intoler-

93

ance in these states can seriously doubt that these proportions of the persons supporting Mr. Hoover were so dominated by religious considerations that they would have voted for Governor Smith if he had been a Protestant.[2] Many persons associate religious intolerance in politics exclusively with the southern and border states. As a matter of fact, it is intense and extensive in such northern and western states as those that appear in the foregoing list. The enormous increase in the number of women voters in the rural regions throughout the country is of itself sufficient to account for the percentage of religion-determined votes which have been suggested in this paragraph.

It is my deliberate judgment that the foregoing facts, in conjunction with many others that cannot be presented here, demonstrate that without the religious factor Governor Smith would not have been defeated. At any rate, no intelligent person who rejects this judgment can deny that the religious factor was of widespread and profound importance.

How was this brought about? How did the religious factor become practically operative in the campaign? It appeared in three principal forms. The crudest and coarsest form is illustrated in the "Chamber of Horrors" which was set up at the Democratic National Headquarters just before election. This was an exhibit of pamphlets, cards and newspapers. Here are some of the titles borne by these documents: "Convent Horror, Illustrating What Will Happen to American Womanhood if Smith Is Elected"; "Traffic in Nuns"; "Three Keys to Hell"; "Rum, Romanism and Ruin"; "Thirty Reasons Why a Protestant Should Vote for Alcohol Smith." Lest any reader should conclude that "literature" of this sort would have no effect upon American voters, I call attention to the vast membership once embraced by the Ku Klux Klan. Scurrilous and indecent publications of this sort constituted the principal

---

[2] This was written November 8, 1928. The intervening two years have brought convincing confirmation of this estimate.

reading matter that was cherished and circulated by that precious band of "one hundred per cent Americans."

CHARGES AGAINST CATHOLIC DOCTRINE

A somewhat higher, or less disreputable, method of utilizing religious animosity against Governor Smith is exemplified in a long article printed and circulated by Bishop Cannon in the closing days of the campaign. The title was: *Is Southern Protestantism More Intolerant Than Romanism?*—an irrelevant question which aptly indicates the animus and purpose of the author. The greater part of this article was either completely untrue or gravely misleading. Among the untruths were the following assertions: That according to the Catholic Church no Protestant can be saved; that according to Dr. Ryan the government of the United States is morally obliged to profess and promote the Catholic religion; that a Catholic's religious belief "compels him not to follow his conscience, no matter what it may dictate"; that the Catholic "brands all non-Catholic marriages as adulterous and the children of such marriages as illegitimate"; that Pope Pius IX pronounced education outside of the Catholic Church, including our public school system, "a damnable heresy." The misleading statements included references to Masonry, Bible societies, the Y. M. C. A., the reception of the Papal Legate by Mayor Walker and Governor Smith, misused quotations from a chapter contributed by me to the volume, *The State and the Church,* and characterization of two Catholic papers from which quotations were made as "official organs of the Roman Catholic Church." Just how Bishop Cannon could reconcile statements and actions of this sort with his sense of justice and decency, I am unable to imagine. If he really believed that he was stating the truth and the adequate truth, his condition of mind is a sad and disturbing reflection upon his education. However, there are thousands upon thousands of Americans whose education has been similarly neglected or perverted.

95

The third method of injecting religion into the campaign is illustrated by an able religious periodical, the *Christian Century*. In an editorial published on October 18, 1928, this publication defends the right of Protestants to vote against Governor Smith on religious grounds; for, says the writer, "They cannot look with unconcern upon the seating of a representative of an alien culture, of a mediæval Latin mentality, of an undemocratic hierarchy and of a foreign potentate in the great office of the President of the United States." The evident intention of this sort of appeal is to emphasize and deplore the prestige which might come to the Catholic Church in America following the entrance of one of her sons into the White House. Indirect influence of this sort is apparently regarded as the exclusive prerogative of the Protestant churches. If a high class journal, which prides itself as "liberal" could conscientiously use this sort of argument, the same is probably true of thousands upon thousands of educated Protestants.

Happily, the one argument which enjoys any real plausibility received little or no attention during the campaign. That is the contention raised by Mr. Charles C. Marshall and others that danger to American institutions is latent in the Catholic doctrine of the union of Church and State. For some reason, possibly because the intolerant-minded persons retained a modicum of common sense, this fantastic and remote "menace" was not frequently exploited.

Elementary justice and gratitude demand that recognition should be made here of the splendid statements condemning religious animosity in the campaign by many prominent Americans, such as John W. Davis, Raymond B. Fosdick, Henry van Dyke, John Dewey, Rabbi Stephen S. Wise, Edward T. Devine and many others. These men spoke according to the noblest American traditions. In this connection, I cannot pass over the fine address, to which I had the privilege of listening, delivered by Miss Virginia Gildersleeve, Dean of Barnard College, and daughter of the man who for many years was the distinguished head of the Department of Greek at Johns Hopkins University. Miss Gildersleeve defended the thesis that Governor Smith was by all vital tests an educated man. In effect, her address was a most convincing rebuke to and refutation of the snobbishness referred to above as one of the factors in the campaign against Governor Smith. It was peculiarly appropriate as coming from a woman.

CATHOLIC CHURCH NOT IN POLITICS

In the editorial of the *Christian Century,* of which mention has already been made, it was asserted that, "The Roman Catholic Church in this campaign is in politics up to the hilt," and "The Roman Catholic Church will go to the polls almost as one man and vote for Mr. Smith." Both of these statements are false. If the assertion that the Catholic Church is in politics means anything it means that the Church as an organization, through its responsible officials, took part in the recent political campaign. That statement is directly contrary to the fact. No bishop, I am certain, and no priest, so far as I am aware, advocated the election of Governor Smith either from the pulpit or in any other public or general or official manner. Nor did the Church go to the polls either "as one man" or in any other capacity. I have before me a considerable list of very prominent Catholics who supported Mr. Hoover and I am persuaded on the basis of the election returns that a considerable number of Catholics in more than one American city gave their votes to the Republican candidate. Several of my own friends made this choice. Concerning the attitude of the Catholic clergy during the campaign, I would submit a brief quotation from a letter written to the New York *Sun,* October 20, by Ellery Sedgwick, the editor of the *Atlantic Monthly.*

> May I be allowed to bear public and admiring testimony to the dignity, the forbearance and the good citizenship of the Roman Catholic clergy in America? I doubt indeed whether our history affords an instance

of a large and cohesive body of men who, under the bitterest provocation, have better kept their self-control and self-respect. . . . This Church, quite alien to most of us, has taught us a lesson in manners and in morals. It is a commonplace of such reasonable conversation as is still conducted during this campaign that had the Catholic clergy thrown themselves into the hurly-burly after the pattern of their Methodist brothers the Republic would have rocked on its foundations.

Among the millions of Catholics who participated in the election, I venture to say that not one voted *against* Mr. Hoover. A similar statement cannot be made concerning some hundreds of thousands whose support he received. Catholics voted for Governor Smith either for party reasons, or because they regarded him as the more suitable candidate, or because they were glad to be able to vote for a fellow Catholic, or because they resented the effort to defeat him on account of his religion, or because they wished to disprove and destroy the unwritten tradition that no Catholic is fit to be or can be elected President of the United States. All these classes of Catholics believed that he was qualified for the great office which he sought; consequently they were not acting as bad citizens. Thousands of high-minded Protestants voted for Smith for these same reasons.

While I am disappointed and disillusioned on account of the injection of religious intolerance into the campaign, I am not discouraged. Nor have I the heart to attribute moral blame to the great majority of my fellow countrymen and women who voted against Governor Smith mainly or exclusively because he is a Catholic. They are inheritors of a long anti-Catholic tradition, compact of misrepresentation and falsehood. They have never had adequate opportunity to learn the facts about the Catholic Church. But I cannot feel so indulgent toward the men who have exploited religious intolerance in the campaign

98

from their pulpits, from the platform and by the written and printed word. Most of these men know better or are culpably ignorant. If the disgraceful history of the recent campaign in this matter is not to be repeated, there will be required a long, a comprehensive and an intensive campaign of education to enlighten those that sit in darkness.

Obviously, I am not pleased with the results of the election. As a Catholic, I cannot be expected to rejoice that some millions of my countrymen would put upon me and my co-religionists the brand of civic inferiority. As an American, I cannot feel proud that the spirit of the Sixth Amendment to the Constitution is thus flouted and violated. As a believer in personal freedom and political honesty, I cannot feel cheerful over the prospect of four more years of the arrogant, despotic and hypocritical domination from which we are suffering by the grace of the Anti-Saloon League. As a democrat and a lover of justice, I cannot look with complacency upon a President-elect who, judged by his campaign addresses, believes that the economic welfare of the masses should be confided, practically without reservation, to the care of corporate business, in the naïve faith that corporate business will dispense and hand down universal justice. This is industrial feudalism. Possibly it may turn out to be benevolent. In any case it will do violence to the most fundamental and valuable traditions of the America that we have known and loved.

10. Assaults Upon Democracy

THIS topic has been suggested by *An American's Catechism on Democracy*. In itself, it has little or no merit but it is fairly typical of the attacks upon and objections to Catholic democratic theory which have not infrequently been made during the last few years. Although the pamphlet seems to have been sent to a considerable number of the Catholic clergy, it does not disclose the name of either the author, the publisher or the printer. This complete and mystifying anonymity seems to imply that the author is lacking either in courage or in an adequate sense of humor.

On page 2 we find this question: "But are we not all equal because we all partake of the same nature?" The answer ought to be either "yes" or "no," but the author apparently had not the courage to reply with a forthright negative. Instead he disposes of the question by a smart and tricky assertion: "Similarity does not imply equality." Here he overreached himself; for similarity does imply equality under whatever aspect it exists. If I say that a monkey is similar to a man because he has two hands, I imply that the monkey is equal to the man in that particular; that is, in so far as both possess two hands. I do not commit myself to the proposition that the hands are in all details equal.

Of course, the correct answer to the question is in the affirmative. In more than one place St. Thomas declares that "all men are by nature equal." Indeed, this doctrine was "a commonplace of the Schoolmen."[1] The natural equality of men consists in the fact that they are equal as persons; that is, that they all possess intrinsic worth, are equally sacred and equal in the possession of certain natural

---

[1] Alfred O'Rahilly in *Studies*, March, 1920, p. 14.

rights, particularly those of life, liberty, physical integrity, marriage, access to the bounty of the earth and opportunity for reasonable life and for development of personality. While natural rights are not always equal in *content*, they are always equally inviolable, and in every case they include that minimum of goods and immunities which is necessary for the attainment of the individual's proper end. The equality existing among men is, therefore, very considerable and vastly more important than their inequalities.

In the answer to the next question the author rejects democracy because it implies "that all men are equal," a fact which he thinks he has got rid of by his evasive statement about "similarity." The equality which we have just set forth is a sound and adequate basis for democracy.

On pages 3 and 4 the *Catechism* rejects the doctrine of equality and political democracy defended by Cardinal Bellarmine. The author denies that men have the right to confer ruling authority upon the person whom they designate. God, he declares, "has predestined every man for a suitable position in society. He knows perfectly who is best fitted to carry out His wishes and to exercise authority in any state." The author seems to be playing with the thought that God rather than the multitude ought to appoint political rulers. Undoubtedly, that would be a much better arrangement for the welfare of society, just as a divine choice of spouses would be more conducive to happy families than the prevailing method of free choice on the part of each. Unfortunately, the author provides us with no formula by which we can ascertain either the persons whom God knows to be fittest to rule or the husbands who would provide the happiest marriages for Mary and Jane and Catherine. In the absence of such a revelation, the rulers must somehow be a matter of human choice. Who is to exercise that choice? Who has a right to exercise it? These are crucial questions which the critics of democracy never face honestly. They do not dare to assert, for example, that the ruler has a right to choose himself and

101

impose himself upon the community by force. Nor do they venture to assert that there exists in every community some *élite* persons to whom God has committed the right of designation. If they were entirely frank, the critics would admit that Bellarmine was correct, that the right to determine the form of government, designate the persons and transfer to them the ruling authority belongs to the whole body of the people. Where else can this right be found? Cathrein does, indeed, contend that in a very primitive society where only one man was capable of carrying on the government, that unique person would have a right to rule, regardless of the wishes of the community.[2] This claim may be conceded as often as Father Cathrein can extract from the pages of history a political community where governing capacity was all concentrated in one man.

On page 5, the pamphlet asserts that Cardinal Bellarmine was wrong because he asserted that all men have equal rights to elect the ruler. The great Cardinal never made any such claim either explicitly or by implication. What he said was that the right to designate and to confer authority upon the ruler rested in "the whole multitude," that is, in the community as a whole. He did not assert that all the individuals possessed that right equally. That was the theory of Rousseau, not of Bellarmine or any other Catholic defender of fundamental democracy.

On the same page we are told that all men are born "subject to constituted authority." Bellarmine never denied this truth, although he pointed out, with St. Thomas and Schoolmen generally, that men have a right to disobey and get rid of "constituted authority" when it degenerates into tyranny. The traditional doctrine on this subject is well summarized by Cardinal Billot, S.J.:

> If at any time the public good requires a new form of government and a new designation of rulers, no pre-existing right of any person or of any family can validly prohibit this change. The right to create a

[2] *Philosophia Moralis*, p. 376.

102

new legitimate government inheres in the community habitually or potentially.[3]

Apparently the author of the *Catechism* does not accept the traditional Catholic teaching on the right to expel tyrants.

On page 8, the *Catechism* informs us that "democracy, in the sense of a government by the people, as a depositary of God's authority, is untenable." This assertion is, as it was meant to be, directly contrary to the teaching of Bellarmine. The doctrine that the people are the depositary (not source) of political authority, which they confer upon the rulers whom they designate, is also closely associated with the name of another great Jesuit, Francisco Suarez; indeed, it is sometimes referred to as "the Jesuit theory." As a matter of fact, it should be called the doctrine of the Scholastics. It was taught by St. Thomas, as he is interpreted by all the authoritative commentators.[4] Professor O'Rahilly cites sixty theologians and canonists who defended this view between the thirteenth century and the seventeenth.[5] The first prominent Catholic writer to reject the traditional doctrine seems to have been Haller, in 1820. About thirty years later he was followed by the Italian Jesuit, Taparelli. Since then it would seem that the majority of Catholic writers on ethics have rejected the ancient doctrine. By a strange irony some of the most prominent among the dissenters are Jesuits. The traditional teaching, which the author of the *Catechism* rejects, is thus summarized by Professor O'Rahilly:

Sovereignty is an essential attribute of the people, as constituting a corporate entity; it is radically and fundamentally inalienable, but for convenience and

---

[3] *De Ecclesia Christi*, sec. 1, chap. 3.
[4] *Summa Theologica*, 1.2, q. 90, a. 3.
[5] *Studies*, March, 1921, p. 43. In the *Irish Theological Quarterly*, October, 1920, the same writer informs us: "I have made a laborious investigation of every accessible Catholic philosopher and theologian from the thirteenth to the nineteenth century. Here is the significant result: fifty-two writers prior to Suarez and eighty-seven after him uphold the principle that government is based on the consent of the governed; sixty-five do not discuss the subject at all; and only seven Gallicans, of very doubtful orthodoxy, reject the principle" (p. 303).

103

efficiency it may be transferred, by and with the consent of the community, for such time and under such conditions as the people deem expedient for the public good. The ultimate test of the juridical validity of any system of government is the consent of the governed."[6]

The next paragraph in the *Catechism* after the one just considered makes the bald assertion that the traditional doctrine "has been condemned by the Church's highest teachers, including Popes Leo XIII and Pius X." Then follow some passages from the document in which Pius X condemned *Le Sillon*.[7] These excerpts include the following quotation which Pope Pius made from the encyclical *Diuturnum Illud* of his immediate predecessor, Pope Leo XIII:

It is necessary to remark here that those who preside over the government of the state may, in certain cases, be chosen by the will and judgment of the multitude without repugnance or opposition to Catholic doctrine. But if this choice marks out the governor, it does not confer upon him the authority to govern; it does not delegate the power, it designates the person who will be invested with it.

On its face, the passage just quoted looks like a repudiation of the doctrine of Bellarmine. The context, however, shows that these words were directed against non-Catholic writers who were following in the footsteps of the "philosophers" of the eighteenth century, of whom the best known is Rousseau. It is preposterous to assume that Pope Leo intended to condemn a doctrine which had been uniformly held by Catholic authorities for upwards of six centuries. Had he entertained the idea of any such drastic action, he would have made his purpose abundantly clear. Referring to the extraordinary assumption that such was Pope Leo's intention, Cardinal Billot declared:

---

[6] *Op. cit.*, p. 49.
[7] *Acta Ap. Sedis* 2 (1910), 616.

We reply that these words merely set forth the pure and simple doctrine of faith against the pressure of innovation with which many were infatuated in the sixteenth century, and which, in the eighteenth century, led to the monstrous error of *The Social Contract*. . . . In a word, the Pope denies what has been unanimously denied at all times by Catholic theologians.[8]

Professor O'Rahilly cites twenty-four writers who discuss this declaration of Pope Leo and who all agree that it was in no sense a condemnation of Bellarmine or any other exponent of the traditional doctrine.

As for the statements by Pope Pius X in the document condemning *Le Sillon,* they were likewise directed against the theory of Rousseau.

According to *Le Sillon,* authority continues to reside in the people after it has been transferred to the ruler: and so to reside in the people that every individual citizen is a sort of king. According to Suarez, the people are the first recipient of authority. They transfer it to the ruler; and after they have transferred it to the ruler it is no longer *formally* in the people but only *radically* or *habitually.* . . . According to *Le Sillon,* the ruler is the mere mandatory or instrument of the people. He is, therefore, wholly dependent on the will of the people in the use or exercise of his authority. It is not his own, he cannot use it as his own. He can do nothing without the consent of the people. According to Suarez, authority is indeed conferred on the ruler by the consent of the people. But he is not the mere mandatory or instrument of the people. He is the minister of God in things temporal. In the use or exercise of authority he is not dependent on the will of the people.[9]

---

[8] *Loc. cit.*

[9] Edward Masterson, S.J., in the *Irish Theological Quarterly*, October, 1921, p. 315. In this and the April, 1921, issue of the same magazine, the writer attacks with devastating effect the assumption that either Leo XIII in his *Diuturnum Illud* or Pius X in the condemnation of *Le Sillon* repudiated or had any intention of repudiating the traditional doctrine as taught by Suarez and Bellarmine and all the rest.

Notwithstanding this and many other clear expositions of the difference between the traditional doctrine and that of *Le Sillon*, a Catholic writer is occasionally found who asserts that the two doctrines are identical and that, in explicitly condemning the latter, Pope Pius X implicitly repudiated the former. Happily these men possess no doctrinal authority and very little authority as private teachers. Notwithstanding the alleged condemnation of the traditional doctrine of Suarez and Bellarmine by two Popes, it continues to be taught in Rome at the Gregorian University, the Carmelite International College and the Benedictine Scholasticate of San Anselmo. In view of these facts, no Catholic who holds to the traditional doctrine need be disturbed by such a brazen charge of unorthodoxy as that contained in *An American's Catechism on Democracy*.

Following the quotation from Pope Pius X, the *Catechism* dogmatically asserts: "So Blessed Cardinal Bellarmine, S.J., was mistaken in this point as well as in his bold statement that all men are free and equal." The first part of this sentence has been sufficiently considered in the preceding paragraphs. A cursory reading has failed to reveal any passage in which the great Cardinal asserted that all men are "free." If he did make the statement, we may feel quite confident that he restricted its meaning in conformity with the facts and right reason. At any rate, we are certain that he did not, as did Rousseau, declare that men were free to set up or not to set up a government; for he says that, whether they will or no, men must be governed by somebody and that they are obliged to transfer the governing authority to some person or to a few persons.[10] As we have seen, he affirmed the common teaching of the Schoolmen that all men are equal. Of course, he was right in the sense in which he understood and defended human equality.

The last assertion of this egregious *Catechism* that we shall consider is that "our Declaration of Independence

[10]*De Laicis*, chap. VI, note 1; chap V.

106

was signed by many good and intelligent men, and yet it contains the false statement we have discussed." The writer does not make it quite clear which one of the statements that he denominated "false" he refers to in this passage; nor does it matter. All the statements in the Declaration which he could possibly have in mind are true: namely, that all men are created equal, that all are endowed by their Creator with certain indestructible rights, that governments derive their just powers from the consent of the governed and that when any government becomes destructive of the ends for which government exists, the people have a right to alter or abolish it and set up a new government. As we have seen in the foregoing paragraphs, all these propositions are in accord with the traditional Catholic doctrine concerning human equality and natural rights, including that of determining the form of government and transferring authority to the ruler, together with the right of making "a new form of government and a new designation of rulers when that is required by the common good and social tranquillity."[11] The author of the *Catechism* is consistently wrong from first to last.

While the *Catechism* is brazen in its effrontery, crude in its composition and puerile in its arguments, it typifies in a general way the assaults upon the ethical basis of democracy which have been made in recent years. Practically all the first class writers, such as Taparelli, Meyer and Cathrein, who refused to accept fully the traditional doctrine as expounded by Bellarmine and Suarez, went no further than to assert that the people had no right to transfer the governing authority, but only the right to designate the governors. This difference in theory amounts to little in practice. If popular choice is necessary to give a man the right to rule, the consent of the people is evidently at the basis of all legitimate government. The hypothesis of a society in which only one man can be found who is fit to govern, may be passed over as negligible, since Cathrein

---

[11] Cardinal Billot, *loc. cit.*

himself admits that outside of patriarchal times it is "perhaps rarely" verified.[12] The significant attacks upon the democratic principle come from those who contend that the ruler may legitimately be designated by "accomplished facts." They would lay the groundwork for justifying almost any form of forcible usurpation, whether by a domestic dictator or a foreign conqueror. Against this insidious repudiation of the traditional Catholic doctrine all its adherents and all lovers of human rights should be constantly on guard.

So much for the principles of democracy in Catholic teaching. Attacks upon the efficiency of democratic institutions and representative government have likewise been frequent in recent years. They have varied from dignified and supposedly scientific presentations, such as that by Faguet in *The Cult of Incompetence* to flippant and intemperate diatribes such as those of Mencken in *Notes on Democracy*. They all agree in the assertion that democratic government works badly in our time. To this general proposition all students of contemporary political institutions would assent, in substance. The inference, however, that democracy should be abolished does not follow any more than that drawn by the Socialists from the fact that the institution of private property is vitiated by grave abuses.

There is one question which the opponents of democratic institutions, if they are political realists, ought frankly to face. It is this: "What are you going to put in the place of representative government?" I do not recall any of the critics of democracy who have seriously and systematically attempted to answer.

As already noted, the crucial question concerning the form of government is: Who shall designate the governing authority? Under democratic constitutions the designation is ultimately made by popular suffrage, more or less widely

---

[12]*Op. cit.*, p. 381. Recall the words of Cassius to Brutus:
"When went there by an age, since the great flood,
But it was famed with more than with one man."

distributed and, let us admit, more or less badly exercised. Only two other methods are practically available: that some strong man should choose himself and rule as dictator, or that the ruler should be chosen by some select group, some kind of oligarchy. As a permanent institution, dictatorship would probably be rejected by the most virulent critics of popular government. Giving the power of designation to an oligarchy seems to have been accomplished in the new Constitution adopted for the people of Italy by Mussolini. The Fascist organization seems to have the elective power which under democratic governments reposes in the whole people. Other special groups might conceivably be intrusted with this authority. In the United States, for example, the executive and legislative officials might be chosen by the Ku Klux Klan, or the Knights of Columbus, or the Masons, or the Rotary Clubs, or the Chambers of Commerce, or groups of University professors, or some other select element of the population. Do the critics of democracy seriously prefer such a method of selection or of election to the method of popular choice? If they shrink from accepting the only practicable substitutes for democratic government, they ought, as honest and sincere men, to devote a share of their attention to proposals for improving and modifying democratic institutions, instead of spending their time upon the easy task of merely destructive criticism.

This paper could not be more appropriately concluded than with a reference to St. Thomas Aquinas. He is often represented as preferring monarchy to any other form of government. Nevertheless, the régime for which he expressed preference was a very limited and qualified sort of monarchy.

> The best arrangement of rulers in any city or kingdom is had when one man is according to merit set at the head to preside over all, and under him are others ruling according to merit; yet such a régime is

109

the concern of all because the rulers are not only elected from all but also elected by all.[18]

Evidently this sort of government would be more accurately described as a democracy than as a monarchy. Not only those immediately under the supreme official *(principantes)*, but the presiding official himself, would be chosen at some kind of popular election. With probably the majority of the political writers of the Middle Ages, St. Thomas preferred an elective to a hereditary monarch. His formula for the best system of government does not differ essentially from that which is actualized in our own federal and state systems.

---

[18] 1-2, q. 105, A.1.

Part III

ECONOMIC QUESTIONS

11. Public Utility Rate Regulation

THE articles by Professor Philip Cabot[1] on public utilities and rate regulation are sufficiently fundamental—not to say revolutionary—to deserve a critical examination. He not only questions the efficacy of regulation in practice but attacks the underlying theory. Public utilities, he maintains, are in the main not of a monopolistic character; even to the extent that they enjoy monopoly power, they can be best regulated on the assumption that they are subject to indirect competition; therefore, the commissions should aim at regulating prices rather than profits.

The success of regulation is today questioned by many persons who would not agree with the central thesis maintained by Professor Cabot. Some of these are believers in public ownership, while others reject that alternative, holding that the necessary and sufficient remedy is to be found in better laws, better technique and more efficient personnel for the regulating commissions. Professor Cabot's criticism assails the central principle or aim of regulation, namely, service at cost through limitation of profits. The attempt to reduce this principle to practice permits, according to his contention, excessive operating costs and excessive rate bases. Since the managers are restricted to a definite rate on investment, they have no incentive to reduce operating costs, which often amount to 75 per cent of the gross earnings. Savings in operating expenses would provoke reductions in rates by the regulating commissions, leaving the companies with no more net profits than they enjoyed under higher rates and less efficient operating methods. In the second place, the present system of regulation encourages the adoption of excessive rate bases through ex-

[1] *Harvard Business Review*, April and July, 1929.

113

cessive construction costs and excessive valuations. The higher the rate base, the higher the profits for the companies. In other words, the companies lose nothing from inefficient operating methods, while they gain from unduly high rate bases. The consumer suffers from both these factors.

OBVIOUS CORRECTIVES

Inefficient operating methods and excessive operating costs could be prevented through adequate supervision by the regulating authorities. Proper systems of accounting and the requirement of comprehensive reports could be imposed upon the utility companies. Apparently no general attempt has yet been made to secure these results. "Only thirty-two states have authorized their commissions to control the accounting of the utility companies in all its phases, yet even in these states control of accounting methods has not been altogether successful . . . Failure to supervise the accounts of utilities is one of the primary weaknesses of state commissions."[2] Until a systematic and wholehearted attempt is made to correct these conditions, the charge that the present theory of regulation necessarily permits or condones financial irregularities and wasteful operation will remain unproved.

As to excessive construction costs, excessive prices paid for utility properties and all other methods of inflating capitalization, the obvious preventive is supervision and control of the securities issued to cover these expenditures. Apparently many of the regulating commissions are unable to exercise this control because they lack the legal authority or the money or the ability or the good-will. In all such cases, the evil results to the consumer are clearly due to deficiency of regulation in practice rather than to any defect in the theory or the institution.

Excessive burdens on the consumer, on account of excessive valuations and costly litigation over valuations, are

---

[2]Mosher and Others, *Electric Utilities—The Crisis in Public Control*, p. 29.

114

real and of considerable magnitude. They will be greatly increased if the Supreme Court should definitely confirm the policy and rules laid down in the Indianapolis Water Company case. In that event, regulation will have failed, not because of anything in the process itself, but because of an ethical theory of value imposed upon the commissions by the Supreme Court. The only adequate relief from that evil condition would come through public ownership and operation. Even if the utilities had to be purchased at reproduction cost, or at some figure approaching that level, there would be a definite gain for the consumer. The rates which he would be called upon to pay could be lower than under private operation because of the lower rate of interest at which the public authorities could obtain the necessary capital for purchasing the properties. At present a rate of 7 per cent is common, while 8 per cent is not unknown in the "fair rates" fixed by the courts. In the Indianapolis Water Company case the Supreme Court allowed a valuation of $19,000,000 and a rate of 7 per cent. Even if the city of Indianapolis had to pay that amount for the property, it would be able to effect a considerable saving to the users of water ($380,000 annually), inasmuch as it probably could obtain money at 5 per cent.

Professor Cabot would reject this proposal as a general remedy for excessive valuation on two grounds: first, that public operation is less efficient than private operation and second, that all the utilities except water companies are competitive and can best serve the public by being treated and regulated on this assumption. The first of these objections is sufficiently refuted by the achievements of the Ontario Hydro-electric, the Port of New York Authority and a large number of successful municipal utilities throughout the United States and Europe. The second objection involves the central thesis of Professor Cabot's constructive proposals and will be dealt with in later paragraphs of this paper.

Although he points out the evil effects of excessive valu-

115

ations, he rejects the rule of prudent investment. His reasons, however, are not ethical but purely economic. Prudent investment as a rate base would not, he maintains, bring about "stability in terms of purchasing power, the only kind of stability in the markets in which these public-utility services must be sold." One might inquire why such stability is any more necessary for the utilities than it is for the concerns that produce wheat, shoes, steel or any other commodity. The owners of all these run the risk of finding that their dollars have fallen or risen in purchasing power between the beginning and the end of any year. From this point of view Professor Cabot's argument has very wide scope and by implication calls for a stabilized dollar. At any rate, his assumption that, because utility rates on the prudent investment basis are lower than "the index figure for other services and commodities," they would greatly accentuate a general level of high prices, is pretty far fetched. No matter upon what basis rates be fixed, whether prudent investment or reproduction cost or some point between these, the demand for utility products and services would increase to some extent during a boom period. The utility companies would be compelled to enlarge their plants and facilities accordingly. That the amount of demand and the consequent enlargement of plant would be so much greater in case of a low than in case of a high rate base as to cause a notable rise in the general price level seems to be entirely improbable. When prices are rising, all the available capital is put to some productive use. If it were not put into public utilities, it would be employed to inflate production in some other field.

A VALID OBJECTION

There is one fundamental respect in which Professor Cabot's attack upon the prevailing theory and practice of regulation is valid. It has to do neither with ineffective regulation nor with juridically imposed rules of valuation. In fact, the more effective the regulation, the more powerful

116

will be the temptation confronting utility managers to follow the undesirable course indicated. Regulation necessarily discourages managerial initiative, efficiency and progress, since it aims at transferring these gains sooner or later from the utility to the consumers in the form of lower rates. For example, a utility company may, through improved methods of management, be able to earn 12 per cent on its valuation; as soon as this becomes known to a vigilant commission the latter will reduce rates to such a level as to enable the company to earn only 7 per cent or 8 per cent. If the company is forever prevented from earning more than a fair rate of return, regardless of its savings through greater efficiency, why should it strive to be efficient? Why should its managers not content themselves with that mediocre and routine kind of operation which will enable them to obtain just the allotted rate of return?

To this objection there are two answers. First, not all the gains of efficiency can be immediately transferred by the commission to the consumer. The fact that the company is enabled through improved methods of operation to make more than the allotted rate of profit does not become known to the commission until the end of the fiscal year. Hence, the gains of efficiency produced during the preceding months are secure in the treasury of the company. Even if the commission should immediately take steps to reduce rates, some time must elapse before they go into effect. In the meantime the company will still be reaping the unusual profits due to unusual efficiency. After the new rates go into effect, the company will have the opportunity to reap new gains through additional improvements until such time as the commission takes cognizance of the new situation and makes a further reduction in service rates. Whether this opportunity of securing temporary gains will provide a sufficient incentive to managerial efficiency and progress depends upon circumstances; upon the energy and initiative of the managers as well as upon the speed with which the commission moves to capture the new gains. At any rate,

117

the opportunity is of sufficient importance to weaken considerably the contention that regulation necessarily destroys all incentive to efficient management.

The second answer to the objection is that managers should be permitted to retain from year to year a definite part of the gains of efficiency. This principle is recognized in the recapture clauses of the Transportation Act which permit a railway company to keep for itself one-half of the net profits above 6 per cent. There is no reason why the method should not be applied to all public utilities. It is entirely sound, both ethically and economically.

Almost all the objections, observations and arguments dealt with in the foregoing paragraphs have been set forth in many other places than in the articles by Professor Cabot. The really distinctive and challenging feature of these two articles is his attack upon the regulatory principle of service at cost. This principle assumes that prices are determined by cost, whereas, says Professor Cabot, "some of the shrewdest merchants of our time tell us that the fact is exactly opposite—that prices determine costs—not costs prices." Therefore, he suggests that "the attempt to regulate profits be abandoned, and that instead profits might be regulated indirectly, as they are now in the competitive trades, through the skilful regulation of price."

PRICES AND COSTS

The assumption that prices determine costs is a very misleading species of half-truth. "Some of the shrewdest merchants" may, indeed, give expression to this formula, but all they mean is that a reduction of prices is sometimes followed by such an increase in demand as to justify reductions in costs through quantity production. Henry Ford and his low-priced cars provide the best known example of this sequence. Even in such cases it is not accurate to say that prices determine costs. Low prices may be regarded as the psychological cause of enlarged demand, which may, in turn, be designated as the psychological cause of mass

118

production; the latter is the efficient and objective cause of low costs, which, in turn, become the psychological cause of low prices. By a psychological cause is meant, of course, a factor which produces its effect through the human mind and the human will. As between costs and prices, therefore, the true causal relation runs from the former to the latter. No matter how great the depths into which prices and costs have fallen, the latter still set the limits to the process of descent. The most efficient quantity producers will not continue operating unless they obtain sufficiently high prices to cover all their costs of production.

"The cost of a cotton mill," says Professor Cabot, "has no influence on the price of sheets." This is another half-truth. It applies only to *some* cotton mills. It cannot truthfully be predicated of the most efficient concerns operated by the most efficient managers. If the latter cannot sell their products at a sufficiently high price to provide normal returns on the money invested in their mills, they may, indeed, be content for a time with returns that merely cover the cost of operation. If this happens, the higher-cost mills will cease to produce. As a consequence, the supply of cotton sheets will decrease sufficiently to provoke an increase in price. The higher prices will enable the most efficient mills to cover all their costs of production, including the current cost of capital.

All this is elementary, but it seems worth stating in view of the implications of the language used by Professor Cabot. The costs of operating public utilities cannot be reduced arbitrarily and indefinitely through the simple device of reducing prices. As a matter of fact, the possible range of the method, even in actually competitive industries, is not very extensive. When all its possibilities have been utilized, the fundamental fact remains that the lower limits of prices are fixed by costs.

The goal which Professor Cabot sets before the regulating commissions is prices fixed "at the point which would give the largest volume of service at the greatest total

119

profit." Undoubtedly the utilities do seek this end, however clumsily and ineffectually. According to Professor Cabot, a more intelligent pursuit of the end would give lower rates to the consumer. He would have this more intelligent course revealed to and imposed upon the utilities by the regulating commissions. If this proposed identification of producers' and consumers' interests is feasible, why has it not been accomplished by the utility companies themselves? Why do they not reduce rates sufficiently to justify "the largest volume of service at the greatest total profit"? Professor Cabot replies: "Many men are blind to their own best interests and to the interest of those they serve." Let us concede that this is true, not only of "many," but of the majority of public-utility managers. Nevertheless, the enlightened minority should be able to see the greater profits to be derived from mass production and lower prices. Such a minority exists and functions in every private industry. How comes it that universal blindness in this respect afflicts the public utilities and only the public utilities? The assumption is extremely improbable.

THE QUESTION OF MONOPOLY

Professor Cabot ties up his assumption about the elasticity and docility of prices with his contention that public utilities are not monopolistic. In this connection he mentions particularly electric, gas, telegraph and telephone companies. Under all four heads his arguments are unconvincing for the following reasons:

In cities where both gas and electricity are furnished by the same company, there is not even potential competition in street lighting, except in so far as it is always possible for the municipality to establish a plant of its own. The check which this possibility places upon extortion is not of itself sufficient to protect the public.

Speaking of the telephone business, Professor Cabot says: "The temptation to use monopoly power to limit production, which is the only way in which monopoly

120

power can be abused, has disappeared." One would like to see the concrete evidence for this statement. Does Professor Cabot maintain that the telephone companies could never nor anywhere reduce charges and at the same time obtain fair profits on their investment? Or that they always refrain from unnecessary and unjustifiable rate increases? His observation about limiting production is misleading. A monopoly does not limit production for the sake of limitation. Its primary aim is maximum net profits and it strives to fix prices accordingly. If it finds that its maximum production cannot be sold at the price which will bring maximum net profits, it will limit production accordingly. Professor Cabot brings no evidence tending to show that the telephone companies are not limiting production in this sense and to this extent.

Equally unsupported is his assertion concerning the telegraph companies. "No one can deny that the telegraph business is competitive; in fact, in this field government rate regulation has all but disappeared." If Professor Cabot infers the presence of competition from the absence of regulation he is guilty of an astonishing *non sequitur*. "Government rate regulation," whether federal or state, has never been a serious factor in the telegraph industry. The impending introduction of a bill in the United States Senate to meet this deficiency indicates that some members of the Upper House of Congress reject Professor Cabot's assumption of competition. We all know that there is no competition in rates between the two great telegraph companies.

THE QUESTION OF SUBSTITUTES

However, Professor Cabot's argument for a change in the principle of regulation is not based upon the claim that the utilities face *direct* competition with regard to their respective products or services. He attributes their alleged competitive character to the availability of substitutes. "It is assumed," he says, "by utility commissions that where

121

monopoly exists competition cannot control prices, but it is my sincere belief that this assumption is unwarranted and that the markets for utility services are now truly competitive." He adds: "This is the nub of the whole question and it is here that I part company from most, if not from all, writers on this subject."

Despite Professor Cabot's argument, it would seem that the other economic writers may safely and logically continue to entertain their opinions. He gives no convincing evidence that the substitutes for utility products are capable of preventing the imposition of extortionate rates by the companies. To be sure, there are actual or potential substitutes for all such products except water. Were it not for the prohibition laws, Professor Cabot might not have conceded even this exception; for beer and wine might conceivably supplement rain and snow for beverage purposes, while some chemical substitutes might be invented to supplant the other uses of water. The trouble is that the process of substitution cannot begin soon enough. Consider a typical example:

The street-car fare in the District of Columbia for several years was eight cents. For more than two years the railway companies sought an increase on the plea that they were not obtaining a reasonable return on the fair value of their properties. The valuation which they desired is approximately equal to the cost of reproduction. They did not deny that eight cents would yield a just profit on the prudent investment or the historical cost. According to Professor Cabot, both the public-utility commission and the street-railway companies ought to abandon the cost-of-service principle entirely and fix rates on the basis of the competition that is possible through substitution. Undoubtedly this factor does operate. Competition by automobiles had a good deal to do with the increase of fares from six to eight cents and it continued in such force that the companies demanded and have obtained a rate of ten cents. The competition by substitution has caused an increase rather than a decrease in the price which the community must pay for street-car service. While the companies realize that the higher fare is followed by some further increase in substitution and some further decrease in the number of persons using the street cars, they believe that these changes will not be sufficiently great to prevent an increase in net profits. In this instance, therefore, the competitive effect of substitution is altogether unfavorable to the public, inasmuch as it very considerably increases the amount that they must pay for riding on street cars.

Professor Cabot lays great stress upon the "elasticity of demand" as evidence that competition by substitution is a reality. Undoubtedly, the demand for street-railway service is elastic. A decrease in the fare will be followed by an increase in patronage. Some persons who now walk will then ride and some persons who now use automobiles will revert to the street cars. When the fare is increased, some who have been riding will walk while others will use automobiles. In themselves, however, these facts give no support to Professor Cabot's contention that competition by substitution can be manipulated so as to bring greater profits to the utilities and at the same time lower prices to the consumers. This could happen only where substitution would be sufficiently elastic and sufficiently prompt to keep prices at the lowest, instead of permitting them to reach the highest level of the practicable range. Not the fact but the degree of elasticity in the demand is the decisive consideration. In some cities, for example, New York and San Francisco, the street-car fare is five cents; in Boston and Washington it is ten cents. Every conceivable rate between these two extremes is in force in one or more American cities. Five cents is probably the lowest and ten cents the highest profitable rate attainable anywhere. If Professor Cabot's theory were consistent with the welfare of the car riders, the companies ought to desire the five-cent rate everywhere. As a matter of fact, some of them prefer double that rate, since they find that competition by substitution does not become effective or threatening below that level. In the absence of regulation on the cost-of-service principle, other companies would no doubt exact a ten-cent fare, as do those in Boston and Washington. At least it is safe to say that most of them would be charging more than is now permitted to them by the commissions, for they could profitably do so despite the effect of competition by substitution.

Conceivably the street-railway companies might make more money by attracting larger patronage through lower fares, but the hypothesis is extremely improbable. The companies seem to have had plenty of experience to warrant the conclusion that the greatest net profits are obtained not from prices which attract the largest demand but from prices which are considerably above that level. And no amount of "skilful regulation of price" by utility commissions would seem to be capable of changing the essential factors of the situation. What is true of street railways applies to many other utilities. Men will no doubt return to oil lamps rather than pay enormous prices for gas and electricity, but the majority of them will pay much higher prices than are necessary to attract the maximum demand or to return a fair rate of interest on the invested capital. In the field of electric *power* it is quite possible that low or moderate prices would prove the most profitable, but the reason is that the competition of other kinds of power is really elastic and promptly operative. Wherever such competitive sources of power give substantially as good services as electricity at a cost very little greater; that is, wherever the service and cost of the substitute are approximately equal to the service and cost provided by the product of the public utility, competition exerts a satisfying influence upon prices. Where these features do not characterize the substitutes, as in the case, for example, of electricity for domestic lighting purposes, their potential competition will not guarantee reasonable charges to the consumer nor "the largest volume of service at the lowest profitable price."

124

PUBLIC UTILITY RATE REGULATION

THE PROCEDURE RECOMMENDED TO THE COMMISSIONS

"Perhaps in the long run," says Professor Cabot, "competition by substitution might achieve the desired result—namely, the greatest service to the public at the best prices—but it seems to me entirely clear, as I shall try to show, that state regulation skilfully applied will reach this goal more certainly and more rapidly than *laissez-faire.*" Following is a summary of his proposed changes in the methods of regulation:

Since the reasonable prices which the law requires are competitive prices, the objective of regulation should be the prices which would obtain under a system of free competition. To attain this end the commission should have before it the records of the company for the past years, showing, first, the money received under each rate schedule, the prices charged under each classification and the quantities sold; second, the money paid out to produce and deliver the total quantities, including fixed charges, taxes, depreciation allowances, interest and dividends. "And it is important to understand clearly the exact nature of these charges." The companies must also be required to make known their plans for the future and to present estimates showing the quantities and profits expected under present rates and those expected under a change in rates.

In determining rates, the commission will disregard entirely "the cost or value of the company's property devoted to the public service." Instead, they will "charge each class of customers as nearly as possible what the service is worth to that class." The worth of the service is determined in each case by what the consumer is willing to pay rather than turn to a substitute. If any class is paying substantially less than that rate, the company will be unable to serve some other class which is unwilling to pay the then lowest profitable price. However, the increase in prices must not be carried so far that it will reduce the quantity to such an extent as to cause a decrease in the *total* profit. In determining the rate schedule, however, the rate making body must not "attribute certain expenses and certain rates of profit to certain customer groups. . . . In all public utilities the income and the expenses are joint, and any attempt to allocate costs or profits will lead to error." Hence "the aim of the company and the commission alike must be maximum volume and maximum aggregate profit. . . . If this method is patiently and skilfully applied, the result will be the best prices for the buyers considered as a whole. . . . To sum up, the ideal is to have large producers with long views which will lead them to seek maximum total and minimum unit profits; in short, managers who manage according to modern instead of medieval methods."

With the suggestion that the companies be required to adopt better accounting systems and budget making and in general to provide the commissions with more comprehensive information, all authorities on utility regulation would be disposed to agree. But Professor Cabot's outline of the method which the commissions should follow in utilizing this information for the regulation of public-utility prices seems to be very vulnerable. His proposals seem inapplicable to any utility which is required to sell its services at uniform prices to all persons. Such are street railways, steam railroads, interurban lines and automobile buses of all sorts. In none of these utilities would it be practical to raise fares as high as the traffic would bear to one class of patrons and reduce them to another class in order to get the benefit of mass production at low rates, low unit costs and high aggregate profits. The latter part of the method is already exemplified in the excursion rates offered by the railroads at certain seasons, on week-ends and for the delegates to conventions. While the other part of the plan is theoretically open to the utilities that we are now considering, it would scarcely bring about "the best prices for the buyers considered as a whole." An increase in passenger rates up to the point just beyond which the diminished demand would bring about a fall in net profits, would cost the majority of patrons more for this service than they pay at present, while a considerable minority would be impelled to curtail their use of the carriers.

To be sure, if a general reduction of rates should be followed by an increased volume of both business and profits, this particular "skilful regulation of prices" would justify itself to both the companies and the public; but the companies and commissions seem to be persuaded that these beneficent results would not come about. There is no need of discussing Professor Cabot's plan in relation to the transportation of freight, in view of the settled policy of the law concerning discrimination among different classes of shippers. In so far as the method is practically available, it is already applied in a very complex system of freight classifications.

Professor Cabot seems to have in mind chiefly the sale of electric current. The demand for all the domestic uses of electricity could be greatly increased by lower prices, and the same is true of electricity for power purposes. He thinks that in both these cases lower rates would result in low unit costs and greater profits. If this opinion is correct, the only important service for which higher rates could profitably be imposed is that involved in the use of domestic lighting, inasmuch as this, according to Professor Cabot, is not truly competitive. To compel this part of the service to bear the whole burden of increased prices for the benefit of all other services would not seem to be particularly wise or just.

The telephone industry could bear a limited application of the proposed method. Residence telephones might be required to pay the maximum prices that could be imposed without causing a decrease in total profits, while the rates might be lowered to business concerns; or the procedure might be reversed. Similar classifications might be made in the telegraph industry. Messages originating in business establishments might be subjected to higher rates in order that private messages could be sent at lower rates; or the opposite course might be followed. Another conceivable re-

127

course would be to impose high charges upon the wealthiest patrons of telephones and telegraphs, while giving the benefit of lower rates to all persons in medium and moderate circumstances. While this method is not unknown in the medical profession, it is scarcely practicable in any of the public utilities. The conclusion indicated by this brief survey is that Professor Cabot's method of manipulating rates would not bring us nearer to the goal, "the best prices for buyers considered as a whole."

This and two or three other formulas employed by Professor Cabot aptly illustrate the vagueness and inconclusiveness of his arguments. What really does he mean by "the best prices for buyers considered as a whole"? The lowest average unit price? If this is what he means, does he assume that it will be lower than the average unit price under the present system of regulation? Unless this result is produced, the new method of regulation can scarcely be regarded as beneficial to the consumer. Even if average prices are to be reduced, there remains the question of justice to those groups of consumers who will be required to pay the highest price that can be exacted from them consistently with the highest total profit. These groups may be compelled to pay prices out of all proportion to the cost of the services which they obtain. Indeed, the value of the service, as measured by the utmost price that a group will pay rather than turn to a substitute, might make possible the crudest kind of extortion. In a public service, is no account to be taken of the needs and capacities of the various classes? Professor Cabot makes a telling point when he urges that rate hearings include testimony of non-users as to why they do not use utility services. But the implication is that the prices are too high in all such cases. Perhaps the formula that we are considering means that the *majority* of the consumers are to enjoy lower rates than they do at present. Even so, the injustice to the minority still remains.

The aim of both the commission and the company should be, he says, "maximum volume and maximum aggregate profit." Wherein does this differ from the practical rule adopted by monopolies always and everywhere? They seek maximum net profit. Any volume of business that brings less than this may be too large, or, perhaps, too small. Here again Professor Cabot has permitted himself to be seduced by a slogan. He seems to think that the words "maximum volume" have an absolute character, whereas they are necessarily relative to the other part of the phrase, "maximum aggregate profit." In order to obtain the latter, the companies and the commissions may find it necessary to keep the former considerably below the amount that is produced under a system of regulation on the basis of cost.

"Maximum total and minimum unit of profit" is the ideal which Professor Cabot would have the producers pursue. This pursuit would be helpful to the consumers, subject to two conditions: first, that certain groups are not compelled to pay extortionate prices on the basis of "what the service is worth to them" and second, that "maximum unit profits" are to be lower than those prevailing under the existing system of regulation. The companies may find, as they often have found, that maximum total profit is consistent with minimum unit profit only in so far as the latter is determined by the former. Sometimes, at least, the maximum total profit is obtained through unit profits which are higher than they would have been had the companies been aiming only at moderate total profits. Professor Cabot has adduced no evidence nor any objective argument to warrant the conclusion that in pursuing this "ideal" the companies would perform "the greatest service to the public at the best prices." Indeed, maximum total and minimum unit profit may be equivalent to maximum volume and maximum aggregate profit.

A SUMMARY CRITICISM

Let us try to sum up as briefly as possible our criticisms of Professor Cabot's assumptions and proposals. He brings forward no facts to show that any considerable amount of public utility products are subject to prompt and adequate competition by substitutes. If such competition really existed, the consumers would not need protection through any sort of public regulation. Prices and rates would be kept down to reasonable levels, as in private industries which are genuinely competitive. So much for his assumptions of fact. As regards his proposals for a new method of regulation, the suggestion of raising prices to all those groups of consumers who are willing to pay more rather than go without the service, and raising them sufficiently to produce maximum profits, involves a degree of injustice that is ethically abhorrent and socially impossible. His recommendation for reductions in rates in order to utilize the advantages of mass production is undoubtedly sound within certain limits, but it is attainable without any change in the principle or methods of regulation. His suggestion that, instead of determining rates according to a fair return on the investment, the commissions should "aim to increase aggregate profits," on the theory that "profit is the measure of benefit to the community," is new and extraordinary. It assumes that maximum profits will always be more beneficial to the community than any smaller volume of profits. Surely this is a naïve act of faith. Surely it is discredited by all the experience that has been accumulated in the operation of public utilities, both with and without regulation. In a word, what Professor Cabot did in these two articles was to combine a few isolated facts with a large amount of hypothesis and speculation. The result is an unconvincing picture of what might happen in certain improbable contingencies.

A PROGRAM OF REGULATION

At the beginning of this paper it was noted that the existing regulation of public utilities is far from giving general satisfaction. According to some critics, it has utterly failed and is incapable of any considerable improvement. Pronouncements of this sort are misleading and

130

futile. There are only two alternatives to regulation: namely, complete license for the monopolistic utilities to exploit and oppress the consumers, and public ownership and operation. The former is a counsel of despair which will hardly be heard by men who still cherish freedom. The second is, and unfortunately will remain for many years to come, incapable of general adoption. Therefore, the practical question concerns such improvement in the methods of regulation as will provide the maximum protection to the consumers that is consistent with fair treatment of the utilities.

Regulation of rates has two phases, the process itself and the conditions within which it is restricted as regards the rate base and the fair return. The regulating commissions should possess all the legal authorization, all the funds and all the personnel that are necessary to insure the following: the use of proper accounting systems by the companies; the rendering of adequate reports and the disclosure of complete information concerning company receipts, expenditures, operations and plans; the enforcement of managerial efficiency, and rigid control of security issues. In all probability, there is not one state commission which is equipped according to all these specifications. Several of them are wanting in the majority of the commissions. One defect is particularly conspicuous in relation to electric utilities. Inasmuch as the state commissions have little or no control over the management fees exacted by holding companies from the operating companies, they are unable to exercise full control over operating expenses. The profits of the holding companies from engineering, construction and finance enter into the fixed capital accounts of the operating companies. Since the state commissions cannot pass authoritative judgment on the reasonableness of these charges, they lack adequate control over the issuing of securities. Apparently, the interstate character of the holding companies renders them immune to state control in their relations with the operating companies. "There is evidence that present methods of commission regulation are totally ineffective in dealing with the special problems of the holding company and that the entire system of commission regulation of utility companies may be circumvented and destroyed unless means are found to render it more effective in this direction."[3] The companies engaged in the interstate transmission of electric current are likewise beyond the jurisdiction of the state commissions. Both kinds of organization should be brought under Federal control through some such agency as that proposed in the bill introduced by Senator Couzens.

However, it is under the second phase of regulation that its defects have become most manifest and irritating. The commissions are required to fix charges sufficiently high to enable the utilities to obtain a fair rate of return on the fair value of their properties. Now the fair value of a public utility, if correctly estimated, would be identical with the amount of money prudently invested therein. This is the measure of capital value upon which the vast majority of savers and investors are satisfied to obtain the competitive rate of interest. The vast majority of men who had invested money in private industries before 1914 do not find that those investments have since increased in value to such an extent that they now equal the present cost of reproduction. The vast majority are lucky if the present value of their investments is as high as it was previous to 1914.

Nevertheless, certain decisions of the United States Supreme Court rendered since the beginning of 1923, particularly in the cases of the Southwestern Bell Telephone Company, the Bluefield Water Works, the Indianapolis Water Company and the O'Fallon, have practically deprived the commissions of the power to determine the rate base by the rule of prudent investment or historical cost. The most urgent requisite in this field is the enactment by the state legislatures and by Congress of laws providing specific rules of valuation. These rules should be such as to withstand the scrutiny of the Supreme Court and at the

---

[3]Mosher and others, *Electric Utilities—The Crisis in Public Control*, pp. 123-124.

132

same time to yield only as much as is absolutely necessary to the rule of reproduction cost. Possibly the Court would uphold a law which would establish as a valuation base prudent investment plus subsequent increases in the value of lands owned by the utility, or prudent investment plus a specified maximum percentage on account of the rise in the price level. Since the Court has steadfastly refused, even in the O'Fallon case, to specify the weight which should be accorded to reproduction cost in the valuation of utility properties, it might be satisfied with these concessions. Perhaps if Congress had introduced some such specific rule of valuation into the Transportation Act, the Court would not have set aside the ruling of the Interstate Commerce Commission in the O'Fallon case. At any rate, the primary need in the field of regulation today is legislation which will specifically define the rule of valuation and the rate base, thus rendering unnecessary any further valuations and any further litigation about valuations.

The fair percentage of return is likewise a problem for the legislative bodies. It should not exceed 7 per cent. At that rate, abundant money can be found by the utility companies for refinancing and for expansion. Neither in economics nor in morals is there any good reason why they should receive a higher rate than is sufficient to attract new capital.

Possibly the increased cost of effective regulation, according to the specifications of the foregoing paragraphs, would provoke a wide-spread demand for public ownership and operation. That would not be an undesirable outcome. Regardless of the efficiency or inefficiency of regulation, public ownership of public utilities ought to be adopted by the cities and the states wherever conditions are favorable and public opinion is sufficiently educated. Finally, the federal government ought to establish a sufficient degree of public operation in connection with such projects as Muscle Shoals and Boulder Dam to act as a check upon private operation and to set up standards of what is fair and attainable in both service and price.

12. The Ethics of Public Utility Valuation

A. THE JUDICIAL THEORY OF VALUATION

ABOUT thirty years ago the distinguished economic historian, William J. Ashley, now Sir William Ashley, in an address on American trusts made this statement:

> It may be the result of my *penchant* for the things mediæval but I cannot help thinking that the economist may soon find himself confronted in modern life with some of the ideas underlying the old demand for "just prices" and "reasonable wages," which he has been accustomed to regard as quite out of place in political economy.[1]

This expectation has been pretty generally fulfilled. For many years the economist no less than the moralist has been dealing with such concepts as "reasonable wages," "living wages," "fair wages," "reasonable prices" and "reasonable charges." The ethical aspects of prices and charges have always been of interest to the consumer. Just wages and just prices have forced themselves upon the consideration of the business man. No longer does anyone pretend to deal with either wages or prices on the old assumption that competition is a universally satisfactory regulator.

In this paper I intend to discuss the question of reasonable prices in relation to one class of goods only, the services performed and provided by public utilities. As briefly as is consistent with clearness, I shall examine the morality of the rules and factors which govern and determine public utility rates and charges.

---

[1] *Surveys, Historic and Economic*, p. 389.

134

Nevertheless the function of rate making is purely legislative in its character, and this is true whether it is exercised directly by the legislature or by some subordinate or administrative body to whom the power of fixing rates in detail has been delegated.

This sentence was uttered by the Supreme Court itself in the Knoxville Water case. It is found, substantially, in several other decisions of that body. What the court really does in such cases is to decide whether existing rates or contemplated rates are so low as to violate the "due process" clause of the Fifth and Fourteenth Amendments to the Constitution. By this clause Congress and the states, respectively, are forbidden to deprive any person of property "without due process of law." Rates fixed by public authority which are not sufficient to yield a fair rate of interest, are construed by the courts as contrary to this constitutional provision.

In order to ascertain whether legally fixed rates and charges will afford a fair return, the courts endeavor to ascertain the fairness of the valuation which is put upon the property by the rate fixing authority. Hence, the most fundamental and most important question is that of valuation. If it is low a given set of charges may yield a high rate of interest; if it is high the same charges may fail to provide a fair return.

In order to appreciate the authority which the courts now exercise over rate fixing and valuation it will be helpful to review briefly the development of the judicial doctrine since the Supreme Court first passed upon rate regulation, in the case of *Munn vs. Illinois* (1876). The process of development has included not only theories of valuation but interpretations of the "due process" clause. In his dissenting opinion in the District of Columbia Minimum Wage case, Mr. Justice Holmes pointed out that the word "liberty," in the "due process" clause, had undergone a judicial expansion within the lifetime of himself and his colleagues, from "liberty to follow the ordinary

135

callings" to "liberty of contract." The word "property" has suffered an analogous and equally great development. As now interpreted in rate making cases, the right of property is not merely the right to compensation when property is taken by the government, but the right to receive a reasonable rate of interest. The investor in public utilities now enjoys judicial protection not only against deprivation of the substance of his property, but against legally fixed rates which are inadequate to provide a *fair rate of interest* on the *value* of his investment.

The development of the judicial doctrine of valuation has been equally fundamental and far-reaching. The first decision by the Supreme Court on the right of public authorities to fix rates for public service concerns was rendered in the so-called Granger cases, the first of which, as noted above, was that of *Munn* vs. *Illinois*. In this decision the Court flatly declared that reasonable compensation for the use of public utility property was "a legislative and not a judicial question." While affirming the principle that property cannot be taken without due process of law, the Court clearly intimated that "due process" referred only to a judicial proceeding, and declared that the law itself which fixed the rates could be changed at the will of the legislature. Admitting that this legislative power could be abused, the Court, nevertheless, declared that for protection against such abuses "the people must resort to the polls, not the courts." The same judicial doctrine was laid down in several cases in the following ten years. Most of these decisions, however, were accompanied by dissenting opinions which proclaimed the right of the Court to review the rates fixed by the legislature or its subordinate agencies, and to determine whether these rates were reasonable.

In the Commission cases, which came before the Supreme Court some ten years after Munn, the Court gave expression to certain *dicta* which approved the doctrine laid down in the previous *dissenting* opinions. Under the guise of

136

regulating rates, said the Court, the states may not confiscate property. Here we have an implied reversal of the doctrine of the Granger cases. The Court now asserts its right to pass upon the reasonableness of rates fixed by the legislative authority, and expands the "due process" clause to include the doctrine that imposition of inadequate rates upon public utility concerns is equivalent to "taking property without just compensation." In the Chicago, Milwaukee and St. Paul Railway case (1890) the question of judicial review was squarely presented to the Court for the first time. It was answered as follows:

> The question of the reasonableness of a rate of charge for transportation by a railroad company, . . . is eminently a question for judicial investigation, requiring due process of law for its determination.

Inasmuch as this statement occurs in the decision itself and not merely in the *dicta*, it constitutes an explicit reversal of the doctrine laid down in the Granger cases. The opinion of the minority has become the doctrine of the Court.

In *Reagan* vs. *The Farmers Loan and Trust Company*, the Court admitted the right of the legislature to protect the public by fixing maximum rates, but reaffirmed without limitation its own right to review rates and to establish a minimum binding upon the legislature. What is that minimum? This question the Court does not answer more definitely than by the general statement that the public utility is entitled to "some compensation." Upon what basis is the compensation to be reckoned? Upon the value of the property, answers the Court. How is the value to be determined? Apparently, by actual cost and prudent investment. Nevertheless, the question of value was not formally nor comprehensively discussed.

In *Smyth* vs. *Ames* (1898) the Court for the first time undertook to state, at least in general terms, the method of valuing public utility property and to lay down compre-

137

hensive guidance for determining the constitutional rights of public utilities as regards rates and charges. While asserting that the interests of the public are paramount to the interests of the utility, the Court declared that the latter had a right to "a fair return on the value of that which is employed for the convenience of the public." Five years later, in the case of *San Diego Land and Town Company* vs. *National City*, the Court, Justice Holmes writing the opinion, repeated this formula in the following terms:

> What the company is entitled to demand, in order that it may have just compensation, is a fair return on the reasonable value of the property at the time it is being used for the public.

In only slightly varying phraseology this rule has been frequently repeated in subsequent decisions.

How did the Court define "reasonable value"? It enumerated no less than six factors which the legislature should consider in valuing public utility property. Apparently fearful lest it might have omitted some relevant consideration, the Court added: "We do not say that there may not be others." Of the six factors which it did specify only two have continued to retain importance in the judicial review of rate making cases. These are "original cost" and "present cost of construction." Although there is ample reason for believing that by "present cost of construction" the Court merely meant to introduce a check upon *excessive* original cost, in recent decisions it has made this phrase completely synonymous with present cost of reproduction. Nevertheless, the Court did not, in *Smyth* vs. *Ames*, give any indication of the relative weight which should be assigned either the original or present cost or any of the other factors which it prescribed. All were to be considered and apparently to be accorded some influence in valuation, but the relative degree of influence to be assigned to each was left completely undetermined.

Subsequent decisions have failed to supply a definite

138

rule. The most that they have done is to indicate a trend away from original cost and toward reproduction cost, although the latter trend has not been steady and uniform. The first important case following *Smyth* vs. *Ames* was that of *Willcox* vs. *Consolidated Gas Company* (1908). In the decision of the Supreme Court, we find this sentence:

> If the property which legally enters into the consideration of the question of rates has increased in value since it was acquired the company is entitled to the benefit of such increase.

However, this statement was of no great importance in that particular case, since the property of the gas company had not greatly increased in value.

In the Second Minnesota Rate cases (1913), the Court said:

> It is clear that in ascertaining the present value we are not limited to the consideration of the amount to the actual investment. . . . The property is held in private ownership and it is that property and not the original cost of it of which the owner may not be deprived without due process of law.

In the decision itself, however, very little recognition, except in regard to land, was given to the great increase in prices which had taken place since the railroads were constructed.

In the year 1923, the Supreme Court decided three cases, in each of which the question of original cost versus reproduction was clearly presented. The first of these was the Southwestern Bell Telephone case. Here the Court affirmed the order of the lower court which had set aside the rates fixed by the Public Service Commission of the state of Missouri. It declared that the Public Service Commission should have taken into account the increase in prices since 1913. In its own valuation, however, the Court allowed an addition of only 25 per cent to original cost, whereas

139

prices had increased 100 per cent. In the Bluefield Water Works case, the Court rejected the valuation made by the Public Service Commission of West Virginia, likewise on the ground that the Commission had made no allowance for the increase in prices; but the Court did not say whether the company should receive the full benefit of that increase. In the Georgia Railway and Power Company case, the Court approved rates which made no allowance for the general increase in prices but only for the rise in the value of land, and included this statement in the written opinion:

> The refusal of the Commission and of the lower court to hold that, for rate making purposes, the physical properties of a utility must be valued at replacement cost, less depreciation, was clearly correct.

The opinion was written by Justice Brandeis, who had dissented from the decisions in the two former cases. In all three he consistently opposed reproduction cost. Justice McKenna vigorously dissented in the Georgia case, on the ground that the decision there was inconsistent with the other two. Undoubtedly, the premises and arguments in the first two decisions are irreconcilable with those in the third. Mr. John Bauer has tried to reconcile the decisions themselves and from his analysis has drawn this inference and forecast:

> Rates will not be nullified unless they fail to bring a fair return on the actual investment.[2]

We shall see that his fame as a prophet has been seriously affected by the decision of the Supreme Court in the case of the Indianapolis Water Company.

---

[2]*Effective Regulation of Public Utilities*, p. 102.

140

B. THE INDIANAPOLIS WATER
COMPANY CASE

The actual investment in the Indianapolis Water Works plus the appreciation in the value of the company's land was certainly not more than $12,750,000. Although the Public Service Commission of Indiana had fixed rates sufficient to yield 7 per cent on $15,260,000, plus some increase in land values, the water company secured an injunction in the federal district court, restraining the Commission and the city of Indianapolis from putting into effect the proposed rates. In granting the petition, the district court declared that the Commission's valuation of the property was more than $3,500,000 too low and that the fair value "was and is not less than $19,000,000." From the decisions in the Southwestern Bell Telephone and the Bluefield Water Works cases the district court concluded that reproduction cost should be given "dominant consideration."

The decision of the district court and the valuation allowed by it were sustained by the Supreme Court of the United States. Justice Butler wrote the opinion, with Justice Holmes concurring in the result but apparently not in the argument, and Justices Brandeis and Stone dissenting. Recurring to the so-called rule laid down in *Smyth* vs. *Ames,* the Court in the Indianapolis case points out that both the original cost and the present reproduction cost must be considered.

But this does not mean that the original cost or the present cost or some figure arbitrarily chosen between these points is to be taken as the measure. The weight to be given to such cost figures and other items

141

or classes of evidence is to be determined in the light of the facts of the case in hand.

Here we have two important statements: first, the valuation must be fixed somewhere between actual cost and present reproduction cost; second, the exact point of its location depends upon the "facts of the case." According to the Court, the average price level for the ten years ending with 1921, which would give a valuation of about $14,-750,000, was "too low." The average price level for ten years ending with 1923, which would give a valuation of about $17,000,000, was pronounced "substantially less than the amount fairly attributable to the physical elements of the property."

Upon what basis, whether of fact or of fairness, did the Court declare that these valuations were too low? The only facts which it adduced are those which describe the great increase in prices which had taken place since 1914 and the consequent great increase in present reproduction cost, but these give no real help toward finding the answer to the question, "at what point between original cost and reproduction cost should valuation be fixed?" The answer depends entirely upon one's conception of fairness. Apparently, the Supreme Court held with the lower court that reproduction cost should be given "dominant consideration" and that the valuation should approach *much* more nearly to present reproduction cost than to original cost. Hence, the Court rejected valuations of $15,000,000 and $17,000,000, and sustained one of $19,000,000. Indeed, the Court intimated that a higher figure than $19,000,000 would be entirely justified. Obviously, these are purely ethical judgments, not necessary conclusions from any set of economic facts.

At this point it will be helpful to state in summary form the various valuation figures involved in this case:

THE ETHICS OF PUBLIC UTILITY VALUATION

TABLE I

Actual cost of property .... $10,434,254[3]
Actual cost, plus increase in land value 12,750,000
Valuation by Public Service Commission ... 15,260,000
Valuation sustained by Supreme Court 19,000,000
Present cost of reproduction, not more than . 21,750,000[4]
Valuation if original cost and reproduction
    cost had been given equal weight 16,092,124

The salient facts shown by this table are that the Court was not satisfied with the Commission's allowance of 46 per cent above original cost, nor with 50 per cent of the difference between original and reproduction cost, but sustained a valuation which is 82 per cent above original cost and which includes 75 per cent of the difference between original and reproduction cost. Previous to this decision the Supreme Court had never allowed as much as half of this difference. There is no doubt that it gave "dominant consideration" to reproduction cost!

The final valuation of the railroads of the country by

---

[3] According to the record of the case, as presented in the opinion of the Supreme Court (pp. 2, 3, 4, 5), the actual cost comprised the following items:
    Money invested to Jan. 1, 1917 .... $8,000,000
    Capital additions, Jan. 1, 1917—Oct. 31, 1922 1,639,146
    Capital additions, Oct. 31, 1922—Dec. 31, 1923 795,105

       Total $10,434,251
According to the Public Service Commission (p. 7 of Court opinion) "the fair original cost of the physical property was from 12 to 20 per cent less than the $14,904,000 used as a basis herein." The latter figure is the cost of reproduction based upon average prices for the ten-year period ending with 1921. Twelve per cent less would be $13,115,520; 20 per cent less would be $11,923,200. Since the lower of these estimates is $1,488,949 more than original cost, as disclosed by the record, it must include the increase in the value of the Company's land to January 1, 1917. At any rate, it seems fair to adopt an estimate somewhere within the Commission's "12 to 20 per cent less than $14,904,000." The sum, $12,750,000, adopted above in the text, is equivalent to a deduction of 14.5 per cent, and is much nearer to the higher than to the lower of the two estimates. It is sufficiently generous to the company.

[4] The cost of reproduction, January 1, 1924, received three different estimates (p. 14 of the Court's opinion):
    By the Commission's engineer $19,500,000
    By one of the Company's engineering firms 21,898,000
    By the other of the Company's engineering firms 22,669,000
The figure adopted by me ($21,750,000) is $2,250,000 above the lowest of these estimates, only $148,000 below the second highest, $919,000 below the highest, and $665,500 above the figure that would be obtained by "splitting the difference" between the lowest and the highest. The $21,750,000 is probably high enough to cover cash working capital. It may also be large enough to include franchise rights and "going value," although neither of these has any ethical claim to be considered. Incidentally, the enormous difference between the lowest and the highest estimates of the engineers powerfully illustrates the uncertainties and guess-work character of reproduction cost as a method of estimating value.

the Interstate Commerce Commission has been authoritatively forecast as $22,300,000,000.[5] It takes no account of the increase in prices since 1914, except as regards land. Should "dominant consideration" of reproduction cost, as exemplified in the Indianapolis case, be applied in equal measure to the railroads, their valuation would be lifted from $22,300,000,000 to somewhere between $32,000,-000,000 and $35,000,000,000. The valuation of other public utilities, municipal and national, would likewise be greatly increased. The resultant tax upon the public in the form of higher rates, in order to provide a fair return upon these increased valuations, would be enormous. Undoubtedly, they would provoke an agitation for public ownership of public utilities vastly greater than anything that this country has hitherto known.

Let us see what the Supreme Court valuation means to the owners of the Indianapolis Water Company.

TABLE II

Valuation sustained by Supreme Court	$19,000,000
Amount of bonds and preferred stock	10,247,300[6]
Company's equity in the valuation	$8,752,700
Returns available for interest and dividends ($19,000,000 x 7%)	$1,330,000
Interest to holders of bonds and preferred stock (4½ to 6%)	524,383
Interest remaining for owners of common stock	$805,617
On $8,752,700 this amount is equivalent to a rate of	9.2%
Actual investment in concern, including enhanced value of land	$12,750,000
Amount of bonds and preferred stock	10,247,300
Company's equity in actual investment, plus increase in land value	$2,502,700
On this amount $805,617 is equivalent to a rate of	32.1%

[5] *Bulletin Railroad and Utilities Commissioners*, Jan. 13, 1927.
[6] Cf. *Moody's Public Utilities*, 1926, pp. 332, 333.

Therefore, to say that the company is allowed 7 per cent on the valuation of its property is to tell only a part of the story. The owners of the company are due to get the astounding rate of more than 32 per cent on their actual investment and also on the increase in the value of their land.

Now let us try to get some idea of the gains which the valuation rule of the Indianapolis case decision would bring to the owners of the railroads. As stated above, it would add from ten to thirteen billions to the valuation made by the Interstate Commerce Commission. At 5¾ per cent, the legal rate of return allowed by Congress, an added valuation of $13,000,000,000 would yield annual interest to the amount of $747,500,000. In 1924, the total amount of dividends paid on railway stock was $385,129,890. The sum of these two items is $1,132,-629,890. This total is equivalent to 18.5 per cent on the dividend paying stock ($6,042,267,916), or 15 per cent on all the common stock outstanding, good, bad and in-different ($7,538,994,845).

No matter what theory of valuation is applied to a public utility, the rate of return on the valuation does not give us an adequate idea of the rate of return to the owners. The bonds and preferred stock always call for a lower interest rate than that allowed on the valuation, and the difference is obtained by the owners of the concern in addition to the full rate on their own portion of the investment. For example, a city lighting plant is valued at $10,000,-000, which is the actual cost of construction. Half the money required to build it was derived from the sale of bonds and preferred stock, on which the average rate of interest is 5 per cent. Hence, holders of these securities receive an annual return of $250,000. The other half of the capital was provided by the owners of the common stock. As the return on the valuation is 7 per cent, the total amount available for interest and dividend payments is $700,000. Deducting the amount due to the holders

145

of bonds and preferred stock, we have a remainder of $450,000 for the owners of the concern. On their investment of $5,000,000 this means an interest rate of 9 per cent.

Obviously, the greater the portion of the investment in bonds and preferred stock the greater will be the excess over the stipulated rate of return which will go to the owners. According to John Bauer, "fully 75 per cent of the actual moneys expended in property through security issues have come from bonds and only 25 per cent from stock."[7] Applying the 75-25 proportion to the example considered in the second last paragraph, we see that the actual return on the owners' proportion of the investment reaches the attractive figure of 13 per cent.

From the foregoing examples we learn how misleading is the assumption that a fixed rate of return on the valuation provides only that rate of interest to the owners of a public utility. It always yields more. How much more depends first upon the margin between the rate of interest on the bonds and the rate of return for the whole property, and second, upon the bondholders' proportion of the investment. Even when the latter receive as high a rate as 6 per cent and have provided only one-half of the capital, a 7 per cent return upon the whole investment means 8 per cent for the owners of the concern.

All these statements and figures apply to cases where the valuation does not exceed the actual investment. To the extent that the valuation goes beyond that measure, whether on account of higher reproduction cost or through inclusion of "intangible" values, the gain to the owners is still further and correspondingly increased. The first of the tables given in our discussion of the Indianapolis case provides an excellent illustration.

Reference has just been made to "intangible" elements of valuation. The $6,250,000 added by the Court to the actual cost in its valuation of the Indianapolis Water Com-

---

[7] *Op. cit.*, p. 123.

pany was not based entirely upon increased prices and increased reproduction cost. Something less than 10 per cent of the $19,000,000 was inserted "to cover water rights and going value." The Indiana Public Service Commission had included a slightly smaller percentage for these elements. Of the two, "going value" is much the more important. What does it mean? The answers given by the Supreme Court in various decisions have not been uniform, nor satisfactory from the point of view of clearness.

The Court has declared that "going value" is not the same as "good will; nor must it be used to cover past deficiencies or losses in returns." In one case, the Court said that valuation should not be limited to "the bare bones of the plant" and that "the difference between a dead plant and a living one is real value."[8] These are mere figures of speech which yield no definite rule. In the Indianapolis case, the Court quoted with approval the description of "going value" by the Indiana Public Service Commission; that is, earning power, profitable business relations, and exceptional business efficiency. These things, says the Commission, "would be considered by a buyer or seller of the property or by a buyer or seller of its securities."

Undoubtedly, these factors would be considered and would be paid for by a purchaser, if he could be assured that the rates now charged by the water company would not be lowered so far as to leave only a fair rate of return on the physical property. Without this assurance there would be no "going value." The theory adopted by the Commission and approved by the Court could logically be utilized to prevent any regulation of rates, particularly any decrease in rates.

For example, let us take a water company whose rates are not yet regulated by public authority. The existing rates reflect monopoly conditions and exemplify the rule, "all the traffic will bear." They are so high as to yield, let us suppose, 20 per cent on the physical value of the prop-

---

[8] *Omaha vs. Omaha Water Company.*

147

erty. Comes now the public authority threatening to reduce rates to a level that will permit a fair return merely on the value of the physical property. Strong objection is made by the water company on the ground that it will be deprived of that "going value" which exists over and above "the bare bones of the plant." If the old rates are allowed to continue the company can sell the "going value" at a high price. If the threatened rates are put into effect, the "going value" will disappear. Hence, the rates can never be decreased without depriving the company of its property rights!

The truth of the matter is that no valid inference concerning honest values can be drawn from the mere fact that the purchaser is willing to pay more for a public utility than the physical value of its property. Such willingness may mean nothing more than recognition of the fact that the company is an unregulated monopoly. To concede this anti-social advantage to the utility under the cabalistic term, "going value," is to give up the whole case for rate regulation. All that would be necessary to validate any set of monopoly rates and profits would be to compute the capitalized value of the excess returns, add it to the physical value and then point out that the earnings are only a fair return on the inflated capitalization. As Justice Holmes pointed out, in the Cedar Rapids Gas Light case, "going value" may be identical with monopoly power and this is excluded by the very theory of regulation.

So much for earning power as a basis of "going value" in the Indianapolis Water case. Have the other two advantages specified by the Commission, namely, profitable business connections and exceptional business efficiency, any significance that can properly be expressed in terms of value? Undoubtedly they have. In so far as they have not come into existence necessarily and automatically, as from the fact that the people of Indianapolis must have water and can get it nowhere else than through the company, the

148

profitable business connections have probably cost the company some expenditure.

However, if this has already been met out of operating revenues, it should not find a place in the valuation. The outlay involved in acquiring profitable business connections does not belong in the capital account any more than the wages of the meter readers, or any other expenditure that has already been covered by current revenues.

> If the costs of establishing the business and development costs were cared for out of operating expenses through higher rates charged the consumer, no sacrifice has been made by the utility; and such charges should not be included in the rate base. If past consumers have repaid these costs, it is obviously improper to capitalize them against future consumers. In this instance, the investment, if one exists at all, has been made by the consumer.[9]

Apparently this was the situation in the Indianapolis Water Company. All these early costs had been defrayed out of operating revenues provided by the consumers. To include them in the valuation now is to compel the consumers to pay interest on money that they have paid into the coffers of the company.

As for exceptional business efficiency, the Indianapolis Water Company was and is already receiving the benefit of it in the form of unusually high profits. Undoubtedly, these exceptional profits have been created by and ought to be retained by the company; but they ought not to be capitalized and added to the value. If this is done, the company receives two payments for its efficiency; one through its savings in operating expenses, another when it receives interest on the excess capitalization. To sanction this inflation under the mystifying phrase "going value" is to practice fraud upon the public.

Nevertheless, this esoteric and hypothetical entity, which

---

[9]M. C. Waltersdorf in *American Economic Review*, March, 1927, p. 33.

cost the company not a single dollar in capital expenditure, was given a weight of considerably more than a million dollars in the valuation made by the Indiana Public Service Commission. Had "going value" been disregarded, the Commission's valuation of the property would have been about $14,000,000 instead of $15,260,000. In the valuation sustained by the Supreme Court, "going value" was allowed to the extent of something more than $1,500,000. Without it the Court's valuation would probably not have exceeded $17,500,000. One of the company's engineering firms estimated the "going value" at $2,000,000, while the other gave it an allowance of $2,098,000. The inflating capacity of the "going value" concept should be very gratifying to the public utility corporations.

Is "going value," then, utterly devoid of reality or justification? Not necessarily. In the history of many public service corporations are to be found various intangible or overhead construction costs which represent an outlay of money which was quite as real as that embodied in the physical elements of the plant. These intangibles fall mainly under the heads of organization expenses, engineering and superintendence, omissions and contingencies, taxes during construction, and cost of financing. Their importance can be estimated from the fact that John Bauer, who is not inclined to be too friendly to the public utilities, estimates as a fair allowance for all five combined 15 per cent of the entire cost of labor and material.[10] The allowances made by courts and commissions for these items have varied from 5 per cent to twenty per cent of the value of the physical property. When they have not been met out of operating revenue they should be included in the rate base and form part of the valuation upon which the company is entitled to a fair rate of return.

Costs for the development of the business, where reasonable, constitute a charge that in some form

[10] *Op. cit.*, p. 222.

should be borne by the consumers who avail themselves of the service.[11]

Nevertheless, it is highly desirable that these costs should be denominated "intangible value" rather than "going value." The latter term should be incontinently banished from the language of public utility valuation.

[11]Waltersdorf, *op. cit.*, p. 37.

C. THE O'FALLON AND THE NEW YORK
TELEPHONE CASES

In the O'Fallon Railway case (1929) the Supreme Court declared that "the present cost of construction or reproduction is among the elements of value recognized by the law of the land for rate-making purposes, as pointed out many times by the Court." But it refrained from declaring how much weight should be given to this element, whether 25 per cent, or 80 per cent, or any other per cent. The Court did, indeed, allude to this question when it declared: "The weight to be accorded thereto is not the matter before us."

The immediate basis upon which the Court rested its decision in the O'Fallon case was Section 15a of the Transportation Act. This section declares that the Interstate Commerce Commission "shall give due consideration to all the elements of value recognized by the law of the land for rate-making purposes." According to the Supreme Court, the Interstate Commerce Commission failed to carry out this mandate, since it did not give "due consideration," that is, accord any weight, to the cost of reproduction of the artificial part of the O'Fallon properties. That "the law of the land" does recognize this particular element of value is indicated in the decisions of the Supreme Court. In other words, "the law of the land" concerning the rules of valuation means the law as developed by the Court itself. In the valuation of the O'Fallon properties, the Interstate Commerce Commission disregarded this law; consequently its action was set aside by the Court.

The Federal District Court of the Southern District of New York in *New York Telephone Co.* vs. *Prendergast, et al.*, November 11, 1929, rejected the view of the special master that reproduction cost is "equivalent to value," and held that it is merely "evidence of value," citing all the

152

decisions mentioned above and one or two others. Nevertheless, the Court permitted the master's valuation to stand, with certain modifications. Curiously enough, present cost of reproduction does not substantially exceed the original cost of the labor, materials and land. It is the "modifications" made by the Court in the master's valuation figures which render the judicial opinion in this case unusually interesting and illuminating. The "modifications" affect either hypothetical, as distinguished from actual, reproduction costs or intangible, as distinguished from physical, elements of value. Taken together, they throw a glaring, not to say a sinister, light upon the claims and pretensions which the ingenious servitors of the utility companies are able to put forward under the guise of reproduction cost. It is improbable that these claims and pretensions have anywhere else received a more ample presentation.

The following claims were made by the Company but disallowed by the Court:

Promotion expenses	$18,000,000.00
Preliminary organization (about)	4,000,000.00
"Inexperience factor"	17,393,214.00
Going value	25,000,000.00
Cost of financing	22,943,109.00
Bankers checking engineers	2,207,000.00
Interest on preliminary costs	2,554,763.00
Amount by which Company understated depreciation	74,000,000.00
	$166,098,086.00
Less 14.25% to cover property not in New York State	23,668,977.05
	$142,429,108.95

The first two of these items were disallowed by the master as well as by the Court; those remaining were allowed by the master but disallowed by the Court. Under some of the latter heads some allowance was made by the Court; for example, the Company claimed $35,000,000 for "going value" but the Court reduced it to $10,000,000. Al-

153

though making a reserve depreciation on its books of $125,000,000, the Company claimed that the actual depreciation of the property was only $51,000,000. The Court decided that the Company had not proved this contention and that the larger sum must be taken as measuring actual depreciation. Probably the most fantastic claim urged by the company was the "inexperience factor." Certain office materials purchased from the Western Electric Company would cost $17,393,214 more if they had to be obtained from some inexperienced manufacturer! The Court properly held that there was no ground for assuming that in case of reproduction this equipment could not again be bought from the Western Electric Company.

The value which the Court found for the property was $397,207,925.74. The claims of the Company disallowed by the Court aggregated $142,429,108.95. Using hypothetical items of reproduction cost, the Company sought a valuation that was 36 per cent in excess of the judicially determined fair valuation. It desired to collect from the telephone users of New York interest at the rate of 8 per cent on these imaginary values. No more devastating idictment of the theory of reproduction cost could be desired.

To be sure, several of these intangible elements of value represented actual expenditure and would have to be allowed if the property were valued according to original cost or prudent investment. In that case, however, the actual amounts expended would be easily ascertainable. They could not be inflated through imaginary estimates of hypothetical contingencies.

D. JUST VALUATION AND JUST DIVIDENDS

"There is no such thing as value for rate making purposes. There is only one kind of value, namely, economic value, or exchange value."

Such is the position now taken in valuation cases by counsel for public utility companies. Upon it they seem to base their main hope of getting present reproduction cost judicially recognized as the dominant if not the exclusive measure of value.

The simplest refutation of this extraordinary claim is found in the formula which the Supreme Court invariably uses to describe the legal rights of the public companies, "a fair return on the fair value of property." The thing to be ascertained in rate making cases is "fair" value, not exchange value. The former is an ethical concept dependent upon a theory of right; the latter is a conclusion from economic facts. It is determined by such factors as competition, monopoly, and the interplay of supply and demand, not by ethical rules or principles.

The exchange value of any commodity is expressed in the price which it will bring in a market. In the case of capital goods the selling price is determined by the product, the earnings. Capitalize the annual earnings at the prevailing rate of interest and you have the exchange value of the property. For example, if the current rate of interest is 6 per cent, a factory which brings a net return to its owners of $12,000 has a value of $200,000. The factory can be sold for that amount because it produces the current rate of interest on that amount.

Let us apply this calculation to a public utility. A gas company provides its owners a net revenue of $30,000 a year. Capitalized at 6 per cent, this means that the concern has an economic value of $500,000. That is what it will sell for if there is no danger that the earnings will be reduced. Suppose, however, that the city authorities regard the existing gas charges as too high and the company's earnings excessive. Accordingly, they reduce rates to a level which yields a net return of only $24,000. The economic value will then be $400,000, for that is all that the concern will bring in the market.

While the economic value of a public utility is, ideed, determined by its earnings, the earnings themselves are determined by public regulation. Therefore, regulation is the ultimate determinant of the exchange value of public utilities. The earnings and value of an ordinary private business are subject to no such disturbing influence. To put the difference in summary terms: the economic value of a public utility is *estimated* by the same method as that of a private concern, but it is *determined* in part by a factor with which a private concern does not have to contend.

Let us see just how regulation does determine the value of a public utility. It seeks to provide "a fair return on the fair value of the property." The first step, therefore, is to ascertain fair value. This is the process known as valuation. Upon what principle or rule should it be made? If "there is only one kind of value," if fair value is identical with economic value, the valuation authorities must simply capitalize the present earnings at the rate of interest which is currently accepted. But present earnings are what they are because present rates are what they are. If these are lowered the return will be less than fair on the present economic value; if they are raised the return will be more than fair. This conception excludes either a decrease or an increase in rates. The sole function of the regulating authority is to maintain the *status quo!*

Of course, the truth of the matter is that the causal influence in the valuation of public utilities is diametrically opposite to that which governs the value of unregulated concerns. The latter value is determined immediately by earnings, ultimately by the interplay of supply and de- mand. The value of public utilities is likewise determined

156

immediately by earnings, but ultimately by the valuation put upon the property by the regulating authority. Earnings will be high or low according as the valuation is high or low. The valuation is itself determined by the ethical theory adopted by the regulating authority.

However, the public utility lawyers are able to jockey themselves out of this absurd position. They succeed in setting up a proposition which is plausible, or at least not illogical. While economic value is primarily measured by earnings, it finds a secondary or supplementary measure in present cost of reproduction. A competitive concern, say a factory, will sell for the capitalized value of its earnings. It will also sell for the amount of money required to build a new factory having the same earning power. This is the test or measure of economic value which the public utility representatives seem to have in mind when they utter the sententious proposition, "there is only one kind of value."

Nevertheless, this criterion is not valid universally. It is not always true that an old factory, or store or other private business concern will bring a price, allowance being made for depreciation, equivalent to the cost of a new concern having the same productive capacity. The selling price of the old concern will be determined by its earning power, but that will not in every case be equivalent to a reasonable rate of interest on the higher cost of the new establishment. Where real competition exists many of the older concerns will be satisfied with, or will be compelled to accept, prices for their products which will yield only a reasonable rate of interest on their actual cost, not on the higher cost of reproducing them today.

> Earnings of 10 per cent on capital invested cannot be boosted into earnings of 30 per cent by revaluation theories, where less greedy competitors hold down prices to a normal or fair level.[12]

Moreover, the excess cost of establishing equally produc-

---

[12]Donald R. Richberg, *Reply Brief in the O'Fallon Case*, p. 27. Before the Interstate Commerce Commission, 1926.

tive new concerns is frequently less than the increase in the general price level. This is mainly due to improved machinery and better methods of production. In consequence of competition and industrial progress, the economic value of old business concerns is often less than the cost of reproducing them in their present form. The great majority of persons who owned productive properties before 1914 do not today find that these goods are at present worth as much more than their original cost as present prices exceed the prices that prevailed when the properties were constructed or purchased. In the second place, public utilities are in some sense agencies of the state and, therefore, cannot necessarily lay claim to those benefits from price changes which are available to private concerns. Moreover, at least 50 per cent of the capital invested in public utilities has been provided by the purchasers of the bonds. The latter gain nothing from the adoption of the reproduction cost measure of valuation. The same is true of the owners of preferred stock. Why should the owners of the common stock, which is always a minority of the capitalization, receive the special advantage which they seek through the device of valuation based upon enhanced prices?

In any case, the contention that because private concerns are valued at reproduction cost, public utilities ought to receive the same kind of valuation, derives no validity from economics. As it stands it is a purely ethical proposition. It asserts that the analogy of competitive concerns *ought to* determine the value of public utilities. From the viewpoint of ethics this assertion has exactly as much validity as the doctrine of the starvation wage. Men and women do sometimes accept such a wage; therefore it is ethically right. Men have to pay a certain high price to duplicate a public utility; therefore, the existing utility should obtain that measure of valuation. One of these conclusions has as much, and as little, ethical validity as the other.

Examining the question on purely ethical grounds, we see powerful reasons for rejecting reproduction cost and

158

accepting actual cost. When men put money into any productive enterprise, they expect to receive a fair rate of interest on their investment. That is what the average man seeks before everything else. It is his main object when he invests in a public utility; therefore, he has a right to expect that public regulation will not reduce the valuation of the concern below the number of dollars that he has invested. On the other hand, he has no reasonable ground for expecting that his dividend rate will be increased through the operation of any mere valuation theory.

The legal protection now enjoyed by the public utilities is equivalent to a guarantee, not only against confiscation of their capital, but also against being compelled to accept less than a fair rate of interest. The annual rate allowed on their property by the public service commission and the courts is generally higher than the average person obtains from investments of equal security. When the shareholder in a public utility is thus legally assured of a fair rate of interest on the number of dollars that he has invested in the concern, his capital is at least as secure and as lucrative as the investments made by the great majority of persons in private concerns. The latter would be very well satisfied if they had an equal assurance of 7 per cent or even of 6 per cent. So long as the owners of public utilities are assured such rates on the original cost of their property, that is, on the actual amount of money that they have put into these concerns, they will receive fair treatment. So long as the utilities are able to attract new investments at these rates, they will be able to discharge their obligations toward the consumers. In a word, there is no valid ethical reason, nor any sound economic reason, why the utilities should have the benefit of property valuations according to reproduction cost, or according to any other measure that is substantially above the amount of money that has been prudently invested in them. The burden of proof, and it is a very heavy burden, is upon them to show that they are morally entitled to anything more.

159

The Massachusetts practice has always been to enforce actual investment as a measure of valuation and interest return. The same rule is included in the Federal Water Power Act applying to leases of government power sites. No one seriously contends that either of these laws is unfair to investors.

The only ethical argument for reproduction cost is a sort of gamblers' argument. If the price level and therefore the cost of reproduction falls after a utility has been constructed, the valuation and consequently the rate of interest to the investor are lowered. If prices move in the opposite direction valuation and rate of return are increased. In the former case the utility loses and the consumer wins. In the latter case their respective positions are reversed. Therefore, the arrangement is fair to both.

This assumption injects into the public utility business an unnecessary speculative element. There is no doubt that the vast majority of investors would prefer a fair and moderate certain return to a hazardous large return. Undoubtedly, this is a better method for social welfare. Any economic practice which increases the gambling element and the desire to get something for nothing, to gather "windfalls," should not be deliberately fostered by the public authorities.

In the second place, the cost of reproduction rule has not held the balance even as between investor and consumer. It has not distributed the risks equitably. In the period before 1896, when prices were falling, the reductions in valuations, rates, and returns were insignificant as compared with post-war increases in all these items. If we consider the last fifty years and the years immediately ahead of us, we find that the advantages of the reproduction cost rule are practically all on the side of the investor.

It is true that reproduction cost was first urged on behalf of the public and was strongly opposed by the utility corporations. This was during the period of falling prices. Nevertheless, the regulatory commissions made very little headway along this line. The fact that they now oppose what they then advocated should not prejudice their present advocacy of actual investment any more than the reverse attitude of the utility corporations should be a valid objection to their present position. Both parties acted selfishly in both periods.[18]

Probably no disinterested authority on the subject would deny that actual investment is preferable to reproduction cost for valuing all concerns that will be set up in the future, as well as for all additions to existing utility property. Many of the utility representatives hold the same view.

It is urged, however, that past investments in utilities provide a special reason for the rule of reproduction cost. When they were made actual investment had not been adopted as a legal measure of value. Consequently, the average investor had reason to assume that he stood to profit by possible price increases as well as to lose by possible decreases. This was particularly true of land. Moreover, many investors have suffered losses or have failed to get continuously a fair return on their investment owing to the increase of operating costs in recent years; for example, in the street railways and some steam railroads. Therefore, fairness seems to suggest that their experience of evil should be balanced by the benefit which they might obtain through use of the reproduction measure of valuation.

While this claim has some merit, its cogency is greatly exaggerated. In all probability, the great majority of investors in public utilities thought little about possible increases in the value of their property. Their main object was a steady and assured annual return. They hoped, indeed, that the value would not decrease and naturally they were ready to welcome an increase, but the latter was not among their primary aims. Of the investors who have suffered losses through failure to receive the stipulated divi-

---

[18]Probably the ablest and most comprehensive defense of actual investment as against reproduction cost is to be found in the dissenting opinion by Justice Brandeis in the case of the Southwestern Bell Telephone Company.

dends regularly a very large proportion no longer own these securities. Their successors have acquired the stock at a low figure.

In his dissenting opinion from the decision of the majority of the Interstate Commerce Commission in the O'Fallon case, February 15, 1927, Commissioner Woodlock upheld present reproduction cost as a matter of fairness to the investors in railroads. Since the value of the dollar is today much lower than in 1914, a present valuation determined by prices and costs of that date would greatly reduce the purchasing power of both property and earnings. Hence the decrease in the value of the dollar should be offset by an increase in the valuation of the property. A higher valuation would ensure larger earnings. The loss in the purchasing power of the dollars would be made up by the increase in their number. The Commissioner clearly intimated that this had actually occurred to the investors in private, unregulated businesses. Through the increased valuation and earnings of a factory the stockholders can buy as much with their dividends now as they did in 1914.

This assertion is important if true. It is flatly challenged in the supplementary opinion of Commissioner Eastman:

> No proof whatever has been proffered that the returns of investors in private enterprises not subject to public regulation tend to vary in dollars in ratio with the dollar's purchasing power. . . . What proof has been or can be supplied that dividends upon common stock tend to change in rate and amount in proportion to changes in gold dollar purchasing power? The fact is that investors as a group, like various other groups in the community, in general suffer loss with the depreciation of the dollar and gain with its appreciation. That is one of the risks of investment. Why, then, should the government single out one class of investors for special treatment?

A simple and adequate method of testing Commissioner Woodlock's assumption would be to compare the selling prices of the common stock of a considerable number and variety of representative industrial and commercial concerns in the years 1914 and 1926. If substantially all of them show in 1926 an appreciation in value approximating the increase in the general price level, the assumption may be regarded as valid. Private investments have increased in value and their earnings have grown in volume sufficiently to compensate for the depreciated dollar. If, however, no such general trend appears, if the increases are easily explainable by other factors than the rise in the prices of commodities, Commissioner Woodlock's argument loses whatever ethical plausibility it potentially contains.

According to Mr. Richberg, this is the actual situation. Important facts, he says, prove (1) "that investments in private business do *not* increase their earning power proportionately as the dollar declines and (2) that the decline of the dollar brings losses to great groups in the community for which there is no recompense afforded by law and (3) that on the whole the investing group is one group which naturally suffers some loss with the depreciation of the dollar."[14]

Even if the assumption made by Mr. Woodlock and denied by Messrs. Eastman and Richberg were in accord with the facts, it would not compel the conclusion that a valuation on the basis of actual cost or a valuation which disregards the enhancement of prices since 1914, would be unjust to the stockholders. About two-thirds of the investment in railroads and at least that proportion in other public utilities, consists of bonds and preferred stock. Neither the value nor the earnings of these securities would be increased by valuation on the basis of reproduction cost. Why should such increases be given to those investors (the holders of common stock) who have provided only one-

[14]*Op. cit.*, p. 49. For an excellent legal discussion of valuation see Mr. Richberg's *Brief in Behalf of the National Conference on Valuation of American Railroads*, as *Amicus Curiae* in the Supreme Court of the United States, October Term, A. D., 1928.

third of the capital? Their greater risk is amply met by their higher rate of interest.

From the economic and practical point of view, reproduction cost is open to powerful objections. Owing to the inevitable variations in the estimates of prices, expenditures and property elements, the concept itself is indefinite and hypothetical. Sufficient evidence of this uncertainty is found in the great differences in the estimates of reproduction cost submitted by the experts in valuation processes. In the Indianapolis Water case, the estimate by one of the company's engineering firms exceeded the commission engineer's estimate by 16 per cent, and was more than 3 ½ per cent above the figures submitted by the other firm of company engineers. It has been well said that in a large proportion of cases, estimates of reproduction cost are "little more than dignified guesses."[15]

Even if it could be ascertained with the utmost definiteness and without the enormous expense which it generally involves, reproduction cost would be an undesirable measure of valuation. It is highly unstable. It changes with every change in the price level. It calls for a modification of valuation, rates and earnings every time the price level moves upward or downward. The inconveniences and evils that would result from adopting this standard of value are strikingly indicated in the following sentences which occur in the decision of the Interstate Commerce Commission in the O'Fallon case (pp. 31, 32):

Let us consider the effect of applying this doctrine of current reproduction cost to all railroad property in the United States. For convenience in calculation and

---

[15] Summarizing the experience of public utility commissions with reproduction cost, Justice Brandeis wrote the following sentences in his dissenting opinion in the Southwestern Bell Telephone case: "Gradually it came to be realized that the definiteness of the engineer's calculations was delusive; that they rested upon shifting theories; and that their estimates varied so widely as to intensify rather than to allay doubts. . . . The conviction is widespread that a sound conclusion as to the actual value of a utility is not to be reached by a meticulous study of conflicting estimates of the cost of reproducing new the congeries of old machinery and equipment called the plant, and the still more fanciful estimates concerning the value of the intangible elements of an established business."

for want of an accurate figure, we shall assume 18 billions as the value at 1914 unit prices of structures existing on June 31, 1919. The aggregate value which we used in *Ex Parte 74* at the time of the general rate increase of 1920 was $18,900,000,000 for all property used for transportation purposes. But taking 18 billions as a base and applying the bureau's ratios, the value of precisely the same structures would have become 41.4 billions in 1920, 35.1 billions in 1921, 28.3 billions in 1922, and 31.3 billions in 1923. In other words, assuming a static property there would have been a gain of 23.4 billions in 1920, a loss of 6.3 billions in 1921, a further loss of 6.8 billions in 1922 and a gain again of 3 billions in 1923. These huge "profits" and "losses" would have occurred without change in the railroad property used in the public service other than the theoretical and speculative change derived from a shifting of general price levels. . . . During the seven years 1920 to 1926, inclusive, there was an approximate net investment in additions and betterments and new construction of 4 billions. These were paid for at then current prices, all above, in many cases far above, present prices. Assuming that there has since been an average decline in unit price level of 25 per cent, a valuation under the current reproduction cost doctrine would wipe out 1 billion of that additional investment. The effect upon any railroad entirely or largely constructed during the period 1920 to 1926 may be imagined.

A sustained attempt to make valuations and rates conform exactly and promptly to these price fluctuations would obviously have produced vast losses, uncertainty, confusion and inconvenience. Practically speaking, the thing could not have been done. To be sure, the adjustment might be made at long intervals, say once every ten years. But a method which is feasible in inverse ratio to the extent and frequency of its use can scarcely justify itself either theoretically or practically.

While the owners of public utilities cannot as a matter

of strict justice lay claim to valuations on the basis of reproduction cost, general conceptions of fairness as well as of expediency suggest that they should receive the benefit of *some* increase above the actual cost of their property. This would be in accordance with fairness or equity because a very large proportion of other property owners have reaped such an advantage from the rise in prices since 1914. It would be expedient because the courts, particularly the Supreme Court, have in recent years pretty consistently given some weight to present cost of reproduction.

There are two good reasons, however, why the valuations should not be as great as the price increase since the property was constructed: first, public utilities have never, since 1876, been legally recognized as having the same rights to profit by value increases as have private businesses; second, the value increases that are allowed will remain even though prices should afterward fall. For the actual investment method of valuation (which with adjustments is the one here advocated as against reproduction cost) provides that the values thus determined should continue as the rate basis, regardless of subsequent changes in the level of prices. If the stockholders obtain a part of the price advance that has already taken place and if they are protected against a future decline in prices, they will receive abundantly fair treatment.

The most generous method of adjustment is that proposed by John Bauer: add to the actual investment one-half of the amount obtained by multiplying the stockholders' portion by the per cent of subsequent increase in general price level.[16] That is to say, the stockholders would obtain the benefit of one-half the increase in prices, computed, however, on their own portion of the investment, not on the whole investment. For example, a lighting concern has cost $50,000,000 of which one-half has been derived from the sale of bonds and one-half provided by stockholders. Assume that the general level of prices has

---

[16] *Op. cit.*, p. 129.

increased 100 per cent since the plant was constructed. Multiply $25,000,000 by 50 per cent and you have the addition which is to be made to the stockholders' equity and to the total value. Instead of being valued at actual cost the property now has a value of $62,500,000. Since the bondholders never receive the benefit of an increase in prices, there is no reason why they should be considered in this particular adjustment. Since the stockholders have put up only half the money, there is no good reason why they should be allowed the benefit of any price increase on the money furnished by the bondholders.

Another method of giving the stockholders some increase in valuation is to allow them the full advance that has occurred in that portion of their property which consists of land. All the artificial portions would be valued at their actual cost. This is the rule that was applied by the Supreme Court to the railroads involved in the Second Minnesota Rate cases. It has also been adopted, substantially, by the Interstate Commerce Commission in the O'Fallon case and for all the other railroads of the country. "Substantially adopted," because the measure of valuation for the artificial property is not actual cost but reproduction cost as estimated for the year, 1914. This method would probably be more favorable to the railroads than to such utilities as gas plants and street railways.

Still another method would be to allow a higher rate of return on stock which was issued before the great rise in prices than on later issues. Instead of an increase in valuation there would be an increase in the rate of interest. On its face, however, this method seems to be less practicable than either of the other two.

As regards the fair rate of return, we have the opinion of John Bauer that it should be 7 per cent of the total value.[17] In a case where half the investment consisted of bonds paying 6 per cent interest the net return to the stockholders would be 8 per cent. If the rate on the bonds was

---

[17] *Op. cit.*, pp. 256, 257.

167

5 per cent, the stockholders' net return would be 9 per cent. According as the bondholders' portion was greater or less than one-half the total investment, the gain to the stockholders would be greater or less, respectively, than the above figures.

In the New York Telephone case the company demanded 8 per cent. In rejecting this demand the Court declared that the monopolistic character and the constant expansion of the telephone business made it an alluring form of investment. Indeed the language used by the Court in describing the exceptional security attending investment in the New York Telephone Company justified a rate as low as 6 per cent. Certainly the great majority of investors would be quite content with that rate on any property that offered equal security, or an equally solid guarantee that 6 per cent would be forthcoming every year. Nevertheless the Court fixed the rate at 7 per cent on the valuation. Of course, this is equivalent to more than 7 per cent on the common stock, owing to the large portion of the valuation which is represented by bonds upon which the company does not have to pay more than 5 per cent. In all probability, however, the Court felt constrained to allow a 7 per cent return on account of the frequency with which that rate had been named in previous decisions. Congress has already fixed the return for interstate railroads at 6 per cent. Even though a single maximum rate should prove impracticable for all utilities, the legislative bodies could put upon the companies the burden of proving that the legislatively fixed rate was lower than that commonly obtained from investments offering no greater security.

The most discouraging development that has yet occurred in this matter is the decision rendered by the Supreme Court of the United States in *The United Railways and Electric Company of Baltimore* vs. *Harold E. West et al.*, January 6, 1930. No fair objection can be offered to the general principle laid down by the Court:

THE ETHICS OF PUBLIC UTILITY VALUATION

A public utility is entitled to such rates as will permit it to earn a return . . . equal to that generally being made at the same time and in the same general part of the country on investments in other business undertakings which are attended by corresponding risks and uncertainties. . . .

Under the protection of this principle, however, the Court judged that the Baltimore Street Railway Company was entitled to a return of not less than 7.44 per cent on its valuation. As Justice Brandeis showed in his comprehensive and irrefutable dissenting opinion, this conclusion is not adequately supported by the facts.

In view of the fact that the stockholders in a public utility enjoy a substantial degree of legal assurance that they will regularly receive the stipulated rate of return, 7 per cent on the valuation and a substantially larger rate on the net investment seems to exemplify very generous treatment. The question may be raised whether a 6 per cent rate of return would not attract all the money necessary to finance most public utility concerns.

Ever since the Munn case, it has been the theory of the law that regulation of rates for utility services is an ethical process. For upwards of 40 years, the courts have recognized that the related question of valuation is an ethical question. The difference between the theory of original cost and that of reproduction cost is likewise an ethical issue. Indeed, it implies two diametrically opposed doctrines of property rights.

In the Middle Ages the chief function of property was to provide tools whereby men could exercise their labor power. For the most part, property was virtually identical with opportunity to work. Profit from property in the sense of interest on capital was of comparatively slight importance. With the arrival of the machine age capital became the means of obtaining a new and particular kind of income, in addition to and distinct from the rewards of labor. Nevertheless, the great majority of people have con-

169

tinued to regard interest as a moderate gain which supplements wages, or which enables them to make provision against the wants and uncertainties of the future. Indeed, these are the only rational ends of interest.

In recent years, a conception of property has arisen which exceeds all the bounds of custom and decency and justice. Men who hold this concept believe that capital ought to bring unlimited returns. For them there is no such thing as a fair rate of interest. They desire excessive and indefinite rates of interest in order that they may increase as rapidly as possible their capital possessions and their economic power. Typical of their attitude is the defense of reproduction cost recently made by an attorney for, and manager of, a certain western public utility. To the objection that reproduction cost would give certain utilities an interest of 14 per cent on the money that they had invested, he replied in effect: "What of it? They ought to have 40 per cent, if they can get it."

The opposite view is that all the uses of property are subject to the moral law, to the precepts of charity and justice. The Catholic Church proclaims not only the doctrine of just wages for labor and just prices for goods, but of just interest for capital. And just interest is variously defined as "a moderate rate," "the rate which is pronounced fair by competent and fair-minded men," "the rate at which men are generally willing to invest their money," or "the rate which is permitted by the civil law on loans, plus a fair amount for greater risk." There is nothing in the Catholic teaching which sanctions a rate of 32 per cent on a non-competitive investment, even though the rate may be legally established through some hokus-pokus called valuation as in the Indianapolis Water case.

Had Pope Leo XIII foreseen the terms and the implications of the Indianapolis case, he might well have cited them by way of apt illustration when he wrote that penetrating sentence in the fourth paragraph of his *Encyclical*

THE ETHICS OF PUBLIC UTILITY VALUATION

on the Condition of Labor. After enumerating the more specific evils from which the working classes suffer he adds:

> The mischief has been increased by rapacious usury which, although more than once condemned by the Church, is nevertheless *under a different guise* [italics mine] but with like injustice, still practiced by covetous and grasping men.

The valuation of public utilities is one of the most important political and economic questions now before the American people. It will probably remain so for a long time to come. The reasons for this judgment are not far to seek. On a preceding page a general notion was given of the enormous increase in valuation and consequently in rates and charges which will be conceded to the railroads and other public utilities if the decision in the Indianapolis case becomes a controlling precedent. The only bit of silver lining to the cloud is the hope that if the rule of the Indianapolis case receives general application to the public utilities, the people will be compelled to recognize definitely that the policy of regulation has failed. They will realize that the only remedy is in public ownership and operation. When that day comes it will witness such deep and widespread resentment that the people will not tolerate a proposal to buy out the utilities at the inflated valuation.

The utility corporations will be well advised if they refrain from carrying their demands for increased valuation so far as to provoke this measure of popular indignation. In this country the opposition to capital, as such, and to fair interest on capital, is insignificant and negligible. The average person is willing to concede to the owners of capital that rate of annual return which he himself receives or would like to obtain. What the average man resents is special privileges for certain entrenched forms of capital and investment. He does not look with complacency upon the power to take rates of interest which are not justified

171

by labor, or sacrifice, or service. He is unwilling to give any private group of capitalists greater returns than those which can be obtained by them in a competitive market. And he will not indefinitely tolerate the exaction of higher rates either through the devices of monopoly or through the legerdemain of inflated valuation.

13. A Statutory Rule of Valuation

AT present the legal and judicial aspect of valuation is this: Some undefined and undetermined weight must be accorded to reproduction cost. Suppose that in the next railroad valuation case which is to go to the Supreme Court the Interstate Commerce Commission should add 10 per cent to original cost on the theory that this is sufficient recognition of reproduction cost; would the Court nullify this valuation? If it did so, would it provide or suggest some other definite per cent or some general formula or measure by which the Interstate Commerce Commission and the public utility commissions of the states could be guided in subsequent valuations? Probably not. And yet some such definite rule is absolutely essential if the public utility commissions are ever to be enabled to extricate themselves from the present valuation muddle. The only definite guiding knowledge that they now have is derived from decisions of the courts to the effect that the valuation must be somewhere between original cost and reproduction cost, where these differ, and that each individual case must be decided "on its own merits." But the latter formula provides no rational or definite direction. What the commissions are entitled to have is some rule which will enable them to evaluate intelligibly and according to some definite principle the merits of any and every case which they are called upon to consider.

In this predicament relief can come only from the source that ought to have provided it years ago, namely, the Congress and the state legislatures. More than once the Supreme Court has declared that rate making is a legislative function. Since rates cannot be intelligibly or fairly made without guiding rules and principles, the authority which is charged with that function ought to provide these rules

173

and principles. Of course, the legislatures could not do this arbitrarily. They could not lay down rules and principles which would contravene the "due process" clauses of the Constitution as interpreted by the Supreme Court. Within the limits thus far indicated in the decisions construing these clauses, there seems to remain considerable latitude for the legislatures.

January 24, 1930, the Interstate Commerce Commission addressed a letter to Congress suggesting the enactment by that body of "a modified method" of valuation for the railroads. According to this method, the value of any railroad property would be determined at any time by adding to the cost of reproduction in 1914 subsequent increases in the value of the land plus the actual cost of subsequent additions to the property. This suggestion of the Interstate Commerce Commission arises out of two facts—one general, the other particular. The general relevant fact is that the Supreme Court has never declared how much weight should be accorded to reproduction cost when this exceeds original cost. In the Southwestern Bell Telephone case, the Court fixed a valuation which exceeded the original cost by 25 per cent. In *McCardle* vs. *Indianapolis Water Company* the valuation allowed by the Court was approximately 80 per cent above original cost. In the O'Fallon case the Court declared that the Commission should have given consideration to reproduction cost, but failed to specify "the weight to be accorded thereto."

It is now quite obvious that we need never expect any definite action from the federal judiciary. In the absence of positive legislation, the long train of noncommittal decisions shows quite plainly that the uncertainty attending the present method of ascertaining the value of public utility property for rate-making purposes will probably go on indefinitely as long as we leave the final determination of the matter with the Supreme Court.

The refusal of the Court in the O'Fallon case to specify the exact weight to be given to reproduction cost is the

174

particular fact which gave rise to the letter addressed to Congress by the Interstate Commerce Commission. The Commission's valuation of the O'Fallon railroad was set aside because it "gave no consideration to increase in prices since 1914," but the Commission was not informed how large the consideration should have been in order to satisfy the Court.

In its present situation the Commission does not know what percentage of addition on account of increased costs since 1914 will be sufficient to prevent the Court from again setting aside its valuation of the O'Fallon property. Since the Court has studiously refused to lay down a general rule on this point, the Commission properly appeals to Congress.

Now, what the Interstate Commerce Commission tried to do in the O'Fallon case, and what it proposes to have Congress do, is, in effect, practically the same as many economists favoring the so-called "prudent investment" doctrine have been advocating for a long time. I say "practically" because the Commission would have the value of railroads determined by using the reproduction cost as of 1914 as a starting point and adding the cost of subsequent additions. The fact of the matter is that there was not a great difference between "prudent investment cost" and "reproduction cost" in 1914. Prices of raw materials did not skyrocket until the World War came upon us.

There is no reason, therefore, for prudent investment theorists to object to the 1914 basis of the Commission's valuation plan simply because it happens to be labeled "reproduction cost value." Such a plan would unquestionably go a long way towards stabilizing the rate bases of these great transportation agencies and would undoubtedly affect regulatory policies for public utilities generally.

But why did the highest court refuse to approve of such a plan when it was presented for its approval in the O'Fallon case?

The reason given by the Supreme Court for modifying

175

the findings of the Commission in the O'Fallon case was that the Commission had disregarded Paragraph 4, Section 15a of the Interstate Commerce Act, which requires "due consideration to all the elements of value recognized by the law of the land for rate-making purposes, . . ." "The law of the land" is not expressed in any congressional statute. It is found in the decisions of the Supreme Court. Hence the fundamental reason why the Court set aside the valuation of the O'Fallon property made by the Interstate Commerce Commission was that its own rules and decisions had been disregarded by the Commission.

In effect, therefore, the letter of the Commission asked Congress to modify and in part annul the Court's definition of fair value. Now, there is no doubt that *Smyth* vs. *Ames* is the big stumbling block towards stabilizing the rate base by legislative act.

One might say it is the Dred Scott decision of public utility regulation.

Had Congress fixed the rules of valuation before the decision in the case of *Smyth* vs. *Ames,* its action would probably have been followed by a considerable number of decisions which gave specific recognition to cost of reproduction.

One of the most peculiar things about this case of *Smyth* vs. *Ames* was the fact that the so-called present value was urged by the champions of the rate payers as opposed to the "capitalization value" asked for by the railroads. Theoretically capitalization value should be about the same as original cost, but the late William Jennings Bryan, who appeared against the railroads, charged that such a capitalization might be considerably watered and so the highest court was constrained at the insistence of this advocate of the people to decree that present or "real" value should receive consideration for rate-making purposes.

It is a matter of history that the sharp rise in construction costs during the World War brought a corresponding right-about face in the alignment of partisan interests with

176

regard to reproduction cost as a measure for rate valuation. But I comment on this fact parenthetically because it seems to me that what was originally intended by the highest court as a restriction on the composition of utility rate bases has, by virtue of war-time economic fluctuation become a boomerang to the rate payer. I wonder if the literal and consistent reaffirmance of this doctrine by the highest court in later years has been in strict conformity with the intention of the justices that occupied the bench in 1898, not one of whom survives today.

Regardless of such a speculation, however, the fact remains that the Supreme Court once having taken the "present value" stand has hewn to the line. In the face of this history, would the court now uphold a congressional statute which disregarded reproduction cost except in the matter of land?

A definite answer to this question cannot be had except through congressional action. The Supreme Court might refrain from setting aside a law which gave to reproduction cost only that weight which arises out of increased values of land. At any rate, the experiment is well worth making.

Should the Supreme Court fail to sustain the valuation law which the Commission requests, Congress might then pass a statute fixing the definite maximum weight to be accorded in valuation cases to the present cost of reproduction of the artificial property of the railroads. The maximum might be placed at 10 per cent, or 20 per cent, or even 25 per cent. By specifying a maximum rather than a rigid figure, the law would allow the Commission some latitude for making lower allowances in cases where economic conditions, such as competition, rendered impracticable a higher valuation. The important thing, the necessary thing, is that the Commission should have some definite guidance with regard to reproduction cost.

In connection with the letter sent by the Commission to Congress, a dissenting statement was made by Commissioner Woodlock. "Value for rate-making purposes,"

177

he says, "is a fact to be found by a judicial process and not a relation to be fixed by a process of legislation."

This is a curious fallacy. Economic value is indeed a fact which can be judicially ascertained but "value for rate-making purposes" is not economic value; it is "fair value," and this is not an economic fact but an ethical judgment. No amount of economic evidence will suffice to answer the question whether reproduction cost ought or ought not to enter into the valuaton of railroads. No amount of judicial consideration can decide this question without bringing in the ethical notions of the judges. Now the ethical opinions and judgments of Congress may be quite as closely in accord with objective ethical truth as those of the Supreme Court. Contrary to Commissioner Woodlock's view, fair value is "a relation" and not "a fact," *i.e.*, an economic fact.

Commissioner Woodlock declares further that the law of the land governing the valuation of public utility property "rests upon a constitutional and not upon a legislative foundation, . . ."

The constitutional basis for the "law of the land" which recognizes present reproduction cost is rather remote. The Constitution does, indeed, prohibit confiscation of property and this prohibition has been interpreted by the Supreme Court as forbidding the public authorities to fix rates which will give less than a fair return on a fair valuation. Fair valuation has in turn been interpreted by the Court to include a greater or lesser allowance for present cost of reproduction. The last mentioned provision has therefore been judicially read into the Constitution. If a majority of the Supreme Court during the last ten years had held the views on valuation entertained by Justices Holmes, Brandeis and Stone, a different construction would have been judicially put upon the "due process" clause as regards property. In that case, the Constitution and the "law of the land" would have given no recognition to present reproduction costs of artificial property.

178

Consequently there is nothing in the Constitution to prevent Congress from determining the rules of valuation and from defining confiscation as regards the financial returns on public utilities. The real obstacle exists in certain decisions of the Supreme Court. How far these can be "circumvented" by Congressional action as suggested in the letter of the Interstate Commerce Commission can be definitely known only through a favorable response to the suggestion and the subsequent fate of the enactment before the Supreme Court.

Both Congress and the state legislatures should fix the maximum rate of return to be allowed the utilities in rate-making proceedings. This rate should be high enough to attract new capital, but there is no reason why it should be higher.

14. The Problem of Unemployment

A. THE FINDINGS OF THE SENATE COMMITTEE

DURING the early months of 1928 the considerable increase in the number of idle workingmen occasioned a pretty widespread discussion of unemployment. Several debates about it took place in the United States Senate. The number of unemployed was put at 4,000,000 by Senator Wagner and others, while the protagonists of Republican prosperity asserted that this estimate was at least 100 per cent too high. Some of the latter cleverly misrepresented a statement given to the Senate by the Commissioner of Labor Statistics. According to the Commissioner, the number of persons at work in 1928 was 1,874,000 less than in 1925. By the official exponents of prosperity this was set forth as the total number of the unemployed. Such use of the Commissioner's statement could be justified only on the assumption that in 1925 there was absolutely no unemployment, an assumption which was not frankly made by any of Senator Wagner's opponents.

The practical outcome of the Senate discussion was a resolution adopted May 3, 1928, providing for "an analysis and appraisal of reports on unemployment and systems for prevention and relief thereof." In conformity with this resolution, the Senate Committee on Education and Labor, under the chairmanship of Mr. Couzens, held twelve hearings in the months of December, 1928, and January and February, 1929. Business men, industrial engineers, personnel managers, college professors and government officials were heard at length. On March 1, 1929, the Committee made its report, which has since been published by the

180

Government Printing Office in a volume of 530 octavo pages, entitled *Unemployment in the United States.*

In addition to a transcript of the testimony referred to above, the report presents several interesting and important memoranda describing legislation against unemployment in foreign countries, proposed legislation in the United States and provisions obtaining in several American industries for unemployment insurance. There is also a long summary of the testimony at the end of the volume by Dr. Isador Lubin, and thirteen pages of comment at the beginning by the Senate Committee.

These preliminary pages will naturally attract more attention than any other part of the report, since they embody the conclusions reached by the men who conducted the hearings. The most definite recommendation made by the Committee is that the Bureau of the Census should make a count of the number of the unemployed when it takes the decennial census of 1930. This suggestion has been carried out by the Bureau, but the results are unconvincing and unsatisfactory.

Less confident and clear-cut is the language of the Committee concerning employment exchanges. However, it does declare that "efficient public exchanges should replace private exchanges," that the United States Employment Service should be reorganized sufficiently to supervise and co-ordinate the operations of exchanges conducted by the states and municipalities. What the Committee says about the United States Employment Service recalls a statement in the Bishops' Program of Social Reconstruction: "It is the obvious duty of Congress to continue and strengthen this important institution." Unfortunately, Congress did not recognize this duty in the months following the war. As a matter of fact, it almost crippled the Federal Employment Service. Now one of its own committees realizes that this course was unwise. On the other hand, the limitations of public employment exchanges ought to be kept steadily in mind. They can do no more than decrease slightly the

181

volume of unemployment. Very few employers are compelled to cease or even greatly to curtail their business activities because of inability to find employees promptly. There are too many other ways of making their wants known. And obviously employment bureaus cannot increase the number of jobs. What they can do is to reduce the cost and trouble of finding employment and employees, and enable both employer and employee sometimes to make better and more intelligent selections.

In the third place, the Committee recommends at some length stabilization of seasonal employment, quoting the estimate by Sam Lewisohn that the saving possible in this field amounts to $2,000,000,000 annually. Several of the witnesses at the hearings described the success which had attended their efforts to regularize their own businesses. The best-known illustrations of seasonal industries are the building and clothing trades. "Stabilization" describes the process of reducing the number of employed and the amount of production during the busy season of the year, and increasing both during the dull season. Undoubtedly this arrangement is superior in many respects to unbalanced seasonal operation, but its benefits can easily be exaggerated. It does not, except possibly indirectly, increase the total of employment in any industry. All that it does is to distribute the amount of employment and production more evenly throughout the year. Indeed, it reduces the total number of persons who find some employment in the industry, inasmuch as it lessens the demand for labor during the so-called "peak" or busy season. Of course this disadvantage to a small number of part-time workers is more than offset by the benefits of that more steady employment which the arrangement brings to the majority. Steadier operation of the plant likewise benefits the employer, since it reduces operating costs. In the words of Henry S. Dennison before the Committee:

> It is very expensive for management to run a plant full time for eight months and slack time for four, or partly for ten and not at all for two, as a good many

do, for when a plant is shut down overhead expenses continue to go on.

If the employer should pass on these gains to the consumer in the form of lower prices, he could increase somewhat the demand for his product and therefore the number of persons employed. However, none of the exponents of stabilization that appeared before the Committee mentioned this possible outcome.

Outside the seasonal industries stabilization would have no effect whatever. By far the greater part of present unemployment is in the industries that are not seasonal. Industry as a whole is no more seasonal, no more in need of or amenable to stabilization than it was in the first half of 1929; yet unemployment is very much greater. Whatever be the virtues of stabilization in the industries to which it is applicable, it is obviously not a remedy in the non-seasonal industries. It is these that present the great bulk of the existing unemployment.

In recent months the word, "stabilization," has come to be used with reference to a period of years, to the business cycle of boom and depression, instead of to a single year. To stabilize industries in this sense means to keep them in operation regularly year after year, instead of permitting them to undergo periodical slumps as in 1914, 1921 and 1930. Used in this sense, "stabilization" does not describe or suggest a remedy. It merely gives a high-sounding name to the object that is sought. It does not tell us how the object is to be attained. Undoubtedly this long-run stabilization would provide continuous employment, but until those who use the term are able to show us how the thing is to be done, they are simply indulging in misleading platitudes. They are substituting verbalism for thinking and deceiving others if not themselves.

The "prosperity reserve" likewise received strong endorsement from the Committee. This is a recently invented bit of jargon to describe the proposal of concentrating and increasing public works in a time of industrial depression.

183

Undoubtedly, it would counteract considerably the forces making for depression if it were carefully organized and carried out in sufficient volume. The administrative difficulties are, however, very considerable. As commonly set forth, the scheme implies not only an increase of public works in dull times but a slackening of them in very busy times. How are the legislators and other public officials to determine when prosperity is so great as to justify a retrenchment of public expenditures for roads, buildings, *et cetera?* For several years we had loud and positive and authoritative assurances that we were in the midst of great prosperity. Suppose Congress had decided in the winter of 1929 to withhold all appropriations for new Federal projects, and suppose that the states, counties, cities and towns had adopted the same policy. The net effect upon employment would have been grave indeed, for the vast majority of public employees thus displaced would not have been able to find work in private industries. Only when the public authorities are preventing private employers from obtaining men and materials which they urgently need would the slackening of public works be attended by no diminution in the aggregate volume of employment. And it is questionable whether the average legislative body could determine the existence of this condition with sufficient accuracy or sufficient promptness, or discontinue the retrenchment policy soon enough. Let us assume, however, that the condition exists and is wisely dealt with. The workers engaged in public construction could readily find employment in non-public industries. There would be no increase in unemployment. When the depression arrived all the men formerly upon public works would resume operations in that field, together with the additional number required to carry on the public activities which had been neglected during the time of great prosperity. The latter group would represent a net increase in the volume of employment. In the absence of the "prosperity reserve" arrangement, they would not be employed at all.

184

THE PROBLEM OF UNEMPLOYMENT

Such is the theory of the scheme. Its possible good effects would be offset to some extent by its evil influence in exaggerating business activity during a prosperous period, thereby causing excessive expansion and inevitably increasing the depth of the succeeding depression. However, the diminution of public works is no necessary part of a rational project of this sort. That part of the theory which assumes that public works should be retrenched by an equal degree during the first succeeding period of great prosperity had better be thrown overboard entirely. In that case, the much-vaunted "prosperity reserve" would be merely a device for increasing public works when private employment is unusually slack. As such, it is not a new thing under the sun. Many governments, both national and local, have striven to increase the amount of public works in dull times. The only thing new in the proposal, as it is now agitated, is the provision for previous planning and wider use. If it is to produce any considerable number of good results, it should be frankly recognized as committing governments to a very large increase in the amount of public works to be constructed during any period of years which includes a business depression.

In accordance with the immense amount of testimony and information offered at the hearings, the Committee recommends unemployment insurance. But it clearly prefers voluntary and private plans to compulsory and public plans. It rejects "the systems of unemployment insurance now in vogue under foreign governments," and declares that interference by the Federal government in this field "is not necessary nor advisable at this time." However, it does admit by implication the possible value of public insurance, inasmuch as it declares that the study of this problem should be left to the state legislatures. Undoubtedly, the Committee is right in preferring state to national unemployment insurance, but its faith in the possibilities of voluntary and private effort in this field is scarcely justified by experience or by the probabilities.

185

Finally, the Committee gives a qualified endorsement to old-age pensions in the statement that further consideration might well be given to the necessity and advisability of establishing them, "either through private industry, through the states or through the Federal government."

On their face all six of the foregoing recommendations aim at preventing or reducing the hardships of unemployment. A federal census of the unemployed would stimulate constructive action and give valuable guidance by providing adequate information. A comprehensive system of employment exchanges would reduce costs and hardships, and in some degree would lessen the time spent by some wage-earners in search of work. Stabilization of seasonal employment would only indirectly and very slightly reduce the total amount of unemployment during any given year. The "prosperity reserve," with the amendment suggested above, could be so organized as to reduce very considerably the amount of unemployment in periods of depression. Unemployment insurance would relieve an enormous amount of human suffering and it ought to be adopted in every industry. Legislative action, as contemplated in the Huber Bill which nearly became a law in Wisconsin a few years ago, indicates the only adequate method. Both public and private insurance plans could be so organized as to restrict the volume of a depression, by discouraging and preventing over-expansion of plants during especially prosperous periods. From the nature of the case, old-age pensions would not reduce unemployment. They would greatly mitigate its hardships, particularly in our country at the present time when the age limit for employment has been so considerably lowered. If men cannot find jobs after the age of forty-five or fifty, the number of those who may be called the "economically aged" becomes greatly enlarged and the need for old-age pensions greatly intensified.

Although these measures do not seem capable of increasing in any considerable degree the average amount of employment, their beneficent possibilities in other relations are

186

enormous. Their good effects can be comprehensively indicated in the statement that thousands of Americans would have larger and steadier incomes, and would in greater or less degree be relieved from the fear of want and many other demoralizing influences associated with insufficient employment.

The volume, *Unemployment in the United States*, contains one paragraph which gives full recognition to the urgency of the problem and the obligation of society to solve the problem:

> It may as well be remembered that society is going to provide an opportunity for man to sustain himself, or is going to have to sustain man. Society is going to provide opportunity for man to pay his own way or is going to pay for him. Society may as well make every effort to do the job constructively because no society can be strong in which its members are encouraged or forced to adopt the position or place of those seeking charity.

B. TECHNOLOGICAL UNEMPLOYMENT

It is a curious irony that the Senate Committee failed utterly to suggest any specific method for dealing with the precise kind of unemployment which provoked its appointment. The Committee observes correctly that "the causes or the types of unemployment might be divided into three classes: cyclical, seasonal and technological." The outstanding remedy for the first type is, of course, the "prosperity reserve"; for the second, stabilization; but neither of these touches the third type. To it the Committee devotes only two or three short paragraphs and in these it exhibits no adequate comprehension of the phenomenon:

> Technological unemployment covers that vast field where, through one device or another and chiefly through a machine supplanting a human, skilled workers have found that their trade no longer exists and that their skill is no longer needed.

As a matter of fact, the skilled workers who are displaced by new and improved machinery and other forms of efficiency merely constitute a spectacular form of the evil. They are probably a small proportion of the total number of workers who are thrown out of employment by mechanical and technical progress.

Only one member of the Committee, the late Senator Tyson of Tennessee, showed that he had envisaged the problem. Here are the terms in which he formulated it while the Committee was listening to Henry S. Dennison:

> Assuming that the present hours of labor were to continue and full-time employment given to everybody, don't you think that the country would be overstocked in a very short time? . . . The pig-iron industry is now depressed very badly. The textile business is very badly depressed. The coal business is very badly depressed. The woolen business is very

188

badly depressed. Everybody knows that there is overproduction. Now, then, how are you going to remedy
that—by continuing to produce?

Although Mr. Dennison is one of the most enlightened,
humane and progressive employers in the United States, his
answer to these questions was wholly inadequate. It
amounted simply to an act of faith that since the men displaced by machines in years gone by had always found
other employment eventually, the same thing will presumably happen in the present situation. At a later hearing
Senator Tyson returned to this subject, saying:

> If we are to keep taking people into our industry
> and keep them employed we shall have to employ
> them for shorter periods each day. . . . I believe if
> we had seventy hours of work each week as we had
> several generations ago and people worked every day
> with the present amount of machinery, we would
> have 10,000,000 out of work instead of 4,000,000,
> because with the machine process individuals have be-
> come much more efficient than they ever were before.

Among the other witnesses at the hearings, only President Green of the American Federation of Labor, Mr. Sam
A. Lewisohn and Professor John R. Commons had anything to say about technological unemployment. None of
them professed to be able to offer a remedy, except Mr.
Lewisohn, who mentioned stabilization and public labor
exchanges. Obviously both these suggestions are futile.
Professor Commons cited a striking example of displacement of men by machines in the clothing trade. One firm
was able to reduce its force of cutters from 600 to 250. Of
the 350 thus rendered superfluous, 200 quit voluntarily
and the remaining 150 received from the unemployment
insurance fund of the industry $500 each as a sort of "sep-
aration allowance." It is probable that no system of voluntary unemployment insurance could take care of all the
displaced workers at such a cost. Moreover, an allowance of

189

$500 is often an insufficient provision for a man who may find employment only after several months, and then perhaps at a considerably lower rate of pay.

Recent Economic Changes, which is the title of the report of the Committee appointed and headed by Mr. Hoover to study that subject, gives considerable attention to this new kind of unemployment. It states:

> Unemployment can arise as a result of industrial efficiency as well as inefficiency. In the latter case we have seasonal or intermittent unemployment; in the former case, what has come to be known as "technological unemployment" resulting from the introduction of new machinery and processes. . . . This is a serious aspect of unemployment.

Following are some of the striking indications of the vast increase which has taken place in productive efficiency since the year 1919: the average per capita production in all industries increased 39 per cent between 1919 and 1925; the per capita increase in factories was 25 per cent between 1920 and 1927; but the number of workers in the factories was 1,250,000 less in 1928 than in 1923, while the number employed on railroads decreased 150,000. According to the *Industrial Review of the Year* (July, 1928—July, 1929) issued by the Federal Council of Churches, "there were 2,300,000 fewer persons employed in farming, manufacturing, railroading and mining in 1928 than in 1920." In 1928, the *New York Journal of Commerce* declared:

> We are so accustomed to associate unemployment with prostrate industry, closed factories and universal profound depression that it is hard to revise our ideas and grasp the fact that we must also grapple with an unemployment problem that is the direct outcome of prosperity.

The association of prosperity with great unemployment and the responsibility of the former for the latter, are no longer doubted by competent students. One might indeed

190

raise the question whether such a condition can properly be called "prosperity." An affirmative answer would seem to be justified if the term be defined as a condition of industry in which the total production is above the average of any preceding period, and in which the incomes of a very large proportion of the wage-earners are likewise above preceding averages.

"There is nothing new about these problems," says *Recent Economic Changes.* The substitution of machines for men and the displacement of workers by improved productive processes have, indeed, been going on steadily since the beginning of the industrial revolution. Not the problem itself of finding employment for the disemployed, but the magnitude of the thing is new. As shown by the figures quoted above, the process of substitution and displacement has been considerably more rapid in recent years than in any former period. Hence the necessity of what the report calls "an accelerated rate of readjustment." Up to the present the rate has not been adequately "accelerated." In spite of the new occupations that have arisen, mostly as an incident of the general process of invention and mechanization, in hotels, garages, moving picture houses, advertising, selling, bootlegging, road construction, and in factories turning out automobiles, radios, phonographs, electric supplies, silk goods, cigarettes, *et cetera,* unemployment has increased and the average worker has been more than ever out of work. An investigation recently made by the Institute of Economics of the Brookings Institution revealed the fact that the newer industries are not absorbing the jobless as fast as is usually believed. Some 800 displaced workers were studied in three industrial centers. More than one-half of those who succeeded in finding new jobs had been idle for more than three months, while of those still unemployed, about one-half had been out of work for the same length of time. After a rapid survey of the situation, Stuart Chase, in his recent book, *Men and Machines,* puts down this summary judgment:

191

I am seriously afraid that accelerating unemployment is here; that the park bench is destined to grow longer. The advertisers may be able to stimulate new wants that will take care of some of the displaced men, but who is to stimulate the purchasing power that will absorb the commodities new and old?

The outlook would not be so discouraging if we could be certain that the invention of new machines and improved methods would soon come to an end or suffer a considerable slowing down. But there are no definite grounds upon which to base any such expectation. Indeed, some authorities think that these improvements will increase rather than decrease. Writing at the beginning of the year 1929, Dr. William Leiserson forecast the promise of the American industry to its wage-earners as follows:

> Those who are employed shall earn more than ever before; but fewer shall be called to work and more shall be unemployed. Employers have discovered that it is cheaper to pay higher wages to a smaller number of efficient workers than lower wages to a larger number of less efficient. Industry is therefore concentrating its work in the hands of a smaller number of employees. The younger, the more accurate and capable, workers are taught and stimulated by incentive wage payment plans to produce and to earn more, while the older, the slower, and the less efficient workers are weeded out to swell the ranks of the unemployed.

In view of the magnitude and persistence of this new kind of unemployment, it might well be called "chronic." This word has not, indeed, the scientific implications of "technological," but it has much greater practical value. "Technological" tends to "take the curse off" the evil condition which it describes; "chronic" is much more suggestive and much more likely to convey the thought that "something ought to be done about it."

The fundamental cause of the evil is, of course, our old

192

friend "overproduction," or more precisely speaking, a general and constant capacity for overproduction. It is most pronounced in agriculture, coal mining, textiles, the boot and shoe industries and is becoming rather pronounced in the building trades. It is manifested not only by idle men and idle productive instruments but in the greatly increased costs of selling goods, in the prevalence of "high-power salesmanship" and in the enormous outlay for advertising. Perhaps the last mentioned phenomenon is the most conspicuous indication. The proper end of advertising is to supply information, but probably not more than 10 per cent of the "information" currently thrust upon the public is genuine. By far the greater part represents an attempt to persuade the consumers that Brown's product is better than that of Jones. Most of the real information that purchasers need could be obtained from a classified telephone directory, from the classified notices in the newspapers and from trade journals. Another large part of advertising is intended to arouse in the minds of the public a consciousness of needs that they do not now feel. This statement is not to be construed as a condemnation of all that sort of advertising, but merely to emphasize the fact that goods cannot be sold as fast as they can be produced. Hence we have a vast overcapacity to produce and a constant danger that this capacity will be converted into action. The other and more disagreeable side of the picture is widespread unemployment of both the machines and men.

To be sure, traditional and theoretical economics assures us that general overproduction is impossible. A supply of any kind of goods, we are told, is a demand for other goods. In so far as that formula is true it has no practical meaning; in so far as it means anything practical it is untrue. Every supply of goods is, of course, a *potential* demand. It constitutes a power to call for some other kind of goods. But it is not necessarily an actual demand for any kind of goods now existing. For example, the owner of a textile mill does not care to exchange his surplus product

193

for the surplus produced by a farmer. The latter may, indeed, want more clothing, but the former does not want more food. Possibly, he would like to exchange his surplus for a high-priced automobile, but the producer of the automobile does not want more textile goods. Similar statements can truthfully be made concerning the producers of surplus coal and shoes and a great many other products that are turned out faster than they can be sold. When two persons have a surplus of goods on their hands only one may desire the products of the other or neither may desire what the other has to offer. This situation may be general throughout the greater part of industry. All of those having an excess do, indeed, possess the power to obtain some of the other surplus products, but not all desire these surpluses, while those persons who feel a desire for the excessive stocks are without the purchasing power. Owing to this divorce between the desire and the power to consume, it is quite possible that surpluses may exist simultaneously in practically all of the great industries.

For the first time in American history, our unemployed have nowhere to go. If they are in the cities, they cannot flee to the land, because our farms already produce more than can be satisfactorily sold. If they are on the farms, they cannot go to the cities, unless they wish to lengthen the bread lines. Everywhere the power to produce increases faster than the power to consume, and production capacity runs to waste while people starve.

At the present time and during the recent past the excess has taken the form of productive capacity rather than stocks of goods. But the effect upon employment differs only in degree between the one case and the other. *Recent Economic Changes* suggests one remedy. "Wants are almost insatiable; there are new wants which will make way endlessly for newer wants, as fast as they are satisfied." As a general proposition, this is true. Without any change in the present distribution of consuming power all the workers might find employment supplying actual and potential wants if only the latter and the means of supplying them could be developed fast enough. Twenty-five years ago the automobile was generally unknown. Since then, hundreds of thousands of workers have found the means of a livelihood in this industry. To be sure, a great part of the purchasing power expended upon this commodity would have been exchanged for other goods if the automobile had not been invented; nevertheless a great part of the money would not have been spent at all, since its possessors did not desire any other kind of actually known goods. If other inventions as appealing as the automobile should appear next year, undoubtedly they would attract sufficient actual purchasing power to put all idle men and women at work. Of course, these hypothetical commodities would fall under the head of luxuries. Scales of wages need not rise; the total purchasing power in the hands of the working classes need not increase except with the increasing employment; all the workers would be employed in making goods to supply the new wants which had been developed in the possessors of surplus consuming power, that is, the rich and the well-to-do.

However, this picture has two vital defects. In the first place, it is quite unlikely that the requisite new commodities will be invented. More fundamental, is the objection that this would be an undesirable kind of industrial society. The people of our age, even the wealthy, would not be benefited by new luxuries, and the masses ought not to be required to provide superfluous goods for the few, while they themselves are unable to obtain a reasonable amount of necessaries and comforts.

C. HIGHER WAGES

Indirectly and by implication, *Recent Economic Changes* suggests a more acceptable remedy for the kind of unemployment which is now puzzling students of the problem. It endorses "the principle of high wages and low costs as a policy of enlightened industrial practice in a period of stationary cost of living—the recognition of wage earners as the great domestic market." As expressed by Ernest G. Draper at the hearings before the Senate Committee:

> Workers are consumers as well as producers, and to increase the purchasing power of consumers is desirable, not only for the worker himself but for industry and society as a whole.

A considerable proportion of business men have, since the war, become converts to this doctrine. Men who have to produce goods in competition with their fellows have always striven for low costs in order that they might sell at low prices. Until quite recently the great majority have believed that one means of obtaining low production costs was low wages. According to the new theory, it is still desirable to sell the largest possible quantity of goods at the lowest prices and with the lowest production costs, but it is not desirable nor necessary to obtain low costs through low wages. If goods can be manufactured in sufficient quantity, the production cost can be low; but in order to sell all these goods, even at low prices, purchasing power must be widely distributed. Money to buy the goods must exist in the hands not merely of a few well-to-do, but of the masses. The workers must have high wages in order to make their demands for goods effective. Increased power to consume must be extended to the only class that possesses in large measure the unsatisfied desire to consume.

This policy would provide the most humane and the most easily available remedy for the persistent overpro-

196

duction and underconsumption that afflict our industrial system. Instead of seeking to arouse new wants in the jaded appetites of the rich and well-to-do, why not supply the proper and reasonable wants of the toiling masses? Instead of striving to invent new luxuries and create new industries to satisfy wants that are as yet unknown and unfelt, why not provide an effective volume of demand for goods which are already known and desired, which can be produced by industries already established, but now languishing for lack of an adequate market? The masses desire and could use vastly more than they now obtain of the standard necessities and comforts: food, clothing, housing, hospitals and medical service, education, recreation and amusements. We already have the workers and the productive equipment to provide all these goods in vastly increased quantities. The magnitude of the latent demand for them may be appreciated when we reflect that probably the majority of employees, even in the United States, do not obtain adequate living wages. Would not a generous increase in the remuneration of our underpaid toilers be the most direct and the most obvious way to eliminate the evil of idle machines and idle men?

No intelligent student of our economic system doubts the capacity of our industries to satisfy in reasonable measure all these wants for the majority, and to provide a considerable surplus for the economically powerful minority. The extent to which our national production might be increased is not fully indicated by our unused equipment, our unemployed workers and the vast expansion of productive power that is obtainable without any new mechanical inventions. George Soule, in *The Useful Art of Economics,* says:

> In view of the vast array of preventable wastes, it is probably not an exaggeration to say that the national income might be doubled simply by eliminating them, even if inventions and knowledge of better

197

techniques for production should cease to advance today.

Not more productive power but a rational organization of existing power is what we need in order to provide all our people with the material means of well-being and thereby to abolish chronic unemployment.

The better organization that has just been outlined immediately provokes the ancient and facile objection that such a large increase in wages would involve such an increase in production costs as to frustrate the object sought, and that the higher cost of production would cause such a rise in prices that there would be little or no increase in the average demand for goods and for labor. To this objection the obvious answer is that not all the additional outlay for wages would be reflected in prices. The more extensive use and more steady operation of the plant would offset either partially or wholly the higher wage costs. The increased costs, be they great or little, would be defrayed only in part by the wage earners, inasmuch as they are not the only consumers of the goods affected by the increase. In general it should be noted that if this objection were always heeded, it would prevent any increase in wages for any reason whatsoever. Happily, it has not been heeded universally. Dr. Wesley C. Mitchell, who directed the study of recent economic changes, tells us that

American prosperity in 1922-1927 in non-agricultural lines would have been decidedly greater had the six million American farmers been flourishing.

Paraphrasing this statement, we observe that American prosperity would have been decidedly greater during the same period had the ten million or more underpaid American laborers been receiving adequate wages. The economic factors and implications are exactly the same in the two cases. Indeed, *Recent Economic Changes* gives some measure of endorsement to the doctrine and proposal here advocated when it declares that one of the ten outstanding

198

developments in our industrial history since 1920 has been "the recognition of wage earners as the great domestic market." It is too bad that the Committee did not explicitly accept the implications of this recognized fact. Instead of using language which tended to exaggerate the increase which has taken place in wages, it ought to have frankly pointed out that further increases are necessary before a large proportion of the working classes will have satisfactory incomes, and before their effective demand will be sufficiently enlarged to furnish an adequate market for the products of our industries.

The real difficulties confronting the proposal for a better organization of our distributive system, for a better combination of the desire to consume with the power to consume, have to do with the methods for obtaining the requisite increase in wages. While the individual employer may accept the doctrine that high wages and high purchasing power in the hands of labor are good and necessary for industry as a whole, he realizes, or thinks, that relatively low wages would be more profitable in his own business. He believes that this is true at least so long as his competitors fail to adopt the policy of high wages. To meet this difficulty, the only immediately adequate measure would be minimum wage scales fixed by law. Owing to the unfavorable decision of the Supreme Court in the District of Columbia Minimum Wage case, to say nothing of two or three other obstacles, this most important reform is, and for many years to come will remain, impossible of attainment in the United States. The only practical methods now available are increased organization of labor and the economic, social and ethical education of the masters of industry and all other influential groups in our population. While neither of these methods is likely to produce beneficial results rapidly, they have both proved their effectiveness by experience. After all, solid and permanent progress comes slowly in every department of social life.

The foregoing argument has taken no notice of the

thesis upheld in several publications by Foster and Catchings. It is that overproduction, underconsumption and general unemployment come about because industry does not put sufficient money into the hands of the consumers to pay for all the goods produced. This theory has not been considered for two reasons. First, in so far as it deals with the flow of money and credit, it is too difficult either to prove or to refute. In the second place, these authors admit, nay assert, that a great increase in general consuming power could be obtained through a general advance in wages. For example, in a pamphlet reprinted from the *Century Magazine*, July, 1929, these sentences occur:

> Adequate consumption, therefore, does more than anything else to sustain employment. And nothing more is needed to achieve the right rate of consumption than the right flow of money to consumers. Now, the largest part of this flow, and the part that is most promptly spent, is the stream of wages. Nothing, therefore, can go so far toward sustaining trade and employment as increasing the weekly payroll of the country fast enough, and not too fast.

Hence, the first and obvious requisite is to raise wages somehow, with some kind of money. If that measure should fail to increase consuming power sufficiently to take all the goods off the market and keep industry going, the time would then be at hand to consider the problem of increasing consumers' credit. The money phase of the problem, the question how to bring about the right flow of money to the consumers, will then be much more urgent than it is today.

A rationally organized society which found itself able to produce more goods than it could sell and unable to keep all its industries and workers employed would seriously undertake two fundamental investigations. First, it would seek to ascertain whether all its members were provided with a sufficient amount of necessaries and comforts for reasonable living. If it found that millions fell short

200

of that standard it would employ its idle workers and idle machines to produce and distribute the necessary goods. If this plan left some of the workers and some of the machines unemployed, then this rationally organized society would reduce the working time, so that all might be occupied and that none would be engaged in production merely for the sake of production. After all, industry and production are not ends in themselves.

Let us suppose for the moment that we are the responsible representatives of a rationally organized society and that we are attempting to follow out these two lines of inquiry. Do we find that all the inhabitants of this country are already provided with all of the necessaries and comforts needed for rational living? We do not. We find that the average annual income of unskilled laborers in 1929 was little, if any, over $1000 a year, while between $1600 and $1800 is necessary to enable a family of five, including three small children, to live at a minimum of health and decency in any of our large cities. The industrial operations necessary to provide the means of a decent livelihood for these millions would furnish employment for hundreds of thousands who are now unable to find work. Therefore, the first remedy for the unemployment now afflicting us is to increase the wages of our vast army of underpaid workers, thus increasing the demand for goods and providing work for our idle men and our idle machines. If anyone fears that higher wages would raise the price of goods to such an extent as to frustrate this remedy I reply that the same objection has been urged against every increase in wages that has ever been proposed. Another answer is that our industrial resources and powers are undoubtedly sufficient to produce goods adequate to a decent living for all our people and a considerable surplus for a large proportion. If this possibility cannot be realized through the existing system then this system is not worth preserving. It is unworthy of the continued support of a society which has to its credit the great industrial achievements of the American people.

D. REDUCED WORKING TIME

While higher wages for the majority of the laboring class is the primary and direct solution of the problem of chronic or technological unemployment, it is not the only solution. There is an important secondary remedy which would reinforce higher wages and promote a better social order than that which results from the development of new wants. This secondary remedy is a shorter work-day or a shorter work-week, or both. The shorter work-day is sometimes advocated on the ground that it results in as large a production per capita as a longer day. In any industry where this would happen, the shorter work-day would obviously fail to reduce unemployment. What is needed is increased demand for labor, not the ability of labor to turn out more goods in a given number of hours. We should frankly realize that the problem is not one of more productive power but of better distribution of purchasing power. With a shorter work-day or work-week, a given demand for goods would require more laborers, thus decreasing unemployment.

Two situations may be conceived. In the first, labor has shorter hours while the machinery and plants are operated full time; in the second, the plant and the employees are active during a shorter day or a smaller number of days per week. The choice between these methods in any industry should be determined by the amount of demand for its products. At present the building trades in some cities are on a five-day week basis because there is not sufficient demand to require operation for six days. On the other hand, the Ford automobile factory is in good times operated six days in the week, although none of the employees works more than five. This arrangement can easily be substituted for the first whenever the demand warrants the larger use of machinery and plant. Full time for machinery and reduced time for the workers is evidently the more desirable arrangement, for it means not only more workers employed but a more economical use of capital. For example, a plant might be operated for twelve hours a day, six days in the week, and yet employ no laborer for more than six hours per day or five days per week.

The immediate effect of each of these arrangements would be to increase employment. Increased employment would increase the total amount of wages received, not only because more workers would be employed, but because the greater demand for labor would keep wage rates above what they would have been in the absence of increased employment. The increased wages would provide increased purchasing power for the products of many industries, thereby extending further the demand for labor. The order of events would be directly contrary to that set in motion when men are thrown out of work.

The objection that the same or higher wages could not be paid for producing a smaller or the same amount of goods has been dealt with in a preceding paragraph. After all, wages are the money equivalent of goods; if the goods can be produced, their wage equivalent will be potentially available. No competent person doubts that our industries are capable of producing the required volume of goods. The only difficulty is to get into operation the process of converting the goods into wages. The shorter work period for labor seems to provide an effective method.

Indeed, the movement toward this goal is already well under way. The average working time per week per employee in factories decreased 15 per cent between 1900 and 1923. In the last two years considerable progress has been made toward the introduction of the five-day week. President Green of the American Federation of Labor has estimated the number of men who have obtained the five-day week at 500,000. These workers are found chiefly in the building trades, the printing trades, foundries and machine shops, the clothing industries and the automobile industry. In all probability the movement can be extended more rapidly than the movement for higher wages to the underpaid.

As stated in a previous paragraph, the shorter work period "would promote a better social order than that which results from the development of new wants." On the one hand, it would provide the laboring classes with greater leisure and thus make possible the development of a higher intellectual and moral life; on the other hand, it would tend to retard the invention of new luxuries. To be sure, the increased leisure would not immediately be all utilized for intellectual and moral improvement. In all probability the greater part of it would, for a considerable time, be spent uselessly, if not foolishly. However, that is not an argument against the proposal. Men must first get leisure before they can learn to use it wisely. The latter is a problem of education which we have no right to assume is insoluble. The shorter work period would check or retard the production of new luxuries because the workers' increased demand for necessities and comforts would tend to keep capital fully employed in industries that are already established. Since production is justified only as a means to rational and beneficial consumption, it ought to be so organized as to yield the maximum of the good life for all. The elementary necessities and comforts and the material conditions of reasonable leisure and progressive mental and moral development ought to be placed within the reach of all the people, while the supply of useless and harmful luxuries should be kept down to a minimum. Of course, a shorter work period would not entirely prevent the production of luxuries. A vast amount of them would still be demanded by the possessors of unusually large purchasing power. The quantity turned out, however, and the proportion of productive energy thus engaged, would be considerably reduced, while the proportion of productive power used to meet the rational needs of the masses would be considerably greater than is the case in our present arrangements. This would be an immense gain for the good life.

Unfortunately, certain statements in *Recent Economic Changes* tend to endorse the contrary doctrine. By suggestion and by implication they convey the idea that national prosperity and national welfare are dependent upon the indefinite expansion of human wants and the indefinite multiplication of luxuries. In the following section of an editorial by George Russell in the *Irish Statesman,* this construction is unhesitatingly put upon the Committee's language:

> There is an interesting passage in the Report of the Committee on Recent Economic Changes, of which President Hoover is chairman. It speaks of the reaching out for luxuries which make possible the expansion of new industries, and says that the United States has only touched the fringes of its potentialities. Wants, it declares, are insatiable, and one want satisfied makes room for another, and economically there is a boundless field for development. The report seems to suggest that material prosperity is largely based on the limitless desires of humanity for pleasure and luxury, that no great prosperity can be based merely upon the satisfaction of the primary needs for food, shelter and clothing. It suggests that if people are encouraged to have extravagant desires for luxury they will work for these and multitudes of people will be given employment, while the Spartan country will always be poor, however virtuous its people may be.

For the sake of the intellectual, not to say the moral, reputations of the Committee on Recent Economic Changes, let us hope that this interpretation and inference will turn out to have been unforeseen and unintended, however necessarily it may follow according to the strict processes of logic. Charity constrains us to give the Committee the benefit of the doubt. Charity constrains us to assume that

205

on account of their great appreciation of our recent industrial progress and their preoccupation with "prosperity," the members of the Committee failed to perceive the false and disagreeable implications of their loose talk about "insatiable wants." Let us charitably assume that they did not mean to say that genuine prosperity "is largely based on the limitless desires of humanity for pleasure and luxury." Let us charitably assume that they had no intention of identifying this conception of prosperity with industrial sanity, social well-being or desirable human life. Moreover, we will charitably assume that they are not so lacking in economic knowledge or in the capacity for straight economic thinking as to suppose that our industries can be kept going at a reasonable rate or for a reasonable period of time per week only on condition that the multitude shall continue to work eight or ten hours per day in order to satisfy the "extravagant desires for luxury" felt by the economically powerful minority. Let us charitably assume that the members of the Committee merely overlooked the fact that the productive capacity of our men and machines could all be utilized to a reasonable extent in turning out goods for the satisfaction of wants already known and felt, particularly the elementary and rational wants of the majority.

In their preoccupation with a conception of prosperity which logically implies a belief in production for its own sake, the members of the Committee are in line with our baneful tradition of Puritan industrial ethics. Describing this ethical discipline as it was taking final shape at the end of the seventeenth century, R. H. Tawney writes in *Religion and the Rise of Capitalism*:

> The worship of production and ever greater production—the slavish drudgery of the millionaire and his unhappy servants—was to be hallowed by the precepts of the same compelling creed.

Nevertheless, one of the two underlying principles of the Puritan ethics of work and production has been inconti-

206

nently rejected by the Committee as by all American industrialists. George O'Brien says, in *The Economic Effects of the Reformation*:

> The desire for ever-increasing production, which is a feature of the capitalist spirit, was encouraged not only by the Puritan conception of the fulfillment of the vocation, but also by the other branch of Puritan ascetic teaching—namely, the observance of strict frugality and austerity.

Instead of urging men to strive for greater production through "frugality and austerity," the Committee points to the inexhaustible spring of "almost insatiable wants." Whether this new emphasis upon limitless consumption is more rational, or less, than the traditional maxims of frugality and saving, it constitutes, at any rate, eloquent testimony to the capacity of our industries for overproduction.

The program suggested by Stuart Chase is more in harmony with humanity and reason than the suggestions of the Committee on Recent Economic Changes. It is quoted here, not necessarily as correct in detail but as indicating the right approach and method:

> Let me recapitulate. Machinery saves labor in a given process; one man replaces ten. A certain number of these men are needed to build and service the new machine, but some of them are permanently displaced. Now if the articles called for remain the same, and the financial system remains the same, sooner or later half the workers (let us say) in the country can produce what once required the labor of all the workers. The other half are on the park bench. But as an alternative, all can continue to work for half as many hours in the day. Or all can combine to work a full day and produce twice as much. None of these clean-cut alternatives has of course been taken. The ideal result would be something in the nature of hours reduced a third, and output of sound necessities and comforts increased two-thirds. This would end hard work and

207

poverty forever. Instead, hours have fallen a little, output has increased considerably, but the present financial control neither releases sufficient purchasing power to enlarge output as far as the machine is readily capable of enlarging it unhindered, nor promotes the kind of output which necessarily makes for the good life.[1]

The most reassuring and the most significant truths that emerge from an objective study of American conditions today are these: In the United States, at least, the prosperity of the industrial system is consistent with and dependent upon the welfare of the toiling masses. Industrial well-being and the principles of justice can be practically harmonized. The doctrine of the living wage and all the other humane doctrines taught by Pope Leo XIII in his encyclical, *On the Condition of Labor,* can no longer be stigmatized as visionary by any intelligent student of our industrial achievements and potentialities. To establish universal living wages and to abolish all excessive labor, as regards persons, quality and hours, would be the most direct, prompt and effective means of meeting the menace of chronic unemployment and of ensuring prosperity for our industries. The thing can be accomplished if only the masters of industry and of politics will devote to the problem a small part of the energies that they habitually spend in making and selling goods and in pursuing profits.

[1] *Men and Machines,* pp. 215, 216.

E. THE INDUSTRIAL DEPRESSION OF
1929-1931

With the exception of four paragraphs, all the preceding sections of this paper were written in August, 1929. At that time, the downward movement of business activities had not yet become apparent. Nevertheless, the foregoing pages were not written as an academic exercise; for I was well aware, despite all the "ballyhoo" about current prosperity, that unemployment was considerable and extensive and had been so for more than two years. It seemed to me then that displacement of men by machines and the failure of consumption to keep pace with productive capacity were continuously increasing and must in a comparatively short time culminate in an industrial depression.

As a matter of fact, the depression set in imperceptibly in July, 1929, and was plainly evident the following November. The crash of prices on the stock exchange was an effect rather than a cause. It was a cause only in so far as it accelerated somewhat, and temporarily intensified, the downward movement of industrial activity. Of course, it made the depression spectacularly obvious. The depression would probably have been just as general, as profound and as enduring in the absence of the orgy of speculation which reached its peak in the last days of October, 1929.

What has been the course of unemployment since the depression became generally evident? According to the data gathered by the United States Bureau of Labor Statistics, employment declined every month from November, 1929, to January, 1931, inclusive. Although September, 1930, showed an increase of 1 per cent over the preceding month, the gain was due entirely to seasonal changes in three industries, namely, coal mining, canning and retail trade. In all the other industries covered by the Bureau, including manufactures, the downward trend continued in September as

209

it had in every one of the immediately preceding ten months. Between October, 1929, and the end of January, 1931, the level of employment in manufacturing industries fell 25 per cent.[2] Whether the average decline for all industries was as great as 25 per cent is a question which cannot be answered on the basis of available statistics.

How many workers are now out of employment? The decennial census taken in April, 1930, reported the number of persons "able to work, out of work and looking for a job" as about 2,500,000. However, the questionnaire which yielded these figures did not take in those workers who regarded themselves as having a job, but temporarily "laid off," nor those who were employed less than full time. A very large proportion, possibly a majority of those who have been thrown out of work since the preceding October, may have considered themselves in the former class, and therefore, do not appear in the census report of 2,500,000. At any rate, they were sufficiently numerous to bring the total of unemployed persons last April up to somewhere between three and four million. At the present time (February, 1931) it seems well within the bounds of conservative statement to put the number of unemployed well above five million. Employment in manufacturing industries declined 18 per cent between April, 1929, and February, 1931.

What light has the depression thrown upon causes of unemployment? It has confirmed the view of those who hold that the main cause is overproduction and underconsumption, and it has brought to the same view a very large number of thoughtful and competent persons who previously had not accepted this explanation. On a preceding page of this paper a few figures were presented to show the enormous increase which has taken place in the productive capacity of American industries during the last decade. It may be worth while to submit more comprehensive and specific data. They are taken from an article by Stuart

---

[2] *Trend of Employment and Labor Turnover*, U. S. Bureau of Labor Statistics.

THE PROBLEM OF UNEMPLOYMENT

Chase entitled "The Enemy of Prosperity," in *Harper's Magazine*, November, 1930.

In April, 1929, the automobile plants of the United States were capable of producing 8,000,000 units a year. Plant-expansion programs have gone forward since that date. Yet in 1929 the entire world bought only 6,295,000 new cars, including the output of all foreign plants as well as American. To make matters worse, in 1923, 3,000,000 people in the United States became, for the first time in their lives, the proud owners of new cars, whereas in 1929, the potential market had been so far exploited that there were only 500,000 such persons. A lush virgin territory has been reduced to cut-over lands; a *new* market has largely given way to a *replacement* market.

. . . The most immediately critical factor in the whole "overproduction" situation, to my mind, is *excess plant capacity*—which means more mills, more mines, more machines, aye, more farmers' fields— than can be used. Not only is this equipment almost always in excess of purchasing power, but frequently, if you please, *it is in excess of consumption requirements, granted unlimited purchasing power.* American shoe factories are equipped to turn out almost 900,000,000 pairs of shoes a year. At present we buy about 300,000,000 pairs—two and one-half pairs per capita. There is admittedly a considerable shortage of shoes, but could we wear out, or even amuse ourselves with, five pairs per capita? I doubt it. For myself two pairs a year satisfy both utility and style. Yet if we doubled shoe consumption—gorging the great American foot as it were—one-third of the present shoe factory equipment would still lie idle. There are more shoe factories than we have any conceivable need for, either here or in Utopia.

Untold plants, furthermore, have expanded to meet a peak demand—a demand which never comes again. Thus during the War new coal mines were opened right and left. After the War demand fell away by

211

100,000,000 tons, and will probably never climb again to the dizzy peak of almost 600,000,000 tons. The War is responsible for current excess capacity in many industries.

An able management engineer, Mr. Wallace Clark, finds his clients [in the textile industry] normally operating at 40 per cent to 60 per cent of capacity. The printing trades are 50 per cent overequipped, while paper mills are now suffering acutely from overproduction. The steel industry was rated in 1929 at 62,000,000 tons. Production in that abnormally busy year ran to 56,000,000 tons, yet extension programs for 1930 call for 4,000,000 tons of additional capacity. . . .

The machine-tool industry has operated at 65 per cent of capacity for the last ten years. Oil refineries do somewhat better at 76 per cent, according to Mr. J. E. Pogue. Plants manufacturing gas function at 66 per cent. Flour mills, says the Federal Trade Commission, utilize only 40 per cent of their capacity on the average (due partly, of course, to peak demands in grinding cereals).

The acute presence of overproduction throughout industry, even as we noted it in motor cars and agriculture at the beginning, is only too manifest. It is needless to document it with additional figures. Every other business man you meet on the street is lying awake at night trying to work out a plan to come to terms with his competitors; to formulate an agreement, legal or illegal, whereby price cutting may be mitigated, territories divided, marginal mills closed down, and some sort of order and reasonable security established in what is now a roaring chaos. In the last month I have happened to be an innocent bystander in the formation of three such agreements. The whole merger movement, basically, is a flight—often with all the earmarks of panic—from overproduction.

As Mr. Chase points out, some of this excessive capacity is absolute. In the case of shoe factories and agriculture, for example, it would be too great for the demand even though

212

all persons had money enough to buy as much of these goods as they desired. In the majority of industries, however, the excessive productive capacity is only relative; that is, it is greater than the amount of goods that can be sold with the present distribution of purchasing power. More ground, more houses, more automobiles and more comforts and luxuries of a hundred sorts would find a market if those who now desire these things had the money to buy them. For this condition, the obvious and only remedy is a redistribution of purchasing power. To some extent this means taking some buying power from those who now have it and do not desire to exchange it for more consumption goods because they already have sufficient. In any case, it means giving more purchasing power to those who desire more necessaries, comforts and luxuries than they are now able to purchase. This redistribution could be brought about directly through increases in the wages of the majority of workers and indirectly through reducing working hours without any reduction in wages. Apparently these measures have won the assent or, at least the sympathetic attention of a considerable number of prominent persons during the last five years. Following is an extract from an editorial in a recent issue of an ultra-conservative metropolitan newspaper:

> Attempts to solve the problem of too many goods by curtailment of production is a negative approach. Of course, many adjustments will have to be made, and producers in some fields will have to be shifted to others. But the constructive solution lies in development of the earning, and, consequently, the purchasing power of the masses.

Obviously, a general increase in wages would not be achieved as easily or as soon as a reduction in the hours of labor. Hence the number of industrial and other leaders who have become converted to the latter proposal is much larger than that of those who heartily accept the former. Probably the most conspicuous among those advocating

213

reduced working time are Vice-President Curtis and John J. Raskob, both of whom have come out for the five-day week, specifying that there should be no reduction in weekly wages. Both these remedies are fundamental and adapted to changes over a period of years. Except in a minor degree, they could not be put into operation during the existing depression. In other words, they are preventives rather than immediate relief measures.

In dealing with the present evil situation have the masters of industry and of government exhibited conspicuous wisdom? They have not. In the existing emergency only two comprehensive and adequate remedies are available, namely, legal compulsory insurance against unemployment and a very large program of public works. Few, if any, of our leaders either in politics or in industry have lent a sympathetic ear to unemployment insurance. Mr. Hoover was a strong advocate of the public works proposal before he became President. He also made large promises and large gestures in that direction in the White House conferences with business leaders in November, 1929. Nevertheless, the amount of money actually expended for public works by the federal government during the first six months of 1930 was only about $1,500,000 above similar expenditures in the first half of the preceding year. At the beginning of November, 1930, the Emergency Committee on Unemployment, appointed some three weeks earlier by the President, announced that current public works projects aggregated almost $1,000,000,000. However, more than half of this sum is accounted for by works already in process of construction. The remainder will be spread over so long a time that it will provide very little more employment than was obtained from public works during the same length of time in previous years. A more exact notion of the insignificant achievements of the federal government in this respect can be derived from the announcement of the Committee that the number of persons employed directly or indirectly by the federal govern-

214

ment had increased between January 1 and November 1, 1930, by 43,000 persons. When due allowance is made for the reduction made in employees and in materials by the various departments of the federal government in pursuance of the economy program adopted in the summer of 1930 (for example, the curtailment of the mail service and the increased tasks laid upon post office employees), it is probable that the amount of employment directly and indirectly provided by the federal government during the first ten months of 1930 actually underwent a decrease.

What does the Emergency Committee on Unemployment purpose to do? It will press for action on government work, federal, state and municipal; encourage industrial corporations to begin projects that they have been planning; stimulate the home owner to undertake needed repairs; set up volunteer employment agencies, and urge all persons who have the money to increase their purchases of goods. The first of these proposals will not provide many new jobs in the winter of 1930-31, because the total amount of public money already appropriated is relatively small and new appropriations (even if they are made in large volume) cannot become available for actual expenditure before spring. Industrial corporations cannot fairly be expected to engage in much new construction. The amount of employment that can be provided through domestic repairs is insignificant. New employment agencies will not create new jobs. The recommendation for larger buying is the best of the five. If all who are financially able to do so would heed it, their action would provide more employment than all the other plans put together. In any case, it is an implicit admission that underconsumption is the true explanation of unemployment and industrial depression.

A special writer on one of the Washington newspapers soberly referred to the published proposals and recommendations of the Emergency Committee on Unemployment as "efforts of the Administration to create a psychology of

215

optimism throughout the nation in the face of business depression and unemployment." Unfortunately, this "psychological creation" is likely to be the principal achievement of the Committee.

What might have been done to check the depression and the continuous increase in unemployment? Congress could have provided for a vast bond issue to be expended on public buildings, road construction, improvement of navigation, electric power plants and flood control. This should have been done during the special session in the spring of 1929 or, at the latest, soon after the beginning of the regular session the following December. However, Congress did not even discuss the subject. It adjourned in July, 1930, without even enacting the Wagner bills for unemployment insurance and a very mild installment of the "prosperity reserve." President Hoover was equally indifferent, not to say unfriendly, to the public works proposal. (A more detailed presentation of his failure in this respect will be found in the last paper of this volume.)

As already noted, appropriations for public works cannot be made available in time to reduce unemployment in the winter of 1930-31. They could, however, give a powerful impetus to any movement that may be under way in the spring toward recovery from the depression. After all, there is no certainty that business will of itself be able to bring about a revival next spring any more than last spring. Indeed, recovery might be more difficult in the spring of 1931 than twelve months earlier on account of the intervening decline in employment and in the purchasing power of the masses. Even now, therefore, it is not too late for Congress to authorize large bond issues for large public works. Even though a revival of business next spring were possible without these measures, they would be of great benefit to the community and would postpone the coming of another period of overproduction, underconsumption and depression.

The reason why neither Congress, nor the President,

216

nor business leaders have adopted this obvious remedy is easily understood. They fear increased federal taxation, especially higher income and inheritance taxes. Nevertheless, the measure that we are discussing is not only the scientifically correct one, but is in thorough accord with the principles of what the Schoolmen call "distributive justice." There exists in the community sufficient purchasing power and sufficient desire to take off the market by far the greater part of the goods that our industries are capable of producing. The reason why this does not happen is that the power and the desire are not combined in the same persons. Those who would like to consume more have not the money, those who have the money lack the desire. Increased income and inheritance taxes would make for a better distribution of purchasing power by transferring it from those who do not to those who do want more of the necessaries and comforts of life. It would exemplify the formula of distributive justice, namely, that governments should distribute burdens according to capacities and benefits according to needs.

15. The Clergy and the Labor Question

It is clear then that some men are free by nature and others are slaves, and that in the case of the latter the lot of slavery is both advantageous and just.[1]

Slavery has been introduced through human reason for the welfare of human life.[2]

That this man rather than another should be a slave . . . is reasonable inasmuch as it is good for him to be governed by a man wiser than himself and good for the latter to be assisted by the former.[3]

THE first of these sentences was written by the greatest philosopher of antiquity, the man whom Dante called "the master of them that know"; the second and third sentences are from the pen of the greatest of Christian philosophers, indeed, the greatest philosopher of all time. The significance of these quotations lies in the fact that the classes that they discuss were the true economic analogues of our present wage earners. While there were free artisans when Aristotle wrote, as well as in the thirteenth century, they were to a great extent business men rather than wage earners, inasmuch as they sold their products rather than their labor. The laboring class of today sells only its labor; the corresponding industrial class in former times exchanged its labor for a livelihood in a condition of servile subjection.

It is true that the slaves whom St. Thomas knew were in reality serfs and that they were protected in the enjoyment of certain rights, such as those of life, sustenance, marriage, and parental control. In these respects, they were immeasurably better off than the slaves of Aristotle's time,

---

[1] Aristotle, *Politics*, Book I, chap. 5.
[2] *Summa Theologica*, 1ᵐᵃ 2ᵃᵉ, q. 94, a. 5.
[3] *Op. cit.*, 2ᵃ 2ᵃᵉ, q. 57, a. 3.

and even better off than those black bondsmen who were comprised in the "peculiar institution" which existed in our southern states down to January 1, 1863. Nevertheless, as pointed out by Father Bede Jarrett, O.P., the slavery defended by St. Thomas "really meant slavery in all essentials, and not mere subordination of a worker to his master."[4] The essential fact for our purpose is that both Aristotle and St. Thomas looked upon slavery as natural and necessary for the enslaved persons themselves and for society. The former went so far as to assert that some persons are naturally as inferior to others as the body is to the soul. In *De Regimine Principum,* St. Thomas declared that "some men cannot follow reason and are fitly slaves, and this is called a slavery by natural right."[5] Taken as they stand, both these assertions are inaccurate, although in different measure. That of Aristotle is simply false, for no such degree of inferiority ever existed in any group of human beings outside an insane asylum. St. Thomas's statement is surely a grave exaggeration. The intellectual inferiority and dependence which he mentions have existed in particular groups and in particular social conditions. It could never have been necessarily true of any group throughout several generations. Even though certain persons were intellectually incapable of maintaining themselves in any other condition than slavery, their children or their grandchildren could have been made self-dependent through education and economic opportunity. And it is abundantly clear that the statement of St. Thomas could not have been fairly applied to the serfs of his own time. Their servile condition was not due to a natural or congenital inability to "follow reason."

What is the explanation of the grave errors made by these two great minds on the question of slavery? Undoubtedly, a large part of it is to be found in the fact that slavery was a contemporary, long established and generally

[4] *Social Theories of the Middle Ages,* p. 101.
[5] Book II, cap. 10.

219

recognized institution. To the vast majority of persons, even in the Christian thirteenth century, slavery, or serfdom, seemed to be a necessary element in society. Its victims were illiterate, economically helpless and in other respects apparently inferior to the more fortunate social classes. In such situations the more fortunate persons have always been prone to look upon these kinds of inferiority as the reflection and outcome of an incapacity of nature. In some minds this false inference is due to careless observation and thinking; in others it is, to a large extent, produced by unquiet consciences, inasmuch as they feel the need of justifying somehow their unfair treatment of their fellows. Of course, the fundamental and sufficient cause of slavery in the Middle Ages, as in every other age, was human greed and the desire of the powerful to lord it over and exploit the weak. This is not the place to examine the question whether the institution of slavery was necessary for social welfare in the Middle Ages or whether it could safely have been abolished sooner. Under this head much nonsense has been written in the attempts to extenuate the failure to condemn slavery or to do anything for its abolition on the part of those who might reasonably have been expected to concern themselves. As a matter of fact, the institution could, in every country where it existed, have been abolished with entire safety to society many decades before it actually came to an end. Even if we assume its necessity as a social institution, we do not understand why it should have included the same persons and their descendants for generations. Why was not the burden shifted to and distributed among other elements of the population? This would have been in accord with the principles of distributive justice. To be sure, this dictate of social and distributive justice could be comfortably ignored by persons who held that the actually enslaved persons belonged in that condition by nature.

The other reason why Aristotle and St. Thomas committed this grave mistake concerning the natural inferiority of the slave classes lies in their failure to examine adequately the pertinent facts. Had they done so, they would have found that the inequality and inferiority which they attributed to nature was due entirely, at least as regards the great majority, to social environment and lack of opportunity. Had St. Thomas applied to a concrete study of the serfs of his time, their antecedents, native abilities and social handicaps, the time and genius that he bestowed upon the study of a hundred other questions, he could scarcely have accepted the dictum of Aristotle and the current assumptions of his time, concerning the natural unfitness of vast classes of his fellow beings for any other condition than that of slavery.

No priest or bishop would make those assertions his own today, even with regard to that race which emerged from slavery in the United States less than three-quarters of a century ago. The moral principles concerning human equality and human rights have not changed since the days of St. Thomas and no modern ecclesiastic knows them as well as St. Thomas knew them. The advantage which the modern moralist possesses with regard to the subject under discussion is a wider knowledge of the facts. Our observation of the enslaved classes throughout the world and of their emancipated descendants convinces us that they have sufficient power of reason, given adequate opportunity, to be their own economic masters. Hence, we should regard as preposterous the assumption that certain races are essentially and perpetually unable to take care of themselves in a condition of economic freedom.

The Thomistic teaching on slavery has been dwelt on at considerable length in this paper because it involves an important lesson for the moralists and religious guides of our own time. The spokesmen for the laboring classes have always taken advantage of Labor Day, not only to describe the achievements of the labor movement, but to make known their grievances, claims and aspirations. The grievances may be real or unreal; the claims, just or unjust;

221

the aspirations, reasonable or unreasonable. We cannot decide these questions unless we have adequate knowledge of industrial facts. We cannot reach true and fruitful conclusions by any amount of deductive reasoning from first principles. The general principles are true, indeed, but they are practically useless unless they are applied specifically to the actual conditions and relations of industry. Unless we know the facts, we cannot apply the principles.

Fifty years ago the majority of labor leaders in every country were persuaded that the Catholic Church was out of sympathy with the aspirations of the laboring classes and, as between them and the employing classes, that it was in favor of the latter. Nor were these assumptions and conclusions entirely devoid of foundation. Churchmen were sometimes silent when they ought to have had something to say about unjust industrial conditions. When they did speak, they sometimes made unfair and incorrect pronouncements upon the justice of certain working-class claims and the morality of certain proposed remedies for industrial evils. Their denunciation of Socialism and other false remedies was more frequent than their acknowledgment of the need for some reform, or their advocacy of sound reforms. The great majority of these mistakes were due to lack of comprehensive knowledge of the facts of industry.

Happily, a great change for the better has taken place in the attitude of the labor unions. The change is most strikingly illustrated in a recent address delivered by Albert Thomas at an international labor conference held in Geneva. Mr. Thomas is a very able man. He is also a Socialist. If he were addressing a similar international gathering twenty-five or thirty years ago, he probably would have denounced the "Black International," *i.e.* the Catholic Church, as the natural and traditional enemy of the working classes. On the present occasion, he emphasized the necessity of observing sympathetically the attitude of religious bodies in our time toward labor. This attitude,

222

he said, could become a means of great assistance to the labor movement. He summarized for his audience, not only the teaching of Leo XIII, but the Pastoral Letters of bishops in many countries, laying particular stress upon the American Bishops' Program of Social Reconstruction.

Now we all must realize that the happy conditions which Mr. Thomas described and the happy change in the attitude of men like himself toward the Church, are due almost entirely to Pope Leo's Encyclical on Labor. This great pontiff enunciated no new principles of justice or charity in relation to industry. The general principles which he laid down had long been commonplaces of Catholic moral theology. The new thing that he did was to consider comprehensively the facts of present-day industry, and to apply the traditional principles specifically to these facts. At the beginning of the Encyclical, he declared that the condition of the working classes had come to be little better than that of slavery. This was a statement of fact, not a repetition of a general principle. It was not arrived at by deductive reasoning. Throughout the Encyclical, he deals constantly with the actual conditions of labor in all its relations. Hence the concreteness and usefulness of his moral pronouncements.

While the clergy have given much more attention to industrial conditions and have a much better understanding of them than in the years which preceded the appearance of the Encyclical on Labor, there is still great room for improvement. While our seminaries devote much more time than formerly to the consideration of these questions, only a few of the students become deeply and sympathetically interested. Smaller still is the number of those who continue their interest after they have left the seminary. Our industrial relations and their moral aspects are exceedingly complex. It is much more difficult to obtain an adequate grasp of the present industrial system and to pass correct moral judgments upon its many characteristic practices than was the case in the simpler industrial organization of the Middle Ages. Hence, it is quite natural that many priests should become bewildered and discouraged when they are confronted with the more intricate facts and relations of industry. Nevertheless, those who appreciate the importance of the subject will not be deterred by mere difficulties. They will take advantage of the practical contacts with industry which they can easily obtain, which, indeed, are frequently forced upon them, in the ordinary course of their parochial work. They have here a laboratory in which they can test and apply the general principles with which they became familiar in the class room. A single important labor dispute will present all the facts, conditions and questions which are necessary to convert one's abstract knowledge into concrete knowledge. No priest whose mind is eager and whose will is healthy will neglect such opportunities.

In the United States at the present time we are in danger of yielding to a false sense of industrial security. Strikes have become relatively infrequent, class feeling has apparently diminished, Socialism, which troubled us so greatly a few years ago, has all but disappeared, and the skilled section of the laboring classes enjoys comparatively great prosperity. To assume that this is an adequate picture of labor conditions is to deceive ourselves. These are facts, indeed, but to know them alone is to have only one-sided knowledge. Conclusions drawn from these alone are liable to be as inadequate, essentially as false, as the generalizations which medieval writers made about slavery and serfdom upon the basis of a one-sided observation of these institutions.

Despite the fact that here in the United States the wage-earning class as a whole is better off than any other laboring population has ever been, anywhere in the world, our industrial system contains certain grave defects and presents certain menacing features. As regards wages, no competent authority denies that an annual income of $1600 a year is necessary for the decent support of a husband and wife and three small children in any city of America, or that considerably more than that amount is required in our largest cities. Nor does any well-informed person deny that a very large proportion, probably a majority, of our adult male wage earners receives less than $1600 a year. Some persons who are aware of these facts belittle their importance with the comforting assumption that these underpaid wage earners are somehow made of different clay and therefore can readily get along with less than the normal requisites of life. Other complacent persons reflect that a majority of these underpaid males are probably unmarried and therefore do not need a family wage. All such persons need, first of all, to examine the pertinent facts. They ought to inquire whether it is really true that the underpaid workers and their families differ so greatly from their fellows that they can live decent human lives on less than decent wages. Such an inquiry honestly made would produce disquiet of conscience in any person who is capable of that feeling. A similar reaction would be experienced by any well-disposed person who considered fully the implications of a situation in which a very large number of adult males are compelled through lack of income to forego marriage and family life indefinitely.

Another great evil is economic insecurity. Even in the best times, a considerable number of workers are unemployed, at least temporarily, through no fault of their own. Every few years we experience a period of industrial depression which forces a considerable percentage of the laboring class out of employment for many months. Adequate remedies for this situation are not easy to find. However, there are two measures that would greatly reduce the volume of suffering involved. The first is universal high wages, which would increase the purchasing power of the masses and keep industry going with smaller interruptions than have hitherto been the rule. Depressions occur because our industries are capable of producing more goods than the consuming masses are able to take off the market with

225

their present incomes and purchasing power. The second remedy is insurance against unemployment, which would greatly lessen the inconveniences undergone by persons who are temporarily deprived of regular wages. Sickness and old age are likewise very serious and persistent sources of insecurity. In both cases the universally recognized remedy is insurance. Unfortunately, the comfortable classes and the makers of opinion in our country, including the clergy, have little or no systematic comprehension of the foregoing evils. Until they obtain greater knowledge of the actual facts and acquire a more tender conscience and a greater sense of responsibility, the adoption of the obvious and practical remedies will remain slow and inadequate.

The most fundamental defect in our industrial system and the most fundamental need of the laboring classes are almost entirely overlooked by persons who do not take the trouble to obtain comprehensive knowledge. The defect to which I refer concerns the worker's status. Here in the United States the assumption has been general, until quite recently, that the majority of workers need not remain all their lives in the condition of mere wage earners. According to this traditional assumption, or legend, the great majority of laborers have the opportunity, if they but seize it, of becoming owners of some kind of business, however small, long before they reach the period of old age. Honest and realistic students of our industrial conditions know that this tradition is no longer, if it ever was, in accord with the facts. The great majority, probably 90 per cent, of those who begin life as employees will end it as employees. This is a necessary outcome of our industrial organization with its large, costly and relatively few business concerns. Our industrial system is divided into two classes, a small group which performs all the functions of ownership, control and direction and a very large group which neither owns nor controls, but performs subordinate tasks under the direction of others. As a natural consequence of their position and outlook, the members of the latter class have very little

226

interest in their work or in the prosperity of the concerns by which they are employed. Being for the most part mere executors of industrial orders, they have no opportunity to practice or develop their creative or directive capacities. This condition is an obstacle, not only to industrial efficiency, but to the development of human faculties and the maintenance of human dignity. It is fast creating a kind of industrial feudalism which no believer in democracy and no lover of human progress can contemplate with complacency.

For this condition there are three remedies now well recognized by all thoughtful students, and these remedies have an organic connection with one another. The first is labor sharing in management. Necessarily, it means different things in different industries, but its essential features and ends are the same everywhere. The workers should obtain that measure of control over at least the productive side of industrial management which will arouse their interest in their work and enable them to exercise some of their creative and directive faculties. The men and women who compose our industrial population have not been sharply divided by their Creator into two utterly different classes, one possessing all the managerial ability and the other having no capacity except to do what they are told. In this connection, the words of Dr. Royal Meeker, who was for many years Commissioner of the United States Bureau of Labor and who has been all his life a student of industrial conditions, are highly suggestive:

> I insist that the management, even scientific management, has not a monopoly of all the brains in an establishment. . . . As a worker and a student, I feel that there is a tremendous latent creative force in the workers of today which is not being utilized at all. . . . Here is a vast source of industrial power which has been cut off, isolated, by the transformation of little business into big business. It will be difficult to tap this source, but tap it we must if we are to

227

continue anything resembling the present industrial organization with its large scale production. The good will of the workers is a much more potent force making for industrial efficiency than all the scientific management formulas and systems of production. There is no inherent reason why the good will of the workers should not go hand in hand with scientific management. Until now the workers have had only antagonism for scientific management because the scientific manager never asked them for their opinions or ideas,—he only told them what they were expected to do, and the workers promptly did something else. I have already said that workers are not different from employers. That is precisely what ails them. If employers will only deal fairly and squarely with their employees, let them know all about the business except only those technical processes which must be kept secret, and take them into a real partnership, production will be enormously improved both in quantity and quality.[6]

The assumption of radical mental inferiority in the laboring classes which Dr. Meeker combats in the foregoing quotation, is strikingly similar to the assumption made by many medieval writers about the natural unfitness of slaves and serfs to be anything else but slaves and serfs.

The second change in the status of the worker consists in giving him a share of the profits of industry in addition to his regular wages. There is no doubt that the pursuit of indefinite gain in our competitive industrial society has been a most effective stimulus to invention, efficiency, and achievement. Why should it be restricted to business men and directors of industry? It could be made quite as effective and quite as beneficial to the majority of employees. Therefore, they should be enabled, wherever practicable, to obtain in addition to their wages some share in the surplus profits of industry. Capital must receive a sufficient return to ensure its continued investment; labor should have ade-

[6] *Monthly Labor Review*, February, 1920.

228

quate wages; but the surplus above these funds should be distributed among all those who in any way co-operate actively in the process of production. This arrangement would be a continuous incentive to all workers to make the surplus as large as possible.

The third remedy for the evil that we are now considering is labor sharing in ownership. This can be brought about by two distinct methods. The first is labor ownership of the stock in the corporation. While many large concerns have been encouraging this kind of ownership in the last few years, the great majority of them seem unwilling to let the workers get a sufficient proportion of the stock to give the latter a share in control. This is an undesirable limitation. The other method of worker ownership is obtainable through co-operative industrial societies. This is much more difficult, but it is quite practicable wherever the workers possess the requisite resolution, energy, altruism and patience. At any rate, the traditional Catholic ideal for the working classes is not the status of mere employees, but a condition in which they are also owners, at least in part, of the tools with which they work. Pope Leo XIII was speaking in the line and spirit of that tradition when he declared that "the State should seek to multiply property owners."

The final disturbing element that I wish to consider in the present industrial situation is the condition of labor organizations. The membership of American labor unions constitutes only a small percentage of our wage earners, and for the last few years it has remained almost stationary. On the other hand, there has been a remarkable development of what the employers call "employee representation," but what the labor union leaders stigmatize as "company unions." While these are probably in all cases better than no union at all, they can be genuinely helpful to the worker only in proportion as they become truly representative of their members and independent of employer control. As yet the majority of these organizations

229

have not obtained that representative and independent character. They do not comply with the requirement laid down by Pope Leo XIII: namely, that workingmen's associations should be so organized and maintained as to enable the worker "to better himself to the utmost in body, mind and property." Effective labor unions are still by far the most powerful force in society for the protection of the laborer's rights and the improvement of his condition. No amount of employer benevolence, no diffusion of a sympathetic attitude on the part of the public, no increase of beneficial legislation, can adequately supply for the lack of organization among the workers themselves. Many words will not make this fact clearer. It has been stated with precision and eloquence in the following paragraph by Adams and Sumner:

In the last six centuries the laboring population has risen from a condition of serfdom to a state of political freedom. In this struggle for economic equality, the victories have been won by the wage earners themselves. When they did not pursue their interest they lost their interest. When they forgot to demand their full reward, they failed to receive their full reward. They had occasional encouragement and even an occasional leader from the employing classes, but in the main they fought their way against the opposition and not with the assistance of their employers. Their weapons were the strike and the trade union. When the ponderous machinery of supply and demand was ready to give them a lift, its inertia and initial friction had to be overcome with a strike. When it had begun to thrust wages down, it was prevented from entirely degrading the wage earners by the trade union. Always and everywhere the salvation of the working classes has been collective action; and while the wage system remains, their progress will continue to be dependent upon collective action. . . ."[7]

The condition of the working classes has indeed under-

[7] *Labor Problems*, p. 205.

gone great improvement, not only in the long period of six centuries referred to in the preceding paragraph, but in the century and a half which has elapsed since the Industrial Revolution; but the improvement would have been even greater, much greater, had the clergy taken more interest in the industrial side of the worker's life and had a better knowledge of industrial conditions. Had the clergy been thus alive to their obligation and opportunities, great sections of the laboring classes in several countries of Europe would not have been alienated from the Church. In the United States we are fortunately in a much better situation. Our Catholic workingmen have not in any organized way nor in considerable numbers departed from their Catholic allegiance. Nevertheless, this happy situation will not maintain itself automatically. It will not continue unless the clergy take a sympathetic interest in the economic condition of the workers and equip themselves with that comprehensive knowledge of industrial conditions and relations without which accurate moral judgments are impossible. Hence, I close this paper upon the same note that I struck at its beginning: the necessity of concrete industrial knowledge.

16. Poverty in the United States

TO those who have uncritically accepted the assertions and assumptions which have been current for several years concerning American prosperity, the title of this article will suggest the hackneyed reference to snakes in Ireland. How can poverty coexist with prosperity? Nevertheless economic students and, indeed, all intelligent observers are well aware that the latter does not necessarily exclude the former, particularly when the term "prosperity" is used vaguely and for purposes of propaganda.

The Honorable James J. Davis, then Secretary of Labor in the President's Cabinet, asserted in a letter to a friend in Wales that 86 per cent of the members of the working class in the United States were living in poverty. Mr. Davis is himself a native of Wales. As a matter of fact he was merely quoting, perhaps without using quotation marks, a statement by a Columbia Professor that "about 86 per cent of Americans still are members of families whose incomes are less than two thousand dollars a year, a sum which can be lived on by the average family of five only by the sacrifice of most of the amenities, and even some of the necessaries of life, which would be included in any standard of living calculated to produce conditions of ordinary health and welfare."[1]

One of the significant aspects of the increase in our national wealth and of the improvement in the material conditions of our working people is that the word "poverty," as well as the word "luxury," has become elastic and indefinite in its denotation. In the interest of clearness, therefore, it will be well to introduce some definitions of poverty and some estimates of its extent.

In the year 1904 Robert Hunter published a volume

---

[1] *Industry's Coming of Age*, p. 217.

called *Poverty* in which he used that term to describe the condition of persons who are "unable to obtain those necessaries which will permit them to maintain a state of physical efficiency." This conception is sufficiently definite, even though it considers human beings solely as units of production. Using this standard, Mr. Hunter estimated that not less than ten million inhabitants of the country were in poverty; or about 8 per cent of the population at the time when he wrote. Inasmuch as he was a social worker whose activities had brought him in personal contact with large numbers of the poor and inasmuch as he was a believer in Socialism, his judgment concerning the extent of poverty was not universally accepted.

In the year 1914 Professor Jacob H. Hollander of Johns Hopkins University expressed agreement with Hunter's estimate, but gave a somewhat less precise definition of poverty. He referred to it as the condition of those who have "less than enough food, clothing and shelter." This was in a little book entitled *The Abolition of Poverty*. Two years after its appearance Professor Maurice Parmalee, in a large volume, *Poverty and Social Progress,* likewise accepted Hunter's minimum estimate of the extent of poverty and declared that it was probably too low. He found reasons for thinking that from 5 to 10 per cent of the population were during some period of any year "receiving charitable aid." However, his definition of poverty is more comprehensive than Hunter's. In order to be above the poverty line, a person must possess those goods which are "necessary for a decent and wholesome life and for maintaining the highest physical and mental efficiency."

In the year 1921 Professor John L. Gillin published *Poverty and Destitution,* an octavo volume of more than seven hundred pages. He expressed the opinion that Hunter and Parmalee had exaggerated the number of Americans in poverty and submitted a definition of his own. That man is poor, he said, who does not possess "enough to provide for the physical and mental efficiency of himself and to

233

enable his natural dependents to function usefully according to the standards of his group in society." In the year 1929 Robert Kelso, a social worker of long experience, published a volume called *Poverty*. Although he made no attempt to state the number of persons in that condition, he declared that it had "widespread prevalence" even in the United States. His very long definition may be summarized as follows: Poverty is the condition of a man who has not sufficient means to "ensure continuous bodily and mental fitness to carry on permanently in his occupation and locality, and enable himself and dependents to live and function in their community with decency and self-respect." This definition is more comprehensive than those given by Hunter and Hollander, but seems to be about the same as those of Parmalee and Gillin. The most distinctive additional note is the specification of "decency and self-respect" as necessary attributes of those who are above the condition of poverty. Mr. Kelso clearly indicates that poverty should be regarded as the characteristic of those who are without means for mental, moral and religious improvement. Is this a correct or helpful way of looking at the situation? Does it not seem to confuse the concept of decent living with the concept of a sufficiency which is not, indeed, normal or humanly satisfactory, but which is above the condition ordinarily understood as that of poverty?

At any rate, we have to adopt some fairly precise definition of poverty if we are to discuss it intelligently. The formulation of the "Poverty Level" of family living by Professor Paul H. Douglas in *Wages and the Family* (1925) (p. 5) provides a helpful starting point.

> On this standard, the family is not on a basis of permanent self-support, and exists because of inroads which it makes upon its own health or upon its supply of furniture and goods. The family's dietary is generally appreciably below the standard of 3300 calories which are needed for an adult male at moderately heavy labour. The family is badly over-

crowded and has no resources with which to meet any unexpected expense. While costs necessarily vary from city to city, it is probable that it would cost a family of five between $1000 and $1100 to live on this scale in the larger American cities at the present time.

Inasmuch as the cost of living in the United States is now (January, 1931) about 7 per cent lower than when the foregoing paragraph was written, we shall take $1000 as most nearly expressing the lowest limit of annual earnings which are sufficient to place a family above the poverty line. How many families are there, or how many persons are members of families whose annual incomes are less than $1000 a year?

Nothing like an exact answer can be given owing to the lack of exact data. The best that we can do is to submit estimates which reflect the facts with sufficient accuracy to provide really significant information. The *American Labor Year Book* for 1928 concludes that 7,250,000 male wage-earners of the age of twenty years or over were in the latter part of the year 1927 receiving less than $25 a week. That would be the equivalent of $1200 a year if the unemployment period were assumed to be only two weeks. Of course, the average is considerably higher than two weeks annually. Probably one-half at least of these seven and a quarter million males were married. If they averaged two dependent children each, the total number of persons living in families having family incomes of less than $1250 a year was 14,500,000. What proportion of the married males was in receipt of less than $1000 a year it is impossible to say. In all probability, however, we do not exaggerate if we put the number of Americans living in poverty, according to the definition given by Professor Douglas, at somewhere between ten and twelve million. This is a smaller proportion of the current population than was the ten million estimated as living in poverty by Robert Hunter in the year 1904. The proportion ought to be considerably smaller today, owing to the increase which in the meantime has taken place in the incomes of even the lowest paid laborers.

Speaking of the poorly paid wage-earners of America, in June, 1927, Secretary of Labor James J. Davis said:

> If these underpaid workers were few in number and existed only in scattered instances, the inequality would be less great. But if we count them up, if we think of those in all our industries who may lack mechanical skill but who nevertheless shoulder the heavy weights and do the roughest work, we find a great part of American industry shot through with these unfortunates. It is not an exaggeration to say that we have some millions of these hard-worked but underpaid Americans. Taken together with their families and their dependents, I would venture to say we have among us from ten to fifteen millions of people who do not share as they should in the prosperity enjoyed by the rest of us. Morally, economically, and on the grounds of simple humanity this inequality should not be allowed to exist in this richest nation of history.

It should be noted that $1250 a year is considerably less than the amount necessary to maintain a man and wife and three small children on the "minimum health-and-decency level." In other words, it is considerably less than a living wage. According to Professor Douglas, the cost of providing such a livelihood in the larger American cities is from $1500 to $1800 per year. Moreover, it is to be observed that the 7,250,000 males of twenty years of age and over who are getting less than $1250 per year constitute more than one-third of the total number of male adult laborers. Hence, it is not improbable that one-half the adult male laborers in the United States are receiving less than a family living wage.

Despite this fact and despite the millions of Americans who are still living in poverty, the material condition of the laboring class has improved since the years before the Great War. The most recent figures and estimates on this subject are found in the chapter on "The National Income and Its Distribution" in the second volume of the work entitled *Recent Economic Changes in the United States.* These two volumes constitute the report of the Committee on Recent Economic Changes, which was appointed by Herbert Hoover and of which he was Chairman. The work was published in May, 1929. In the chapter referred to above, it is stated that the average annual remuneration of wage-earners, as measured in purchasing power, was 19 per cent higher in the year 1927 than it was in the year 1913, while the average remuneration of salaried employees increased 14 per cent during the same period. Moreover, the share of the national income received by employees seems to have increased slightly, while that of property owners as such underwent a decrease. In 1913 the "realized income" of wage-earners was 37 per cent of the national income; in 1925 it was 38 per cent. In 1912 the "realized income" of salary receivers was 15 per cent of the national income; in 1925 it was 18 per cent. The total share of all employees increased from 53 to 57 per cent, during those 12 years. This estimate agrees fairly well with that of the Federal Trade Commission for the year 1923, which was 55 per cent. In 1913 the total "realized income" from rents and royalties, interest and dividends amounted to 25 per cent of the national income; in 1925 it had declined to 23 per cent. During the same period, the profits withdrawn by entrepreneurs from business fell from 22 per cent of the whole to 20 per cent. These profits are, of course, a return for labor and risk rather than a return on property.

The diffusion of the shares of joint stock companies among the working classes in the United States has probably received more attention than it deserves. The relatively rapid increase in this sort of ownership since the Great War has occasionally been referred to as a "new industrial revolution." Undoubtedly the number of wage-earners who now own either the stocks or the bonds of business corporations is much greater than it was ten years ago, and undoubtedly many large business concerns have strongly encouraged this form of investment by their employees. Nevertheless, the Federal Trade Commission, in its report on "National Wealth and Income" published in 1926, found that while employees comprised 7.5 per cent of the common-stock owners and 3.5 per cent of the preferred-stock holders in the companies studied, they possessed "only 1.5 per cent of the common stock and 2 per cent of the preferred stock." A study of employee stock ownership made by a department of Princeton University showed that, although the employee stockholders of twenty large corporations comprised 21 per cent of the whole number, their holdings represented only 4.3 per cent of the market value of the stock. So far as we can see, a very long time will elapse before the employees of any large American corporation come to own and control a majority of its shares.

Despite pretty general increases in wages and despite a slight increase in the wage-earners' share of the national income, the contrasts between the very rich and the very poor, the extremes of wealth and poverty, are quite as great and as disturbing as they have ever been in American history. This statement is dramatically illustrated by the juxtaposition of palaces and of hovels in all of our great cities. It is more scientifically indicated in the estimate that 50 per cent of the country's wealth is owned by 1 per cent of the population; 60 per cent by 2 per cent of the population, and 90 per cent by 13 per cent of the population; and that the lower two-thirds of the population "receives virtually no income for owning, for they own virtually nothing."[2]

In the foregoing paragraphs no attempt has been made to describe American poverty in concrete terms of social and living conditions. Under this aspect the poorest classes do not differ greatly from country to country except in degree. Some are more miserable than others, but all are in misery

---

[2] Edie, *Economics: Principles and Problems*, pp. 446, 447.

238

as regards one or more of the essentials of humane and reasonable life. As we have given only one measure of poverty, namely, insufficient income, so we have neglected all other causes than the economic. To be sure, the other causes are as general and as effective in the United States as elsewhere, such as incompetency, vice and misfortune. Here, as in other countries, these factors make a considerable addition to the number of persons whose poverty is due primarily to economic conditions, and they make the poverty of the latter more intense. Nevertheless, the economic factor is the most powerful, the most conspicuous and the most easily measured. The definition of poverty quoted above from Professor Douglas' book is sufficiently precise and the estimate of the number of persons who do not receive enough wages to keep them above that kind of poverty is sufficiently accurate and striking to give the average reader a suggestive, if not a complete, picture of the amount of poverty in the United States. In all probability the majority of those who read these pages will be surprised to learn that American poverty is so extensive.

And yet the greater part of it is unnecessary and indefensible. If our economic system were organized rationally and functioning rationally, no person nor any family in the United States would be compelled to live in poverty on account of lack of income. The vast increase in the productive power of our industries and workers in the last ten years has become one of the commonplaces of our economic literature. No competent authority doubts that we have sufficient natural resources and sufficient productive equipment to provide every man, woman and child in America with means sufficient not only to maintain themselves above the poverty line, but to provide them with the conditions of decent, humane and reasonable life. Nor is this all. Our industries could produce a surplus which would enable a considerable proportion of the population to possess abundant comforts and luxuries and the means and opportunities of higher and more genuine culture than has ever existed since man first appeared on the earth.

As these lines are being written, President Hoover is engaged in several conferences with the masters of industry and the heads of governmental departments in order to explore and, if possible, find the means of preventing an apparently imminent industrial depression or recession. Should these efforts fail, the number of Americans in poverty would for a time be considerably increased and enormous hardships would fall upon other hundreds of thousands.[3] Once again we are threatened with the anomalous contrast of multitudes seeking to produce goods needed by themselves and others, of mechanical equipment that is more than adequate to this end, yet of multitudes in want because the men and the machines cannot be put to work. This predicament constitutes a very severe indictment of the economic intelligence of the richest and most resourceful people of the world.

The cause of the threatened slowing down of our industries is to be found in our excessive capacity for production. Our plants and workers are able to turn out more goods than we can sell. This is true not merely of one or a few, but of all our major industries, from agriculture to automobiles. The process of supplanting men by machines has been so greatly accelerated in the last ten years that a very large number of workers has been constantly disemployed for longer or shorter periods of time and a large proportion of our productive equipment is continuously unused. Mechanical improvements have abolished tasks that were ten years ago performed by upwards of three million human beings, while several of our great industries can produce all the goods that are demanded if they operate steadily for eight to ten months per year. Sooner or later, this excessive potency is converted into excessive actuality, so that superfluous stocks of goods are accumulated with

---

[3] At the end of 1930 we know that "these efforts" did fail.

240

the necessary consequence of diminished production and diminished employment.

Along with the enormous increase in productive power there has taken place an important change in the attitude of American business men. Were it sufficiently developed and courageously acted upon, it would go far toward providing a remedy for the evils that have just been sketched. It is thus described in the report on *Recent Economic Changes:* "The recognition of the principle of high wages and low costs as a policy of enlightened industrial practice in a period of stationary cost of living—the recognition of wage-earners as the great domestic market." Twenty-five years ago both these propositions were ignored or denied by almost all employers in the United States. With a few exceptions, business men held that production and sales could be increased only through diminution of productive costs and selling prices. The purchasing power of the wage-earning class was either assumed or ignored. Today the most enlightened directors of industry realize that the buying power of the wage-earners is a very important part of the consuming power of the whole population and that it automatically increases with increases of wages. These men have become aware that the well-to-do classes are already buying all that they care to buy and that if new sources of demand are to be found they must be sought in the desires of the class that would like to purchase more if only it had the requisite power. The power to consume and the desire to consume must be combined in a much larger proportion of the population than now exemplify that condition if our industries are to be kept going with a fair degree of steadiness and security. If this condition is to be realized, the new attitude of American business men, which is described in the quotation included in this paragraph, will have to become more extensive, more positive and more courageous. They will have to realize that wages in general must go still higher than they have gone, and in the case of the underpaid, a great deal higher.

241

Even if all our workers were receiving living wages, the productive capacity of our industries might still be so great that all the goods could not be sold nor all our labor continuously employed. We could cross that bridge when we came to it. Nevertheless, the manner of crossing is obvious. It is by way of a shorter work-day or a shorter work-week. One of the most baneful assumptions of our materialistic industrial society is that all men should spend at least one-third of the twenty-four hour day in some productive occupation. If all their efforts are not needed to turn out the necessaries and reasonable comforts of life, they should be utilized in the production of luxuries. If men still have leisure, new luxuries must be invented to keep them busy and new wants must be stimulated in the consumers to take the luxuries off the market and keep the industries going. Of course, the true and rational doctrine is that when men have produced sufficient necessaries and reasonable comforts and conveniences to supply all the population, they should spend what time is left in the cultivation of their intellects and wills, in the pursuit of the higher life. If American industries can make the requisite leisure possible, they will have provided at least the opportunity for a more rational society than any people has yet enjoyed. Moreover, a shorter work-day or work-week would reinforce the movement for higher wages and more general employment; for it would require more workers to produce the same amount of goods and thus make labor scarcer and dearer. Indeed, this is the most practical method available for increasing the remuneration and the consuming power of the masses, short of minimum wage legislation.

The argument in the paragraphs immediately preceding refers only to my own country. I shall never forget the wistful tones in which a representative from Japan at the Institute of Pacific Relations in Honolulu in the summer of 1927 addressed the American delegation: "You are an economic world in yourselves. The prosperity of your industries does not depend upon the contingencies of international trade." This is the simple truth. Nine-tenths of the products of our industries are consumed at home. Therefore, we can make any changes that seem good to us in our industrial system, regardless of the industrial policies or performances of other nations. Neither Japan, nor Great Britain, nor France, nor Germany, nor any other great industrial country is in a position to exercise this choice or this power. With regard to their principal industries all these countries have, like the United States, the capacity to produce more goods than they can sell and, therefore, are unable to keep all their workers employed. But these inabilities come not merely from lack of purchasing power in their own people, but also from the inability to find foreign markets. They cannot make sufficient sales in foreign countries because too many of them are trying to sell the same kind of goods. If Japan could keep all her textile mills operating, her people would be much better off. She cannot do so, because her mills must compete with those of China, England, the United States and even India.

For these countries there are apparently only three possible means of escape from the predicament of excessive productive capacity and serious unemployment. They might establish new industries or develop their less important industries so that they would be less dependent upon foreign markets for the products of their main industries. Or they might consign to an international economic committee the power of allotting particular industries to the countries that could carry these on to best advantage. Or they might bring about a redistribution of population so that, for example, the surplus textile operatives in Japan might find employment at some other kind of work in some other country. Obviously, the last mentioned remedy is purely theoretical, while the second is scarcely less so. The United States is not interested in either of these devices, and it is in a position to utilize the first to whatever extent might become necessary.

Part IV

Miscellaneous

17. Catholicism and Liberalism

TWO Roman documents have provoked questions concerning the intellectual integrity of Catholics who profess to be loyal to the Holy See and who call themselves, or are known by others as, "liberals." These documents are: a revised edition of the Index of Prohibited Books and the Encyclical of Pope Pius XI on Education. The former forbids Catholics to read certain proscribed books, while the latter commands them to send their children to Catholic schools. In the subsequent criticism directed at "liberal" Catholics who accept such prohibitions and precepts, one finds a considerable amount of misunderstanding and of inexact language. When these are corrected much of the criticism appears without foundation.

An artificial definiteness has been accorded to the terms "liberal" and "liberalism." Some of the critics assume that any Catholic who accepts the designation "liberal" necessarily uses the word in the sense attached to it by the critics themselves. When we consider the history of these two terms, we are surprised at this assumption. Liberalism may denote a disposition of will, an attitude of mind, or adherence to a set of opinions. Accordingly the liberal is a person who is generous, tolerant and inclined to credit with sincerity those who differ from him; or he is unprejudiced, openminded and friendly to new ideas; or his opinions tend to magnify freedom and to diminish restraint and authority. Liberalism may exist in many fields of thought and discussion: economics, politics, governmental policy, religion, education, science, philosophy, ethical theory and practice, social conventions, *et cetera*. A person can logically and consistently be a liberal in some of these departments and a conservative or authoritarian in others. He can look upon complete and centralized authority as reasonable in some and as unreasonable in others of these spheres of thought and action. For example, he can be a liberal in politics and economics and at the same time an authoritarian in religion. Many men find no difficulty in taking a diametrically opposite position under both these heads.

One of the best known uses of the term "liberalism" is that which has for many years prevailed on the Continent of Europe and in some Latin American countries. Those who profess this variety of liberalism are almost invariably anti-clerical, which is frequently a euphemism for anti-Catholic. On its theoretical side, it denies or minimizes the authority of God and of the Church over the human intellect. On its practical side, it denies or minimizes the authority of God and of the Church over human conduct. Both the theoretical and practical forms of Continental liberalism exhibit several degrees—from the complete denial of divine authority, doctrinal and legislative, to the rejection of Church authority outside those principles of faith and morals which enjoy the prerogative of infallibility.

Now it is this species of liberalism which the European ecclesiastic usually has in mind when he employs the term without qualification. Probably this is the kind that Cardinal Merry del Val was thinking of when he referred recently to "that moral pestilence known as liberalism." The editorial entitled "A Moral Pestilence," in the *Nation,* December 25, 1929, declares that the doctrine of the Catholic Church "is unalterably opposed to very nearly every tenet of the liberal creed." If the "liberal creed" is identical with the liberalism described above, the assertion just quoted is obviously correct. Were the Church to accept or even to compromise with this kind of liberalism, it would commit intellectual and moral suicide.

It should be evident that this species of liberalism cannot be accepted by any Catholic who is at once loyal to his Church and adequately instructed. There have, indeed, been Catholics, particularly on the Continent, who designated themselves as "Liberal Catholics," precisely in order to express their adherence to a mild form of the liberalism that we are now discussing. While accepting the authority of the Church in matters of faith and morals which had been defined *ex cathedra,* they denied the right of the Pope to impose as of obligation doctrinal declarations or disciplinary rules which do not enjoy infallibility. Belonging to, or closely akin to, this class are those American Catholics whom the *Nation* calls "liberals" and whom it thus describes in the editorial referred to above: "Their sentiments are known by their conduct; they disobey many of the commands of the Church, and they are willing to explain away many of its doctrines." If the disobedience of these persons is based not upon human weakness but upon deliberate rejection of the divine right of the Church to impose precepts of morality and discipline, they are not faithful Catholics. A similar statement applies to the device of "explaining away" Church doctrines. Both these attitudes have been condemned on various occasions by more than one Pope. An American Catholic who practices or professes this degree of liberalism is either intellectually dishonest or inadequately instructed.

When the writer of the *Nation* editorial speaks of "the liberal creed," perhaps he does not wish to include the cruder and more extreme forms of Continental liberalism; for example, the denial of the right of God Himself to impose restraints upon intellect, conscience or conduct. Perhaps, he desires to emphasize what are sometimes called "modern liberties"; that is, freedom of opinion, of teaching, of speech, of writing and of printing. Undoubtedly, the Catholic Church does reject unlimited freedom in all these spheres. She denies the moral right of men to accept or to profess false opinions or to propagate doctrines or practices which are contrary to the moral law and therefore opposed to human welfare. She holds that a man has no more right to utter falsehood and wrong than he has to perpetrate them. She maintains that the intellect and the vocal organs are as subject to the moral law as any other human faculty.

As a matter of fact, no government has ever admitted, no modern government admits today, unlimited freedom of expression. Men may not, with legal impunity, calumniate their neighbors, nor publish obscene literature, nor make indecent speeches in public, nor corrupt the morals of the young in the schoolroom. The decision of the Supreme Court in the Espionage Cases (1918), written by Justice Holmes himself, showed that our Federal Constitution restricts very considerably the scope of the guarantee of freedom of speech contained in the First Amendment. Therefore, the principle of absolute and unlimited freedom of expression seems to be rejected by the better and saner part of the community, if not by all but a few extremists.

To be sure, the practical question of drawing the line between reasonable and unreasonable freedom with regard to opinion and expression is one that different persons will answer differently. The way in which it has been answered in the Constitutions and statutes of our federal and state governments is quite satisfactory to American Catholics. They are rarely conspicuous in the groups that appear before Congress and state legislatures seeking diminution of this class of liberties. They perceive no conflict between their Catholicism and the traditional American policy.

So much for definitions and classifications. Our discussion thus far has evidently touched only a few of the accepted uses and kinds of liberals and liberalism. But these are the species that seem to be most frequent in the minds of men who discuss liberalism in relation to the Catholic Church.

Happily it is possible to get away from ambiguous terminology and discuss the actions and attitudes themselves which are called into question. A certain writer seeks to "understand the position of liberal members of the Catholic Church," and to learn the "processes by which the claims of absolutism in religion and relativity in rational thinking are reconciled." Another asks: "By what system of mental partitioning do they [Liberal Catholics] succeed in remaining outwardly good Catholics, when, if they are intellectually honest, they cannot accept their Church's attitude toward the individual's right to read and think for himself?"

"Absolutism in religion" is probably intended to denote that theory or attitude which accepts religious doctrines as certain and recognizes the unconditional authority of the Church to lay down the principles and rules of faith and morals. Surely this attitude is not confined to Catholics nor to the domain of religion. In all probability, the writer of the quoted phrase accepts "absolutism" in mathematics, in physics, in chemistry and perhaps in other sciences. That is, he believes that he can have certainty and not merely "relativity" or probability in these fields. When he uses the phrase "relativity in rational thinking," does he mean that all truth is relative, that there is no such thing as certainty? In other words, is he a complete skeptic or subjectivist? Inasmuch as Catholics, whether they call themselves liberals or not, do not accept this position, they are not called upon to reconcile it with their belief in religious absolutism. Probably the writer merely intends to say that in some fields of thought there is no authority nor any compelling array of evidence to guarantee certainty, that in them men can possess only opinions and greater or less degrees of probability. This statement is true to a greater or less extent of politics, economics, sociology, philosophy, history, and in a large portion of the territory occupied by the physical sciences. The Catholic who accepts this so-called relativity of knowledge, who admits that he cannot have complete certainty throughout these domains, has no difficulty in accepting the absolute truth and absolute authority of the Church in religion and morals. There is no contradiction, because the realities covered by these two classes of thought are different and the appropriate methods and instruments of knowledge are different. To demand or expect identical judgments concerning the knowableness of different kinds of realities is quite unreasonable.

251

The other objector wonders how Liberal Catholics can honestly accept "their Church's attitude toward the individual's right to read and think for himself." In a preceding paragraph this question has in part been answered in the statement that Catholics who refuse to accept the authority of the Church in matters of discipline are not loyal and orthodox Catholics, even though ignorance may prevent them from perceiving this fact. Let us, however, examine on its merits the assumption that the individual has a "right to read and think for himself." Apparently the objector regards this so-called right as an essential element of genuine liberalism. His use of the term is unprecise and ambiguous. He cannot mean *legal* right, for no one denies that the civil law in the United States concedes this. Perhaps he means *moral* right; that is, a right or claim which is in accord with reason, inasmuch as it is necessary or useful for human welfare. As pointed out above, there is no moral right to do wrong. It is wrong for a Catholic to disregard the authority which Christ has conferred upon the Church. The thinking and the reading which the Church forbids is, generally speaking, harmful to the true faith and to sound morality. I say "generally speaking," because the Church does not profess to be infallible in such matters as that which is covered by the Index of Prohibited Books. Nevertheless, faith and morals and truth are safer as a result of the Church's legislation in this field than they would be in the absence of such legislation.

Let us test this question by reference to the works on the Index which are adduced as horrible examples in the *Nation* editorial. Let us leave out of consideration those Catholics who have a special reason for reading these books because they are teachers, or writers, or clergymen; for they will not generally find great difficulty in getting the required permission. Let us take the average Catholic, the average educated Catholic, if you will. I venture to say that such a one could employ his time more profitably in reading other works, say in the same respective fields, than in reading

Gibbon's *Decline and Fall of the Roman Empire,* Darwin's *Origin of Species,* Kant's *Critique* and the works of Maeterlinck. As for *The Book of Common Prayer* and the Protestant versions of the Bible, it is difficult to see what benefit the ordinary Catholic would derive from their perusal. After all, we have incomparably better prayer books of our own, and the Church possessed and preserved the integral Scriptures for many centuries before the emergence of Martin Luther and King James I. A great part, if not the greater part, of the reading done by this generation is sheer waste of time, if not worse. Bertrand Russell's *Marriage and Morality* contains some amazing history and anthropology, some ignorance of the Bible, considerable misrepresentation of Catholic doctrine, much superficial reasoning and immoral ethics. In a word, the book is unscientific. Yet it is and will be accepted unquestioningly by thousands of persons who think that they "think for themselves," and who pride themselves on their intellectual independence. In passing, it is worth while to observe that no previous age has contained more educated men and women who, while rejecting and disdaining religious authority, bow down before the authority of great names. The latter have become the idols of the market place in our modern day.

The *Nation* editorial finds fault with Liberal Catholics who have not repudiated the ban laid by a certain Cardinal upon other than parochial schools. But this is the general and traditional Catholic discipline and it has been restated in the recent Encyclical of Pope Pius XI on Education. Our position is very simple and very logical. We hold that religious training is the most important element in education, that as a rule it cannot be adequately obtained if it is excluded from the school, and that there can be no such thing as a genuinely neutral school. If the school does not teach religion, it shows itself indifferent to religion. This attitude of indifference, insensibly perhaps, but more or less effectively, conveys to the pupil the impression that religion

253

is not an important element in education or in life. Obviously, such a school cannot be completely satisfactory to an intelligent Catholic. Quite as obviously, it is the business of the Church to safeguard the spiritual welfare of her children by appropriate legislation.

The most astonishing and disturbing statement in the *Nation* editorial is that the liberal who is logical "cannot be other than anti-Catholic." This suggests a very illiberal brand of liberalism. To be "anti" is to be opposed; but it implies something more than negative opposition or withholding agreement. Frequently it denotes some measure of hostility. Always it implies that one seeks to thwart the program and purposes of the institution to which one is "anti." The creed of Christian Science I reject utterly, but I am not anti-Christian Science; for its followers do not attack my moral or civil rights. On the other hand, I am anti-Puritan, because Puritanism interferes with my personal liberty by imposing upon me legal prohibition and by designing to deprive me of other liberties.

No such threat is offered by the Catholic Church against the American liberal who refuses to accept her authority. She does not seek to take from him any of his cherished liberties. Why should he scold Catholics merely because they accept what he regards as tyrannical authority? Why can he not permit us to involve ourselves in what seems to him intellectual stultification? Or, does this brand of liberalism insist in saving men against their will from foolish opinions and foolish loyalties? This is the essence of toryism.

At any rate, the position of the intelligent Catholic, whether or not he calls himself a liberal, who wholeheartedly accepts the authority of the Church in faith and morals and discipline is neither disingenuous, nor self-contradictory, nor unreasonable. His interpretation of history impels him to the conclusion that Christ was God and that He endowed the Catholic Church with plenary authority to teach and to govern in spiritual and moral affairs.

254

CATHOLICISM AND LIBERALISM

The non-Catholic may, as he does, reject both the premises and the conclusion of this reasoning, but he cannot fairly accuse those who accept it of either inconsistency or intellectual stultification. And the non-Catholic who professes to be liberal has no valid reason for regarding us from the standpoint of a hostile "anti."

Possibly the foregoing discussion has not provided the kind of answer which the *Nation* and some of its readers seek to their question as to the way in which the Catholic liberal reconciles his liberalism with his religious allegiance. Probably I am not the kind of Catholic liberal that they have had in mind. I have never experienced even a temptation to become a liberal in the sense of rejecting any part of the authority claimed and exercised by my Church. And I strongly doubt that the number of American Catholics who deliberately and knowingly adhere to this form of liberalism is considerable or significant.

Nevertheless, I suppose that I should be classed as a liberal in economics and in politics. As such, I would suggest to the editors of the *Nation* and to all others who desire to see established a reign of wider industrial and political justice that the task before them, before us all, is formidable enough and sufficiently worth while to command our united efforts. This cause will not be served by lecturing, threatening and antagonizing Catholic economic and political liberals, merely because they refuse to accept the anti-Church variety of liberalism. This mistaken and utterly unnecessary course is mainly responsible for the ultra-conservative position taken by many prominent Catholics, lay and clerical, on the Continent of Europe. To protect their religious interests they were compelled to ally themselves with economic and political reactionaries. Should a similar alignment take place in our own beloved country, the blame will surely rest upon those liberals who will not concede to Catholics the right to profess and practice in their own way the religious loyalties which they cherish above everything else in life.

255

18. The New Morality and Its Illusions

THE primary difference between the new and the old morality lies in their respective foundations. The moral system accepted by the young, as well as the old, fifty or seventy-five years ago, was frankly based upon religious authority. The moral law was regarded as a Divine enactment. Right was right, wrong was wrong, good was good, bad was bad—because these concepts were thought to reflect the Divine Reason and to express the Divine decrees. God was looked upon as the foundation, the source, the guarantor and the sanctioner of the entire moral code. All these ethical beliefs, all this ethical teaching was laid down, explained and enforced by living, active organizations. The answer to the question, "How ought I live?" was clearly and authoritatively presented in the teaching of organized religion.

These moral beliefs are today rejected by a large proportion of the American people. That proportion is greater among the educated than among the uneducated. It is probably at least as large among college students as among educated persons who have passed beyond the college years.

Thoughtful persons who have repudiated the old morality feel the necessity of providing a reasoned, if not a rational substitute. They have given us the "new morality." It is not easy to describe because its proponents are not agreed upon even its principal tenets and because very few of them set forth their views clearly and coherently. We can, however, distinguish two main forms or sets of proposals. Neither of them contains anything new. In essence, both are as old as ethical discussion; both can be found in the writings of the ancient Greeks. The two

256

variations that I have in mind may be denominated conveniently as the idealistic and the happiness theories.

The idealistic theory need not detain us long, inasmuch as it does not and will not make any considerable appeal to the vast majority of those who reject the old morality. As fairly typical of the idealistic proposals, I take those offered by Walter Lippmann. About two years ago this writer produced a very readable and in some parts a very thoughtful book, entitled *A Preface to Morals*. In the first part, he describes the decay of the old morality and the unsatisfactory conditions resulting. In the second and third parts he develops the moral system which he recommends to those who no longer accept a moral code based upon religion. The task of the moralist in this generation is, he says, "to show that goodness is victorious vitality, and badness defeated vitality; that sin is the denial and virtue the fulfillment of the promise inherent in the purposes of men." The moralist "must give a true account of that which experience would show is desirable among the choices which are possible and necessary." As a statement of moral ends, these sentences are sufficiently vague. How does he expect these ends to be attained?

His fundamental principle is as vague as his formulation of particular ends. He calls it "high religion" and defines its dominant quality as "disinterestedness." Despite the attractive language in which he describes his proposed code and its applications, his argument is unconvincing. The man who has thrown off authoritative morality and its sanctions will raise the old, old question: "Why should I act disinterestedly when I am persuaded that I shall get more happiness or larger satisfactions out of life by acting selfishly? Disinterested actions may in some circumstances be necessary in order to obtain greater satisfaction later on, but I see no reason why I should make a habit of disinterestedness when I know that it will involve me in many unpleasant experiences. I am willing to consult experience in order to learn what actions are desirable, but

257

you must permit me to make my own choice of the desirable. Exercising this liberty, I do not find that uniform disinterestedness is desirable, either as an end or as a means. I want to be happy and I do not believe that I can attain happiness if I always follow disinterestedness."

Neither Mr. Lippmann nor anyone else can refute this argument. The average person who has rejected the old morality cannot be persuaded that disinterested conduct will bring him the maximum of happiness, as he understands happiness. No doubt a few generous souls will accept Mr. Lippmann's principle because they are so constituted, but the problem facing him is to find a rule of conduct which will appeal to the vast majority. Those forms of the "new morality" that are based upon any sort of idealism may be summarily dismissed as impractical and futile. Here we have one fundamental illusion of the "new morality."

The other form of the "new morality" that I shall discuss is that which places the highest good of man in earthly happiness. In considering this theory, a preliminary fact to be kept in mind is that happiness is always relative to some person or persons. It is not an absolute and independent entity. Even when one aims at the happiness of another in preference to one's own, one is seeking the happiness of a person, not happiness in the abstract. For the believer in a future life, happiness is a sufficiently compelling end; such a person is thinking of his own final happiness. But happiness on earth rests upon an entirely different basis. It must be conceived either in relation to one's self or to society. In the former case, each person will determine for himself whether the happiness that he seeks shall be selfish or unselfish, or a combination of both. Serious and competent moralists realize that the vast majority of persons who deliberately pursue their own happiness degenerate into mere seekers of selfish pleasures. Hence the proponents of the happiness morality would have the individual refrain from pursuing his own happiness or

258

pleasure when these conflict with the happiness of society or mankind.

Fairly representative of the writers who present this view is Durant Drake, Professor of Philosophy at Vassar College. In his work, entitled the *New Morality,* he dogmatically declares:

> What is best in the long run and for the greatest number should rationally take precedence over what chances to be wanted by this or that individual at the moment.

A few pages later he notes this objection:

> After all, happiness is an individual matter; why should one person deprive himself of it for another?

Why, indeed? By way of answer, the best that Professor Drake can do is to point out that men have altruistic as well as self-regarding impulses and to assert that the community must somehow compel persons "to want to be unselfish, or, insofar as this is not feasible, to be afraid or ashamed to be selfish." In the last chapter of his book he lays down the methods for securing this social compulsion. Eugenics, he says, could contribute something, but very little, toward breeding "a race of men who will naturally be more moral." The ethical possibilities of political and social reform move him to assert:

> The secret ballot and the civil service laws are doing more for good government than all the sermons and the moral lessons in the world.

What simple and childlike, not to say childish faith! However, his main reliance seems to be upon moral education, imparted chiefly in the schools, but also through various organizations, such as the Masons, the Knights of Columbus and the Rotary Clubs. Unfortunately, he neglects to inform us just how the schools or any other agency that rejects the old morality are going to find ways and motives to persuade or to compel men to be unselfish.

Having failed to suggest effective ways and motives himself, he passes on the task to institutions and associations. Apparently he has greater faith in these than in his own intelligence or ingenuity. In passing, the fact might be stressed that this exponent of the "new morality" is intrusted with the power and responsibility of teaching philosophy to the young women at Vassar College.

The illusion beneath the happiness morality is obvious. Like that underlying the idealistic morality, it assumes that our selfish impulses can be exorcised or coaxed out by fervent appeals to our altruistic impulses. We are solemnly assured that we ought to be unselfish; when we ask "why?" we receive no convincing reason, only a concatenation of more or less attractive words.

Turning from the illusions which are fundamental to those which are involved in the practical applications of the "new morality," I propose for consideration two provinces of conduct, that of property and that of the relations between the sexes. Inasmuch as I have dismissed the idealistic form as utterly futile for the great majority of persons, my discussion of the applications of the "new morality" will refer to that form which adopts happiness as the end and rule of conduct. In the field of property relations we find the "new morality" interpreted and accepted as authorizing the following aims and practices. Unlimited profits and unlimited rates of interest on capital; in competitive industries all business practices which are not prevented by the civil law or which are not too hazardous; in public utilities every device which enables the corporation to inflate its valuation and to expand the charges imposed upon the public. Labor is too slow a means of getting money. Speculation in price changes is much easier and much more exciting. The laborer need not take any more interest in his work nor work any harder than is necessary in order to hold his job. Mass production will make happiness general because it will provide indefinitely increasing luxuries and will arouse new wants for other luxuries when popular demand fails to take away all the goods that must be sold if the productive machinery is to be kept going.

The old morality condemned all these theories and practices as unjust or uncharitable, or at least as morally unworthy. The happiness morality can offer no logical objection to any of them, except insofar as they may be carried beyond the limits of personal expediency. Nevertheless, all these particular deductions from the "new morality" are illusory, at least in the long run. The position of our great industrial organizations, the position of property itself, will continue to be unstable so long as business continues to seek indefinitely large profits and to maintain what amounts to a system of industrial feudalism. Mass production inevitably leads to decrease of production, and increase of unemployment. The general persuasion that speculation is as normal a method of obtaining wealth as labor produces not only a distaste for work, but a greatly diminished respect for the property rights of those who possess large amounts of material goods. Economic power exerted to the injury of the masses will sooner or later appear to them as endowed with no more sanctity than physical power.

It is in the field of sex relations, however, that the "new morality" is doing the most harm and creating the greatest amount and variety of illusions. Its main tenets in this field are as follows: Divorce should be made very easy, although not quite so easy as in Russia, where it is obtainable by mutual consent of the parties. Birth control is legitimate and desirable, not only in the interest of health, but for economic reasons. Companionate marriage is at least worth serious study as a means of reducing illicit relations and providing a partial sort of family life for those who are unable or unwilling to accept the responsibility of bearing and rearing children. One of the most widely read, if not widely accepted, exponents of the "new morality," Bertrand Russell, would permit extra-marital

261

relations whenever these do not lead to the birth of children. Gilbert Murray observes "in advanced liberal journals a sort of disinterested enthusiasm for sexual misconduct in all its forms."

From both the social and the individual viewpoints every one of these rules, theories and practices is an illusion. When a people deliberately adopts easy divorce, there is no logical halting place this side of divorce by mutual consent. None of our states has yet formally adopted the principle of easy divorce, yet the average throughout the United States is one divorce for every six marriages. Inasmuch as many of the states have a considerably higher rate—for example, Nevada, Wyoming, Oregon, California and Washington have less than four marriages for every divorce —the adoption by all our states of a liberal policy would in a comparatively short time make the divorce rate equal to the marriage rate in the great majority of our population.

Birth control likewise involves a great illusion. All the considerations which are held to justify it by married persons apply logically to the unmarried as well. All the arguments offered for it can be reduced to the proposition that birth control is justified in order to avoid personal inconvenience. No distinction between degrees of inconvenience is logical or effective in the eyes of those who have adopted the happiness morality. Bertrand Russell would permit married persons to practice birth control in their extramarital relations. The disastrous effects of birth control upon any people that adopts it generally are inevitable. According to the population experts, married couples must on the average have three and three-fifths children in order to keep the population merely stationary. It is a matter of common knowledge that no social group that adopts birth control shows nearly that high an average. In fact, the average is nearer two than three and three-fifths. As soon as all, or the great majority, of couples in a country consistently engage in the practice of birth control, the population will begin to decline. Indeed, the birth rate in some of

262

our large cities in the North and West is even now very little in excess of the death rate.

While many advocates of birth control profess not to be alarmed at the prospect of a stationary population, none of them would welcome a declining population, at least for his own country. All would agree with Bertrand Russell that "a diminution, if it continues unchecked, means ultimate extinction and we cannot desire to see the most civilized races in the world disappear." He admits that before very long the birth rate in western Europe and in America will imply a stationary population unless there is intervention by governments. Those peoples that continue to increase in numbers will upset the present balance of power and thus create a grave danger for the nations of western Europe and America. He would meet this crisis through the organization of an International State which would impose birth control propaganda upon the nations that persist in increasing their populations. "Unless this is done," he says, "the peace of the world cannot be secured." The conception of an International State with power to regulate the number of births in the various nations reduces to absurdity the theory and practice of birth control.

Indeed we do not need any more impressive testimony to the illusiveness of the happiness morality than the condition of mind of those who have already given it a trial. I refer to the generation that has approached or reached maturity since the World War. Large numbers of this generation have been in rebellion against the religion and the moral code of their parents, and have substituted therefore the tenets and the implications of the happiness morality; yet, as Mr. Lippmann points out, they are already in a condition of "disillusionment with their own rebellion." No competent observer will dispute this generalization. The persons who have boldly and consistently adopted the happiness morality are neither happy nor satisfied.

In a recent magazine article, Professor John Dewey says that, "the chief intellectual characteristic of the present age

263

is its despair of any constructive philosophy." He means a philosophy of life which includes, of course, a code of ethics. What is his remedy? "A thoroughgoing philosophy of experience framed in the light of science and technique. Faith in the discovery of such a philosophy," he declares, "is neither a dream nor a demonstrated failure." With all due respect to Dr. Dewey's ability and authority, I maintain that the endeavor to get an adequate system of morality out of experience will never be successful. Experience cannot provide us with ultimate ends, or, to use present-day terminology, ultimate values. Experience can tell us, if we are able to interpret it, how to reach certain attainable ends, but it cannot tell us which ends are worth seeking. According to the "new morality" the end is happiness. Those who think that they will find happiness in selfish pleasure, prudently pursued, will never be persuaded by any amount of experience that they are on a wrong road. Dr. Dewey's philosophy of life adds one more to the illusions of the "new morality."

Not the least of its illusions is the assumption that it is scientific and based upon experience, and that the old morality rests merely upon authority. As a matter of fact, the principles of the old morality are scientific, are based upon observation, experience and a long view of consequences. These principles are derived from an adequate consideration of human nature. By this method we obtain a systematized code of morality, based upon nature and reason, and confirmed in large part by revelation. This system is truly scientific, both in its method and in its conclusions. It presents as the immediate rule or norm of conduct the rational nature of man adequately considered. The primary implications of this norm may be summarily stated thus: The rational part of man is higher than the animal part; the human individual is endowed with intrinsic worth and sacredness; all persons are essentially equal; and man is intrinsically superior to the animal creation but completely subordinate to God. The perception of these principles is partly intuitive, as when we assert that men are of equal intrinsic worth, and partly experimental, as when we assert that marriage and property are necessary institutions for human welfare. From these general principles can be derived all of men's particular duties and particular rights.

Precisely because the "new morality" is unscientific, precisely because it ignores important facts of intuition, observation and experience, it is subject to all the illusions that I have pointed out in the foregoing paragraphs. Because the "new morality" ignores the intrinsic distinction between the higher and the lower in the human faculties, it regards man's animal activities as equally important and equally worthy with the activities of his intellect. Because it ignores the intrinsic worth of every human being, it cannot logically require the activities of the selfish will to be subordinated to the activities of the disinterested will. From these fundamental errors it easily passes to the illusion that the lower impulses do not stand in need of discipline; that self-denial has no necessary place in self-development; that in place of self-control we may adopt what Gilbert Murray calls "the vicious dogma of self-expression"; that man can mightily achieve by following the easier way and that his impulses to altruism will automatically confine within due bounds his impulses to selfishness. Hence, we are not surprised when we find that the proponents of the "new morality" would deal with the sex instinct not by rigidly controlling it but by yielding to it, as though the sex appetite were not one of those that "grows by what it feeds on." Hence we are not surprised when we find Bertrand Russell declaring that the sex appetite is, like that for food and drink, "enormously enhanced by abstinence." Hence follows the advocacy of companionate marriage, free relations between unmarried men and women and between the married and the unmarried. The failure of the "new morality" to perceive the sacredness of human personality, and the inviolability of human rights leads its proponents to advocate all sorts of governmental tyranny, of which Bertrand Russell's proposal for the compulsory control of births by an International State, is merely an extreme example. Their superficial analysis of human nature prevents the exponents of the "new morality" from grasping the ample lessons of experience, not only in the matter of sex relations, but in every other problem of life where man's selfish impulses come into conflict with his altruistic impulses. In a word, the "new morality" is fundamentally unscientific and contrary to the most important facts of life and experience.

While the old morality is immediately based upon human nature, its ultimate basis is God. To the person who demands: "Why should I control my lower appetites, why should I act unselfishly rather than selfishly?" the old morality answers: "Because the principles and the intuitions concerning the intrinsic superiority of the higher over the lower faculties and the essential equality of all men are based upon the reason and nature of God; and because the sense of obligation you feel is a reflection of the will of God." In this sense, the old morality is frankly and fundamentally authoritarian. Its principles and sanctions become adequately known to the majority of men through the teachings of organized religion. Today as always, effective morality is generally unattainable without religious teaching.

As a final example of the illusions of the happiness morality, I cannot do better than quote from the *Autobiography* of John Stuart Mill (page 142). After describing the state of despondency into which he fell when he realized that the deliberate pursuit of happiness was unsatisfying, he tells us that he came to the conclusion that happiness

> was only to be attained by not making it the direct end. Those only are happy (I thought) who have their minds fixed on some objective other than their own happiness; on the happiness of others, on the im-

266

provement of mankind, even on some art or pursuit followed not as a means but as itself an ideal end. Aiming thus at something else, they find happiness by the way. . . . Ask yourself whether you are happy and you cease to be so. The only chance is to treat not happiness, but some end external to it, as the purpose of life.

This, let me say in closing, is precisely the method followed by the adherents of the old morality. They find happiness in pursuing an "end external to it," namely, conformity with God's moral law in this life, and union with Him in the life to come.

19. Birth Control

ONLY that is right which agrees with the moral law. Only that agrees with the moral law which agrees with human nature. Birth control is contrary to human nature because it is a perversion. It does not correct nature; it frustrates nature. It abuses a human faculty; it nullifies a human action; it thwarts a human function. It uses the generative faculty in such a way that the primary end of the faculty cannot be attained. The faculty is compelled to defeat itself. This is an inherent contradiction and makes the act intrinsically wrong. To be sure, this argument does not persuade those who identify morality with short-sighted utility. The proposition that frustrative use of the sex faculty is intrinsically immoral is plain; it can no more be proved than the proposition that two plus two equals four.

Happily the intuition which tells us that this practice is immoral, receives abundant support from observation and experience. Birth control is injurious to husband, wife, children, society and the nation.

Self-respect and mutual respect in married couples are injured by birth control practices. Conjugal intercourse is perverted from the noble function of co-operation with the Creator into an ignoble means of sensual gratification. The calculation and artifice employed in birth control are destructive of conjugal reverence. Probably no normal husband or wife ever entered upon this way without moral shock, or continued on it without moral deterioration. Upon the majority of *wives* it has particularly disastrous effects. An unfortunate woman recently executed in New York state for murdering her husband, publicly confessed what the practice of birth control did to her way of life. Here is the substance of her remorseful reflections:

268

BIRTH CONTROL

"Had I, like a Christian and a woman, refused to fall so abominably low as to trifle with the will of God and the law of nature, I would not be where I am and what I am. I would have been tied down to my fireside and my cribside where I belonged, where every married woman belongs. I wouldn't have been gadding about, meeting strangers, with time on my hands for frivolous and sinful pleasures. All the other married women I frolicked with and wasted my years with, were women who had no children or very few. The ones I knew who had three, four, more—tots born close together—didn't burn up their hours like we did. And they were more at peace with themselves, with God and with the world. They were better women, better Christians, and better citizens than we, the set that had plenty of useless time for useless occupations.

"I want to cry aloud, through these bars and past these cold stone walls, out where it can echo against the sky and reach the ears and enter the hearts of all women—birth control is a sin, a crime, and a lurking peril. It is physically and morally obnoxious and it must be black in the sight of God."

It is asserted that birth control will give us a better quality of children. But the practice is fatal to some of the essential moral qualities. Birth control is practiced mainly by those who desire to satisfy more material wants and to escape all hardship. But experience warns us that without capacity for sacrifice we get nowhere and achieve nothing. We cannot have the power to do unless we have the power to do without. Parents who ignore this law deprive themselves of the capacity for endurance and sustained effort. And they deprive their children of the training necessary for acquiring this capacity. The one or two or three children of birth-controlling parents are condemned to an environment which encourages selfishness, flabbiness of will, and mediocrity of intellect. Such children are inferior in most of the qualities of efficient character.

When the opinion becomes generally accepted that birth

control is right, it will be so regarded without as well as within the marriage relation. If it is right in the case of a married couple who seek to avoid the burdens of child bearing and child rearing, why is it not right in the case of unmarried persons who dislike the inconveniences of chastity? Or in the case of the husband who is weary of one woman? Or in the case of the wife who is weary of one man? These inconveniences differ only in degree. Unmarried persons who have sexual intercourse, and escape the consequences through contraceptive methods, do so from the same motive as married persons who practice birth control, that is, to avoid the inconvenience of having children. Once men and women have rejected the principle that birth control is bad in itself and always, once they adopt the opinion that it is good in the presence of hard circumstances, they claim the right to decide for themselves when the circumstances are sufficiently hard. The devastating effect of this persuasion upon social purity and social health needs no formal exposition.

Consider now the effect of birth control upon *national* welfare. The Sixth International Birth Control Conference, held in New York City, in 1925, resolved "that persons whose progeny give promise of being of decided value to the community should be encouraged to bear as large families, properly spaced, as they feasibly can." This is about as foolish and futile a recommendation as ever found expression in a gathering of presumably rational beings. No husband or wife who prefers luxuries to children will make sacrifices for the community or the race or posterity. In order to prevent a decline in its numbers any social group must produce an average of about three and three-fifths children per marriage. No birth control group averages as many as three. No such group ever will reach that average. No proposition in social psychology is more nearly certain than this: When birth control becomes general among all the classes of a nation, that nation will have committed itself to a continuous decline in population.

270

With their customary lack of comprehensive thinking, the advocates of birth control fail to consider this inevitable outcome of their propaganda. Ignoring the pronounced decline in the rate of population increase throughout the Western world in the last forty years, they talk fatuously about the dangers of over-population. At the birth control conference mentioned above, Professor Fairchild declared that the world's population had doubled since the beginning of the nineteenth century, and deplored the results of an equal rate of increase in the next century and a quarter. He did not mention the restriction of immigration to the United States, nor the decline in the average number of children in middle class families in the Middle West from 5.4 in the last generation to 3.3 in the present generation, nor the failure of urban families to average as many as four children.

Equally unscientific is the argument frequently offered that the declining birth rate of the last forty years has been offset by a declining death rate. It is true that the death rate has declined, but this has been due only slightly to the decrease in the birth rate. The vitally important facts are these: The death rate has not been lowered as fast as the birth rate; no low-birth-rate country is increasing as fast in population as it was before the birth rate began to decline; and the nations with fairly high birth rates are increasing faster than those having low birth rates. These facts are available to anyone who takes the trouble to study the sources. The advocates of birth control prefer to ignore them, or to misrepresent them.

One of the most common arguments for birth control is that which stresses the welfare of the working classes. Let them keep their families small, restrict the labor supply and force up wages. It is a delightfully simple remedy. It is also superficial and unjust. Although the productive resources of the world are ample to support all classes in reasonable comfort, the advocates of birth control would deprive the working people of the right to normal family life. In this they are continuing the neo-Malthusian tradition. John Kells Ingram tells us, in his *History of Political Economy*, that the middle classes of England assiduously preached the doctrine of birth control to the working classes in the early part of the nineteenth century. Because they persisted in having large families the working classes were responsible for their own poverty. That was a very comforting doctrine for the exploiters. The bourgeois advocates of birth control are preaching the same gospel to the toiling masses today. They would shift the responsibility for industrial injustice from their own shoulders. They care as little for social justice as they do for fundamental thinking or comprehensive views of social phenomena.

"The law of human progress, what is it but the moral law?" asked Henry George at the close of an eloquent chapter in *Progress and Poverty*. The moral law is the rule of direction and development written by the Creator into the human constitution. We can ignore this rule; we can shut our eyes to the intuitive light by which its fundamental precepts are revealed; we can insist upon waiting for the verdict of experience. In the case of birth control, our skepticism may prove disastrous. Those who have eyes to see need no further experience to convince them that birth control increases selfishness and immorality, decreases the capacity to endure and to achieve, and makes inevitable a declining population. Surely these results are not in accord with the moral law, nor conducive to human welfare.

I shall close this paper by submitting a quotation and a paraphrase which should have particular interest for those who belong to the superior classes. The quotation is from Professor Warren S. Thompson, of Miami University:

> People who wish to play so prominent a part in the affairs of their day that they do not find time for family and children, who are unwilling to partake in the struggles and hardships of the common lot, are doomed to extinction. Those who can make the combination of satisfying their ambition and raising a

272

fair-sized family will survive, and though civilization may change under their guidance, I do not see why we should be exercised for fear it will not be Anglo-Saxon, or Teutonic, or Gallic, as the case may be. If we do not have children it will not affect us or ours, that the present social order which we call Western Civilization will have perished.

More than seventeen centuries ago the great Christian writer, Tertulian, addressed the superior classes of his day, the rulers of the Roman Empire, in these words of triumph: "We are but of yesterday, yet we fill your cities, islands, forts, towns, councils, camps, tribes, decuries, the palace, the senate, the forum; we have left you only the temples." Paraphrasing the statement, those who reject birth control might thus challenge the superior classes of today: "We, too, are of yesterday, but tomorrow we shall be the majority. We shall occupy and dominate every sphere of activity; the farm, the factory, the counting-house, the schools, the professions, the press, the legislature. We shall dominate because we shall have the numbers and the intelligence, and above all, the moral strength to struggle, to endure and to persevere. To you we shall leave the gods and goddesses which you have made to your own image and likeness, the divinities of ease and enjoyment and mediocrity. We shall leave to you the comforts of decadence and the sentence of extinction."

20. Human Sterilization

A. THE MORAL AND SOCIAL ASPECTS

IN *Archiv für Soziale Hygiene und Demographie*, Vol. 4, No. 2, 1929, appears this sentence in an article by Rev. Dr. Josef Mayer: "On the whole, the theological controversy over sterilization has not since progressed far beyond the American discussion." He refers to a discussion which involved a dozen writers, 24 articles, 166 pages and more than 62,000 words in the *American Ecclesiastical Review*, Vols. 42-47, in the years 1910-1912. Among the principal participants were Rev. Stephen M. Donovan, O.F.M., and Rev. Theodore Labouré, O.M.I.; a group of moral theologians connected with Louvain University, including Fathers De Becker and Vermeersch, S.J.; Rev. Albert Schmitt, S.J.; Rev. A. De Smet and Austin O'Malley, M.D. The first two writers defended the proposition that compulsory legal sterilization is sometimes morally justifiable. All the others took the contradictory position except Father De Smet, who seemed to admit that the measure might be morally permissible in the absence of other effective means of preventing the propagation of degenerates. However, he strongly asserted the availability of other remedies, such as prohibiting and making invalid the marriages of persons afflicted with such a heredity and segregating them from intercourse with one another and with society.

It must be kept in mind that the difference of opinion among these writers and among all other Catholic authorities who have discussed the question refers to *sterilization at the command of the state for the prevention of undesirable offspring*. All Catholic moralists admit that sterilization is permissible for the cure of a very serious disease whether of the tissues, as in the case of cancer, or of the

274

nervous system, as in the case of excessive sexual erethism. In such cases the moral principle is that a part of the body may be removed or destroyed for the sake of the whole. On the other hand, all Catholic authorities are agreed that sterilization is never morally lawful merely for the sake of reducing temptations against chastity, nor in order to limit the size of families, nor as a legal penalty for crime. Dangers to chastity can be met by spiritual means; the destruction of fecundity to prevent the birth of normal children involves grave dangers to the race, while sterilization lacks the elements of pain and inconvenience which are necessary to constitute genuine punishment. Even if it were adapted to this end it could be rightfully imposed only upon delinquents and not upon mental defectives.

To the controversy referred to above no less than six articles were contributed by Father Labouré. His argument is substantially the same as that of all other Catholic authorities who have upheld the lawlessness of compulsory legal sterilization for the prevention of degenerate offspring. It may be not unfairly described as an argument from analogy. Just as the individual may submit himself to this operation for the preservation of his bodily health, so he may be compelled by the state to undergo it for the welfare of the body politic. In the second place, it is universally conceded that the state may deprive abnormal individuals of the exercise of other natural rights, such as those of liberty and property. If it may segregate the mentally diseased not only for their own safety but to prevent them from generating their subnormal kind, it may with equal right directly deprive them of the power of procreation. The interference with natural rights is quite as definite and as effective in the one case as in the other.

To the first of these arguments the opponents of compulsory sterilization replied by rejecting the parallel. They asserted that the individual cannot be subordinated to society in the same degree as a diseased member or a pathological condition may be subordinated to the welfare of the individual himself. For the human individual is a person, not a mere instrument to social well being. Father Schmitt made use of what is known in Catholic ethical treatises as the "double effect rule." In substance it prohibits the performance of an action which produces two effects, the one good and the other evil, if the evil effect is the efficient cause of the good effect. In the case of eugenic sterilization, the evil effect of the operation, namely, privation of the generative power, is the efficient cause of the good effect, namely, the prevention of degenerate offspring. Therefore, it is morally unlawful. No such moral effect attaches to sterilization for the bodily welfare of the individual himself; for the evil effect in this case is not the efficient cause but merely the unavoidable *condition* of the good effect. The rejoinder of Father Labouré to this argument was that privation of the generative power is only a physical, not a moral evil, and, therefore, may be utilized as the efficient cause of the good effect, namely, the safety of society. The "double effect rule," he contended, is not properly applicable to legal sterilization. It has application only where there is question of permitting a recognized moral evil, as in the case of the injury to non-combatants incidental to the bombardment of a city. Privation of the generative power is not necessarily a moral evil. To assume that is to beg the question.

With regard to the parallel drawn by Father Labouré and other authors between deprivation of liberty and deprivation of the generative power, their opponents distinguish between privation of the *use* of a right and the destruction of the faculty itself or the right itself. Segregation prevents the use of, but does not destroy, the faculty. Hence it is a much milder attack upon personality than sterilization.

So much for the discussion in the *American Ecclesiastical Review*. As stated above, nothing substantial has since been added to either side of the argument by the moral theologians. Rev. Francis S. Betten, S.J., of Marquette University, published a strong article in the *Catholic Daily Tribune*, September 21, 1929, defending the proposition that compulsory legal sterilization is intrinsically immoral. Rev. Josef Mayer, D.D., upheld the opposite view in what is undoubtedly the ablest, most comprehensive and most scientific work yet written on the subject *(Gesetzliche Unfruchtbarmachung Geisteskranker,* 1927). Rev. Albert Schmitt, S.J., wrote a long review of this book *(Zeitschrift für Katholische Theologie,* 1927) in which he rejected the lawfulness of sterilization. Rev. Charles Bruehl, Ph.D., of St. Charles Seminary, Overbrook, accepted Dr. Mayer's view in his book, *Birth Control and Eugenics* (1928). None of these writers, however, has brought forward an essentially new argument nor any other consideration that seems capable of changing the opinions of his opponents. Dr. Mayer does, indeed, elaborate the argument that a mentally diseased person lacks the natural right of procreation and hence may lawfully be deprived of that faculty for the common good. However, that assumption is implicit in the view that sterilization is lawful. For the state could not licitly destroy the faculty if the individual retained the right thereto.

This difference of opinion among the moral theologians can no longer be maintained in view of the following authoritative declaration by Pope Pius XI in his encyclical on Marriage, issued December 31, 1930:

> Public magistrates have no direct power over the bodies of their subjects, therefore, where no crime has taken place and there is no cause present for grave punishment, they can never directly harm, or tamper with the integrity of the body, either for the reasons of eugenics or for any other reason.

No formal decision has yet been rendered by the Church on the question whether sterilized persons are "canonically impotent"; that is, whether they are incapable of contracting a valid marriage. One of the advantages urged for sterilization over segregation is that it permits at least the milder types of feeble-minded persons to enter the state of matrimony. Presumably this would be beneficial to themselves and it would not be harmful to society. But this benefit would not be available to Catholics if they were incapable of contracting marriage validly according to the laws of the Church.

Sterility is not in itself and always an impediment to valid marriage. The Church sanctions the unions of persons who are rendered sterile by age. Does the sterility induced by a surgical operation create canonical impotency? In the work referred to above, Dr. Josef Mayer gives a good account of the theological and canonical discussion of this question. He divides the various writers into three classes. According to the members of the first group, sterilization entails canonical impotence to both men and women; according to the second opinion, this disability is incurred by a man but not by a woman, while the third group of writers hold that neither a man nor a woman is made incapable of valid marriage by surgical sterilization. While the upholders of the last opinion are considerably less numerous than those adhering to the first or the second, they are of sufficient weight and distinction to justify any Catholic in accepting their view. In theory, therefore, the canonical impotence of sterilized persons, whether men or women, is doubtful. In practice, such persons may contract valid marriages on the authority of Canon 1068 of the New Code, which declares that a doubt, whether of law or of fact, is to be resolved in favor of validity.

Therefore, persons who have been sterilized are permitted to contract marriage if they possess sufficient rationality to give valid consent. Persons who are mentally deranged or diseased to such a degree that their marriages are forbidden on account of incapacity to understand or to fulfil the obligations of the contract remain obviously in the same condition after sterilization. On the other hand, persons

278

who have undergone sterilization after a valid marriage are permitted to continue marital relations.

Such is the present status of the Canon Law and the present practice concerning the marriages of persons who have been sterilized. Should the Church authorities at some future time solve the theoretical question unfavorably to these marriages, the practice would automatically change. Such unions would then be invalid.

Let us consider now the extent and gravity of the social evils arising out of hereditary mental deficiency. Four main questions of fact are involved: the total amount of mental deficiency; whether it is increasing; the proportion of it that is hereditary; and the nature of the social evils for which it is clearly responsible.

The intelligence ratings of the men recruited in the United States Army during the World War occasioned some very pessimistic judgments concerning the amount of mental deficiency in the American people. Certain publicists drew the inference that the area of feeble-mindedness took in almost one-half the population. Did not the Army tests show that 47.3 per cent of the white drafted men had mental ages of less than thirteen years? And was not thirteen the dividing line between the normal and the feeble-minded? Happily this conclusion was discredited generally by its palpable absurdity. Any classification of the distribution of intelligence which attaches the stigma of feeble-mindedness to one-half the population is inherently incorrect, no matter how impressive may be the scientific apparatus upon which it is based. Such classification clearly perverts the concept of "normal" or average intelligence. Even if a very large proportion of our people are unable to pass certain tests of intelligence which are supposed to be attainable by normal persons of thirteen years of age, it does not follow that the majority of them are "social inadequates," or undesirable members of society. There are socially desirable qualities which are not measured by the general intelligence tests and which may be even more valuable than some of the qualities whose absence or undeveloped character is disclosed by Binet-Simon.

According to the calculations of Gosney and Popenoe, there are in the United States about 4,800,000 mentally diseased persons; that is, persons who "before they die will be classified as insane."[1] These are the mentally subnormal whose minds are deranged, who "at sometime had a better mind which has broken down under strain." The same writers give the same estimate of the number of "technically feeble-minded"; that is, those persons who have an intelligence quotient of less than seventy.[2] This general class comprises idiots, imbeciles, and morons. The mentality of idiots is equal to that of children of two or three years of age; that of imbeciles is equal to that of children of the age of three to seven, while morons have a "mental age" of seven to twelve years. The feeble-minded are mentally deficient, not mentally diseased. Their minds have not suffered derangement, but have never been developed in the normal way.

If these estimates are correct, there are upwards of ten million persons in the United States of lower than normal mentality, about equally divided between the mentally deranged and the mentally deficient. For various reasons which need not be discussed here, the problem of sterilization is practically always considered with reference to the latter class, that is, the feeble-minded.

Adopting the criterion given by the Mental Deficiency Committee of the Board of Education and Board of Control in England in 1919 as that "degree of incomplete mental development which renders a person incapable of independent social adaptation and which necessitates external care, supervision and control," Dr. Stanley P. Davies

---

[1] *Sterilization for Human Betterment*, p. 5.
[2] *Idem*, pp. 8, 9.

estimates the number of such persons in the United States at less than one million.[3] He construes this definition as including only the "actually" feeble-minded. Morons he characterizes as "potentially feeble-minded" or "intellectually subnormal." The exclusion of morons from Dr. Davies' definition and their inclusion by Gosney and Popenoe probably explain the great difference between their estimates of the total number of feeble-minded in the United States.[4]

Is the amount of mental subnormality, whether through derangement or under-development, increasing? We do not know. The growth of the number of such persons in institutions may obviously be explained by the fact that a greater proportion of the total number is now confined than formerly. Moreover, some authorities are of the opinion that insanity tends to die out and that the feeble-minded are, contrary to the general assumption a few years ago, less fertile than normal persons. "In the light of such data as are available, the assertion that mentally defective stocks are propagating at such rapid rates that they threaten to swamp civilization appears to belong to the 'legend of the feeble-minded,' as the late Dr. Fernald was wont to call the many misconceptions centering about these handicapped people."[5]

To what extent is feeble-mindedness hereditary? The answers to this question by authoritative writers are both less positive and less alarming than they were twenty years ago. In the Foreword to Dr. Davies' book (p. xi), Dr. Frankwood E. Williams writes: "We have come a long way from the period of 'the menace of the feeble-minded' and the Kallikak family, but the way by which we have actually come is much longer than if it was measured as the

---

[3] *Social Control of the Mentally Deficient*, 1930, p. 6.
[4] See chapter II of Dr. Bernstein's pamphlet, *The Social Care of the Mentally Deficient*, National Catholic Welfare Conference, Washington.
[5] Davies, *op. cit.*, p. 167; Bernstein, *op. cit.*, chap. IV.

crow flies. No expert in the field of mental deficiency would today base his remarks on the 'menace of the feeble-minded' or on the Kallikak family. . . . One may still speak of a 'menace' in referring to the feeble-minded, but it is with an altogether different implication than in 1909. One may possibly still mention the Kallikaks, but it would not be with bated breath." Dr. Davies points out that "the Kallikak family history fitted well into the theories of inheritance of feeble-mindedness that were current at that time. In the light of the latest knowledge of this subject, however, it seems too letter-perfect. In the realm of things human, judging from what is now known of hereditary mechanisms, family histories do not follow such invariably true courses, almost all black on the one side and almost all white on the other."[6]

Some recent writers go so far as to question the application to the feeble-minded of the Mendelian law of heredity. "Of course, if two stocks differ by a single factor only, their progeny would be expected to afford an illustration of simple Mendelian inheritance. But since the inheritance of any human family differs in numerous ways from that of any other and since any change in any part of the germ plasm could scarcely help having a certain influence on the mentality of the individual concerned, it is *a priori* very improbable that the inheritance of mental defects is adequately describable in simple Mendelian terms."[7] According to Dr. S. J. Holmes the inheritance of mental defects is most probably "dependent upon a number of factors instead of a single one."[8] Writing in the *American Mercury*, Vol. XII, page 266, Professor Raymond Pearl declares that "in preaching as they do, that like produces like and that therefore superior people will have superior children and inferior people inferior children, the eugenists

[6]*Op. cit.*, p. 154.
[7]Davenport and Danielson, *The Hill Folk*, p. 7.
[8]*The Trend of the Nation*, p. 34.

are going contrary to the best established facts of genetical science and in the long run are doing their cause harm."

After thirty-eight years of experience in an institution which had dealt with thousands of them, Dr. Walter E. Fernald concluded that fully one-half of all cases of mental deficiency are of the non-hereditary type. Summing up the presentation of recent evidence and recent statements by authorities, Dr. Davies writes: "From these data, it would tentatively appear that one-half or less of the mental deficiencies found among the institutional groups and possibly an even smaller proportion of the mental deficiencies discovered in the community, are of the familial or hereditary type."[9] It is to be noted that Dr. Davies qualifies his conclusion by the word "tentatively." Probably no competent student would feel absolutely certain that his estimate of the proportion of hereditary feeble-mindedness was within 20 per cent of the exact truth.[10]

Descriptions and estimates of the social evils due to mental deficiency have in recent years declined considerably in positiveness and comprehensiveness. This is particularly true with regard to crime. An analysis of four thousand young "repeated offenders" in Chicago and Boston made by Drs. Healy and Bronner showed 13½ per cent of them clearly feeble-minded. Other studies of delinquent groups in other institutions reveal about the same proportion of mental deficients. Obviously the per cent of imprisoned offenders who are feeble-minded is greater than the per cent of all offenders, owing to the fact that a larger proportion of feeble-minded than normal delinquents are apprehended and convicted. According to V. V. Anderson, "not more than 10 per cent of offenders in general are feeble-minded, but this 10 per cent is almost as much trouble as all the rest put together."[11] Summing up his review of recent evidence and estimates, Dr. Davies denies that there was any "inborn

---

[9]*Op. cit.*, p. 163.
[10]See Dr. Hauber's pamphlet, *Inheritance of Mental Defect*, N. C. W. C., and tables in the appendix of Dr. Bernstein's *Social Care of the Mentally Deficient.*
[11]Quoted by Davies, *op. cit.*, p. 175.

or universal or necessary connection between inferior intelligence and social offenses, such as the hasty generalizations of a decade or more ago made out. The mentally deficient probably contribute more than their due proportion to social offenders, not because of any direct relationship between a low intelligence quotient and social misbehavior, but because they are more likely to be underprivileged, coming as they do, in large part, from homes lacking good parental guidance, decent housing, adequate economic resources and a wholesome neighborhood environment."

Another false assumption prevailing pretty widely a few years ago was that the mentally deficient are imposing upon society an intolerable financial burden, that they are unable to make their own living or to contribute a substantial amount thereto. Undoubtedly the latter part of the assumption is true of idiots and imbeciles. However, these constitute not more than 20 or 25 per cent of all the mental deficients. Recent observations and experiments indicate that the majority, possibly a great majority, of morons are capable of providing all or the greater part of their own livelihood. What they need is training, supervision and sympathetic treatment, whether they are segregated in colonies or are members of the general community.[12] Indeed, it has been found that the mentally deficient can perform certain monotonous and routine tasks more satisfactorily than those of normal intelligence. This is an extremely important consideration in an industrial society such as ours where a large proportion of the operations are of a simple repetitive character. Mass production and the automatic machine have provided places for tens of thousands of mentally deficient persons who can operate and tend machines quite as efficiently as, and with less injury to the nervous system than those possessing a much higher degree of general intelligence. A similar statement is true of many forms

---

[12] See chapter III of Bernstein's pamphlet.

284

of unskilled labor and many kinds of domestic service. Ethelbert Stewart, Commissioner of the United States Bureau of Labor Statistics, finds the literature of efficiency and industrial management full of suggestions concerning the preferability of the employment of men and women whose mental age is ten years or less.[18] The conclusion seems to be justified that the mentally deficient who are above the grades of idiots and imbeciles are not a menace to society from the viewpoint of industrial potencies and capacities. In the words of Dr. Davies:

> Experience to date indicates that the large majority of the mentally deficient may be safely and profitably retained as functioning members of society, both from an economic and a social standpoint, provided the group exercises over them a sufficient degree of social control to give them, until they approach adult life, the training suited to their capacities, and continues to furnish throughout their lives the sort of leadership which will foster in them the highest social ideals.

If the mentally deficient do not furnish an unmanageably large proportion of delinquents, particularly of the most harmful delinquents and if on the whole they are sufficiently productive to defray the cost of their maintenance, it is difficult to see why their presence in society should demand such a drastic and revolutionary measure as compulsory sterilization.

This conclusion is greatly strengthened when we consider the very small area within which the method can become operative. Sterilization is not applicable to idiots and imbeciles. For their sake and for the safety of society they should be confined in asylums or in colonies. Thus segregated, they would be unable to reproduce themselves. In general, any mental defective who is incapable of rearing children or managing a family should not be permitted to

18 *Monthly Labor Review,* Vol. XXVII, No. 10.

marry, even if he lives outside an institution. If any such persons have become parents of illegitimate children, they should somehow be prevented from repeating the offense. For them, as for idiots and imbeciles, sterilization would be superfluous. As applied to morons and semi-morons, it is subject to several important limitations. In the first place, mental defectives sometimes produce offspring that are not defective. The arrangement of the defective cells may not be the same in both parents. Whenever this happens, whenever the defective genes derived from the father fail to combine with those derived from the mother in such a way as to produce a pair of defective genes in the child, the latter will not be feeble-minded. This contingency is not at all infrequent, even when both parents are mentally defective. Naturally, it occurs more frequently when the deficiency occurs in only one parent. In a considerable number of cases, therefore, sterilization would prevent the birth of normal as well as of subnormal children.[14]

On the other hand, to sterilize all mental defectives would not put an end to this evil heredity. Mental deficiency may be inherited from parents who are not thus afflicted themselves but who are "carriers"; that is, when they have inherited defective genes which happen to combine in such a way as to give a pair of defective genes to the germ cell of the child. Hence, Dr. A. F. Tredgold, a leading English authority on mental deficiency, declares that "in order to produce any marked decrease in the total number of mental defectives a generation hence, it would be necessary to sterilize or otherwise prevent the propagation of not merely those who are in themselves defectives, but all those who are 'carriers,' that is to say, every person suffering from germ vitiation."[15]

What proportion of those who are capable of transmitting mental deficiency are themselves defective and what

[14] See H. S. Jennings, *The Biological Basis of Human Nature*, chap. I.
[15] Quoted by Davies, *op. cit.*, p. 115.

286

proportion are "carriers?" Dr. H. S. Jennings cites the estimate of R. A. Fisher in *The Journal of Heredity* (Vol. XVIII, pp. 529-531) that about 11 per cent of the feebleminded are derived from feeble-minded parents, while the other 89 per cent have carriers for their parents. Obviously, the reference is only to those mental defectives whose affliction is hereditary. It is estimated that "by entirely excluding the feeble-minded from propagation in the present and future generations, the number of feeble-minded is reduced at the first generation by about 11 per cent; thereafter very little progress is made in reducing their number." To decrease their proportion of the population by 10 per cent would "require about 68 generations or two to three thousand years. . . . In the main the 11 per cent reduction at the first generation is what is accomplished by this measure. The foregoing computations rest on the assumption that the defective genes are widely scattered in the population. If they are not widely scattered, Fisher estimates that the reduction might possibly be 30 to 40 per cent instead of 11 per cent in the first generation."[16] Even if the carriers of hereditary feeble-mindedness could be identified and sterilized along with mental defectives themselves, society would still have to deal with all the cases that are not hereditary. The latter may be more than one-half of the total number. At any rate, no one can prove that as many as one-half of the existing mental defectives have inherited that evil condition. After analyzing the family history of five hundred cases in Surrey, England, the Mental Deficiency Committee of the County Council came to this conclusion in 1926: "It would appear that if every defective now in existence were to be sterilized the result a generation hence would be insignificant."[17]

All talk about a general use of sterilization is theoretical and irrelevant. Compulsory sterilization has never been extended beyond state institutions. So long as the mentally

[16] Jennings, *op. cit.*, pp. 241, 242.
[17] Quoted by Davies, *op. cit.*, p. 116.

287

deficient are segregated they do not need to be sterilized in order to prevent reproduction. Popenoe's suggestion that they might be sterilized and then allowed to marry while remaining confined seems to be without serious merit. At present the proper subjects of the operation are merely those morons who have already been brought within institutions but who would prove to be fairly adequate members of the community if they were deprived of the power of reproduction. They form such an insignificant fraction of the total number of mental defectives (about one in eighty gets into a state institution) that the experiment is not worth one-tenth of the discussion to which it has given rise. The whole number of sterilizations performed in twenty-one states up to January 1, 1928, was 8,515. Of this number 5,820 had taken place in the State of California alone. In the following year, the latter state increased its contribution by 435. The great majority of those subjected to the operation in the California institutions were not feeble-minded at all, but otherwise mentally afflicted, while the total number sterilized in the other twenty states obviously had no perceptible effect upon the existing amount of mental deficiency in those areas.

In reply to this line of argument, Dr. Popenoe declares: "The fact is that there are so many persons who might well be sterilized that the great problem for the next two or three generations will be to find men and money to take care of the most pressing cases. Others may be left until later." The expression "the most pressing cases" is misleading. It suggests that sterilization is the only available remedy and therefore that it should be immediately applied in the cases that are most deserving or most troublesome. As a matter of fact, segregation, supervision and training provide a better and more comprehensive remedy—a remedy which is applicable to all grades of cases. The agitation for sterilization, which confessedly is practicable in only a very small per cent of the cases, tends to delay the adoption of more scientific, humane and comprehensive remedies.

288

It is, indeed, occasionally hinted that compulsory sterilization may some day be applied to the feeble-minded who are outside of institutions. Dr. Popenoe suggests that the operation might be performed upon mental defectives in the public schools at the age of puberty.[18] This proposal sounds very simple, but it may be dismissed as not within the realm of practicability. It is valuable chiefly as an index of the extent to which even the moderate advocates of sterilization are willing to go in disregard of human rights and human personality.

Other extremes and abuses to which the measure is liable deserve brief mention. As late as 1926 one of the most active advocates of sterilization, Dr. Harry H. Laughlin, published the draft of a model eugenical sterilization law which would be applicable to all "the socially inadequate classes." These are the following: "(1) Feeble-minded; (2) insane, including the psychopathic; (3) criminalistic, including the delinquent and wayward; (4) epileptic; (5) inebriate, including drug-habitués; (6) diseased, including the tuberculous, the syphilitic, the leprous, and others with chronic, infectious and legally segregable diseases; (7) blind, including those with seriously impaired vision; (8) deaf, including those with seriously impaired hearing; (9) deformed, including the crippled; and (10) dependent, including orphans, ne'er-do-wells and the homeless, tramps, and paupers."[19]

Some of the early laws on this subject were extremely drastic. That of Nevada included in its scope "persons adjudged guilty of carnal abuse of a female under ten years of age." The Iowa law applied to drunkards. That of Washington was restricted to habitual criminals. While the most recent laws have avoided such extremes and, generally speaking, provide better safeguards against the arbitrary use of the device, this improvement is mainly due to criticism by the opponents of sterilization. Let the opposition

---

[18] *Op. cit.*, p. 133.
[19] *Eugenical Sterilization*, p. 65.

subside and the extremists, such as Laughlin, would readily become once more the dominant exponents and authorities.

Another abuse involved in the policy is the possibility of increased sex offenses by those who have been sterilized and returned to the community. This danger has been well stated by Dr. Charles B. Davenport, one of the most distinguished of American eugenists: "It is urged as one of the advantages of vasectomy that it does not interfere with desire nor its gratification, but only with paternity. But is it a good thing to relieve the sexual act of that responsibility it ought to carry and of which it has hitherto not been entirely free? Is not many a man restrained from licentiousness by recognizing the responsibility of possible parentage? Is not the shame of illicit parentage the fortress of female chastity? Is there any danger that the persons operated upon shall become a peculiar menace to the community through unrestrained dissemination of venereal disease? Will the frequency of the crime of rape be diminished by vasectomy? To many it would seem that to secure to a rapist his eroticism and uninhibited lust while he is released from any responsibility for offspring, is not the way to safeguard female honor."[20] E. S. Gosney declares, indeed, that those sterilized and set at large in California have not shown any increase in sexual promiscuity. However, the time has been too short and the number of those concerned too small to provide a basis for safe generalization.

An incidental abuse attributable to legalized sterilization is voluntary recourse to the operation by persons who wish to avoid parenthood. To be sure, such persons might seek sterilization in any case, but there is no doubt that the sanction given by law has provided them with a considerable measure of suggestion and encouragement.

In view of the serious limitations of compulsory sterilization as briefly noted in the foregoing paragraphs, it is not surprising that in recent years the tendency of the most careful authorities is toward skepticism with regard to the

[20] *Heredity in Relation to Eugenics* (New York, 1911).

290

efficacy of the method. In a letter to the *London Times,* January 20, 1926, the Central Association for Mental Welfare of London made this significant statement:

> In short, the general conclusion arrived at by the most representative body of medical and lay men and women in this country, having a wide practical experience of mental defectives, is that a general policy of sterilization would be ineffective in *Prevention: That the freedom accompanying it would be attended by harm* to the defectives themselves; that it would delay institutional provision for their segregation, which we regard as the only safe remedy for those likely to engage in sexual intercourse; and that, finally it would fail to provide any effectual safeguard either for the defectives or for the community.

Dr. Stanley P. Davies submits the following conclusion:

> To the writer, who has endeavored to weigh available evidence and opinions on all sides of the question, sterilization fails to recommend itself in the present state of our knowledge, as a measure of social control to be *generally* applied to the feeble-minded. From the point of view of succeeding generations, it appears doubtful that sterilization would reduce the number of mental defectives sufficiently to be of any general social significance, or to have any appreciable effect on public expenditures for social control. From the point of view of the present generation, sterilization can in no sense be a substitute for segregation, training and community supervision in the mental deficiency program. All these statements are from the standpoint of sterilization as a *general* procedure.[21]

The enormous influence of a bad environment in producing feeble-mindedness and the great importance therefore of abolishing that kind of environment are emphasized by Dr. Jennings in the following passage: "The great difficulty . . . is that bad living conditions often produce

---

[21]*Op. cit.,* pp. 117, 118.

the same kind of result that bad genes do. Persons may become idle and worthless, insane or criminal or tuberculous —either through bad genes or bad living conditions, or through a combination of both. So long as living conditions are bad, we do not know what ills are due to poor genes. We must therefore correct the bad living conditions, not only for their directly beneficial effect, but also for the sake of eugenics. When this is done, it will be possible to discover what defects are primarily the result of defective genes, and then to plan measures for getting rid of these genes: measures for stopping the propagation of their carriers. That is, as a preliminary to the effective work of eugenics other reforms must be carried through. Measures of public health must be carried out, overwork and bad conditions of living done away with, faults of diet, both quantitative and qualitative, corrected; economic ills conquered, grinding poverty abolished. When these things are done, when the human plant is given conditions under which it can unfold its capabilities without stunting, poisoning and mutilation by the environment, then it will be possible to discover what ills are due primarily to defective genes, and to plan such measures as are possible for their eradication. Acting on such precise knowledge, far more rapid and effective results may be hoped for than from the present blind action in merely encouraging the propagation of certain classes, discouraging that of others."[22]

This brief study may be fittingly concluded by a few summary propositions and a striking quotation. Compulsory legal sterilization is condemned by the supreme authority on morals, our Holy Father, Pope Pius XI. Consequently no Catholic is morally justified in promoting either the enactment or the execution of sterilization laws. This applies to private citizens as well as to public officials and public employees, but especially to legislators, physicians and surgeons.

The social and other inconveniences and evils resulting

[22] Jennings, op. cit., pp. 250, 251.

from feeble-mindedness do not constitute a grave danger to the common welfare. The limitations to the effectiveness of the measure are so great as to render it fatally inadequate as a remedy for feeble-mindedness. Its main limitations are as follows: It is not necessary for those mental defectives who cannot safely be left outside of institutions, nor for those whom the state should not permit to marry on account of their incapacity to bring up a family; not all defectives always produce defective offspring; by far the greater part of inherent defectiveness probably comes from "carriers" and these cannot be identified; possibly one-half and possibly more than that proportion of the feeble-minded have not acquired the defect by inheritance; sterilization is practically applicable only to defectives who have been committed to institutions and these apparently are only one-eightieth of the whole number; the practice is liable to serious abuses, either inherent or incidental; it is opposed by several of the most competent authorities; finally, it tends to prevent the consideration and adoption of genuine remedies which would deal with the feeble-mindedness which is caused by environment as well as that which is inherited.

The ambition of the eugenists reaches still further. When the diagnosis of depravity has been fully perfected, they hope by legal sterilization to eliminate not only idiots and degenerates, but also drunkards, tubercular persons, syphilitics, epileptics, and even the blind, the deaf, hunchbacks, and in a general way all potential parents of inadequate offspring.

. . . In the hands of a people who are conscious of their superiority and are ready to sterilize remorselessly Negroes and Asiatics, or in fact any inferior races, eugenics may eventually relegate the "sacred rights of man" to the limbo of forgotten achievements.[23]

The foregoing extracts from a remarkably penetrating

---

[23] André Siegfried, *America Comes of Age*, pp. 116, 118.

study of American life by a French Protestant describe the logical outcome of the policy of sterilization. Once men reject the truth that the human person is intrinsically sacred, that even his body should be treated with reverence, they can easily persuade themselves that any person may be used in any fashion for the benefit of society. The difference between the social inconveniences arising from the existence of too many imbeciles and that resulting from the presence of too many Negroes, Mexicans or other non-Nordics, is a difference only of degree—possibly in favor of the imbeciles. If sterilization be no degradation of personality, no violation of natural rights, why should it not be applied to all the inferior classes that bring more inconvenience than convenience to the politically dominant *elite?*

B. THE CONSTITUTIONAL ASPECT

The first decision by the Supreme Court of the United States on the constitutionality of legal sterilization of human beings was handed down May 2, 1927, with only Justice Butler dissenting.[24] Both the terms of the law and the history of the person attacking it were favorable to an affirmative decision. The Virginia statute is much narrower in scope than many similar enactments. It applies only to those persons afflicted with "hereditary forms of insanity that are recurrent, idiocy, imbecility, feeble-mindedness or epilepsy," who, if sterilized, could be paroled or discharged and thus become self-supporting. The procedure specified in the law is ample for the protection of all the rights of the inmates which are procedural. A hearing must take place before the board of directors of the hospital or colony, with the inmate or his guardian in attendance; the evidence must be reduced to writing; an appeal must be allowed to the circuit court of the county, which may admit new evidence; finally, there may be an appeal to the supreme court of the state. All these formalities were observed in the case of Carrie Buck, a white woman, who is the feeble-minded daughter of a feeble-minded mother, and is herself the mother of a feeble-minded child. The order for her sterilization was sustained at every step of the proceedings.

R. G. Shelton, who had been appointed her guardian, appealed the case to the Supreme Court of the United States. There the judgment of the Virginia supreme court of appeals was affirmed. Justice Holmes, who wrote the decision of the Supreme Court of the United States, points out that Carrie Buck had obtained the full benefit of "due process of law," so far as procedure was concerned. To the plea that the statute deprived the plaintiff of the "equal

---

[24] *Buck vs. Bell.*

295

protection of the laws," inasmuch as it applies only to those insane, feeble-minded, etc., who are confined in state institutions, Justice Holmes replied: "The law does all that is needed when it does all that it can, indicates a policy, applies to all within the lines and seeks to bring within the lines all similarly situated so far and so fast as its means allow."

Counsel for Carrie Buck before the Supreme Court challenged the law on the further ground that it violates that clause of the Fourteenth Amendment which forbids a state to deprive any person of life or liberty without due process of law. "It violates her bodily integrity," he declared, "and is a deprivation of her life and liberty. . . . The inherent right of the individual to go through life without mutilation of the organs of generation needs no constitutional declaration. That right existed long before the Constitution was framed and was not lost or surrendered to legislative control when the government was created, and is beyond the reach of the police power."

In its decision the Court does not even refer to the claim that the right to life which is protected by the Constitution includes the right to bodily integrity, nor to the claim that the latter right, existing anterior to the Constitution, is beyond the reach of the state's police power. The only statement made by counsel for Carrie Buck which seems to give any support to his interpretation of the constitutional right to life was the following from Justice Field in *Munn* vs. *Illinois:* "The inhibition against its deprivation extends to all those limbs and faculties by which life is enjoyed. The deprivation not only of life, but whatever God has given to everyone with life . . . is protected by the provision in question." The fact that this citation is from a dissenting opinion and is only dictum, probably explains the failure of the Court to consider it in the present case.

Sterilization does involve some deprivation of liberty. This was admitted by counsel for the defendant. He also admitted that the liberty to have children is a right of

296

which a person may not be deprived without due process of law, but he maintained that its deprivation in the case of such persons as Carrie Buck, was in accord with "due process," since it exemplified a proper exercise of the state's police power. Besides, she had already been deprived of that liberty, not only through segregation, but through the Virginia law which forbids mental defectives to marry.

How far may the police power go in restraining individual liberty without violating "due process of law?" Perhaps the most comprehensive answer is that expressed in the famous canon enunciated by John Marshall: "Let the end be legitimate, let it be within the scope of the Constitution, and all means which are appropriate, which are plainly adapted to the end, which are not prohibited, but consist with the letter and spirit of the Constitution are constitutional."

The end of the Virginia sterilization statute evidently is in conformity with this canon and with the definition of the police power, for it is the prevention of that injury to the community which comes from the procreation and existence of the mentally incompetent. Is the means, namely, sterilization through the operation called salpingectomy, "appropriate and plainly adapted to that end?" To some extent. Does the means "consist with the letter and spirit of the Constitution?" Here is the question which touches precisely the individual liberty or individual rights which are guaranteed by the "due process" clause. The answer of the Court is that the state is not forbidden by the Constitution to restrict the liberty of its citizens in the way which the sterilization statute prescribes. The Court points out that "the public welfare may call upon the best citizens for their lives" and refers to the principle enunciated in *Jacobson* vs. *Massachusetts, 197* U. S. 11. "The principle," says the Court, "that sustains compulsory vaccination is broad enough to cover cutting the Fallopian tubes." Hence the Virginia statute was upheld as a legitimate exercise of the police power.

297

One might, however, raise the objection that sterilization is not the *only* means available to the state for securing the end which is sought, namely restricting the number of imbeciles, feeble-minded, etc. Segregation of such persons in institutions and colonies would be equally effective. Inasmuch as Carrie Buck was already in such an institution, the end of the law was attained in her case and in that of others similarly situated. Moreover, segregation is a less fundamental interference with liberty than sterilization. The first of these objections was specifically answered by the Court in *Jacobson* vs. *Massachusetts* when it declared that: "It is no part of the function of a court or jury to determine which of two modes was likely to be the most effective for the protection to the public." Among appropriate means to a legitimate end, therefore, the state may choose the one that seems preferable. In the case that we are considering it chose sterilization because sterilization is less expensive then continued segregation. If it be still contended that the interference with the liberty and physical integrity of the person is so much greater in sterilization than in segregation that the state was bound in harmony with the *spirit* of the Constitution to choose the latter, the obvious answer is that this hypothesis is incapable of demonstration. Even if it had been considered it would probably have been rejected in accordance with the well established rule of interpretation that in case of doubt, presumption favors the statute, not the Constitution.

Still another objection may be raised to the appropriateness of the means provided in the Virginia statute. The Court emphasized the good effects of the law in preventing "those who are manifestly unfit from continuing their kind," but it made no reference to the very serious evil effects. When Carrie Buck is discharged from the State Colony for Epileptics and Feeble-minded, she will be incapable of bearing any more feeble-minded children or any other kind of children, indeed, but she will also be an easier prey for dissolute men. They will have no restraining fear of unpleasant consequences. Moreover, she will become a more active carrier of loathsome disease. Whether these evil consequences of the sterilization statute combined with its deeper assault upon liberty would have been sufficient, if properly presented, to induce the Court to declare that the means provided in the law were not really adapted to securing the end and were not in conformity with the spirit of the Constitution, is a question which has considerable speculative interest. But it has no practical value. No such argument was made by the plaintiff. Therefore, no cognizance was taken of it by the Court.

It is unfortunate that Justice Butler did not write out and publish the reasons for his dissent. On its face the case seems to present no constitutional grounds for invalidating the statute, except those described in the last two paragraphs. Even these points were not formally brought within the Court's consideration.

To be sure, previous decisions could have construed the word "life" or the word "liberty" as including "the right to bodily integrity" mentioned by counsel for Carrie Buck. Had they done so the present case must have been decided differently. It is likewise conceivable that the facts and considerations set forth above might some day be presented to the Court so effectively as to bring about a different decision.

Some Catholics assume that the Constitution protects all natural rights against encroachment by Congress or by the states. This is a complete misconception. What the Constitution protects is certain forms of liberty, certain immunities from arbitrary interference, certain property rights. It does not pretend to safeguard all natural rights, much less to prohibit statutory infringements of the moral law. "Under the principles of judicial review as they have been evolved by the courts, a statute cannot be declared void unless it transgresses some particular provision of the written Constitution."[25] Moreover, the majority of those rights

---

[25] Mott, *Due Process of Law*, p. 271.

which are covered by the Constitution receive from it protection only against Congress, not against the states; for example, those enumerated in the First Amendment. In general, Catholics are too prone to trust to the Supreme Court for protection of their rights and interests instead of actively defending these in legislative bodies before the obnoxious proposals have been enacted into laws. If the decision in the Virginia sterilization case has the effect of dissipating this excessive trust in the Court and arousing Catholics to the necessity of actively opposing such dangerous measures as sterilization before they have taken shape in statutes, it will prove to that extent a blessing.

21. Evolution and Equality

THE concept of equality has not received from Americans a critical consideration "commensurate with the fundamental place it has held in our political and religious and social assumptions." This condition the book before us[1] endeavors to correct. In both its critical and its constructive parts it is so typical of the ideas prevalent in non-Catholic universities and so menacing to human welfare, that it seems to deserve a more extended discussion than that which is attainable in an ordinary book review.

The first four chapters of the volume are descriptive and critical; the last two, doctrinal and constructive. In the former we obtain a historical sketch of equality in America as related to the Declaration of Independence, the institution of slavery, the movement for woman's rights, and the philosophy which until recently has seemed adequate to support equalitarianism. On the assumption that this basis has been discredited, the last two chapters present a new philosophical and sociological basis for the doctrine of equality.

The traditional basis was "a conception of human nature that made the core of personality something transcendently derived. . . ." In other words, it was belief in the intrinsic worth of the human person as possessing a soul made in the image and likeness of God and endowed with certain natural rights. It was a conception derived from and developed by Christianity. According to this conception, the individual was morally immune from attacks upon his life, his liberty and his reasonable minimum of welfare, whether by individuals or by the state.

Scientific progress, particularly in relation to the theory of evolution, has, however, rendered this basis of equality

[1]Prof. T. V. Smith, *The American Philosophy of Equality* (The University of Chicago Press).

no longer available or tenable. "Man is not primarily rational." The human self is not "an independent entity, simple and substantial. . . ." It is merely "a biological organism. . . ." There exists neither a fixed human species nor a fixed human self. Consequently the conception of the person as including a distinct and independent soul, and possessing intrinsic worth is accepted by "few modern students." Nevertheless, the doctrine of equality ought not to be given up. "Needed then by struggling classes [is] a basis for equality that will be at once logically adequate, socially safe and practically effective." This basis must be found in "some new understanding of human nature and of its place in the world."

What is this new foundation for equality which is offered by the author in the name of evolutionary theory and modern philosophy? Well, it is pragmatic instead of ontological. The concept of equality

is functionally useful without being statically true. . . . If equality of treatment produces consequences of maximum desirability it is justified, regardless of whether men are equal in the old sense or not.

In the opinion of Professor Smith, the doctrine of equality is "functionally useful," does produce "consequences of maximum desirability," inasmuch as it is essential to effective co-operation. "Men work together better when they regard themselves as substantially equal." This is true of the family, religion, industry, politics and all other human relations and associations. The twenty-five pages which the author uses to elaborate and illustrate this proposition are surely adequate and ample.

How far is it desirable that men should co-operate or be treated as equals? They should obtain equal opportunities of education, a living wage, a considerable measure of industrial democracy and a better distribution of wealth and income.

Why does Professor Smith regard this amount of

302

equality as desirable? What is its final end? Since equality
is not true in itself nor good in itself; since it is good only
because it is useful, it must find its justification in some
end which is intrinsically good. An indefinite series of ends
is at once illogical and undesirable. The only formulations
of the final end which we find in the book are these incidental expressions: "the good life"; "a happy and efficient
society"; "a happy and efficient social order."

Such is the philosophy of equality which the author
would substitute for that set forth in the Declaration of
Independence and ultimately derived from the natural law
and the teaching of Christianity. In theory it is false; in
practice it is worse than worthless. It begins by confusing
the diverse concepts of truth and utility. The claim of
equality is true, we are informed, "if it functions truly."
Pretentious pragmatic nonsense! Utility means conducive-
ness to an end; truth means conformity with reality. A
doctrine may be false, may have no support in the realm of
objective fact, and yet may be very useful to certain persons. An employer might find it profitable to multiply the
daily wage rate of his employees by three instead of by
six when he makes out their weekly pay checks, but he
would scarcely call the device truthful.

Practically or pragmatically considered, Professor Smith's
basis of equality is pitiable quicksand. Its "functional"
value is a fatal delusion. A considerable degree of equality
is, indeed, a condition of effective co-operation, but what
is the use of effective co-operation? To ensure "a happy
and efficient society"; that is, a society which provides a
generous amount of freedom, education and material well
being for all its component individuals. Such, at least,
seems to be Professor Smith's conception of the desirable
final end. Suppose, however, that the dominant class, or
group, or element, whether it constitutes a majority or a
minority, rejects this conception. Suppose that a determinant plutocracy holds the desirable social order to be
one in which the masses obtain scarcely any education,

merely subsistence wages and practically no control over the labor contract or any other phase of their industrial life. Consider the slave-holding oligarchy which dominated our southern states before the Civil War. In its own eyes it constituted "a happy and efficient society." It needed no doctrine of equality to provide the enforced "co-operation" upon which it was based and which it made "functionally" effective. A dominant plutocracy would be satisfied with similar compulsory "co-operation" and would likewise regard its social order as "happy and efficient."

Upon what logical basis could Professor Smith argue that either of these conceptions of "a happy and efficient society" was false or inadequate? Not on the ground that they do not function; for one of them did function satisfactorily to the dominant class for many generations, while the other has functioned in a considerable degree ever since the industrial revolution, and the term of its functioning has not yet been reached. Professor Smith could not protest that the submerged masses have spiritual souls or intrinsic worth or natural rights; for these metaphysical entities have no place in his philosophy. According to his view, men have no more sacredness than animals, and they are obviously not equal among themselves, either physically or mentally. Why, then, should human individuals not be exploited in the interest of the dominant element, just as the brutes are exploited? Nay, why should not human individuals be killed outright, just as other animals are killed, whenever this action seems to have "functional" value for the ruling class? Should Professor Smith protest that all this is inhumane and contrary to our inherited and accumulated social instincts and sympathies, the dominant class could logically reply that sentiment has no legitimate place in a scientific conception of the universe.

The sober and abiding truth is that the traditional view of equality is the only one which possesses genuine functional value. Since men are equal in the sight of God, have souls made in His image and likeness, they have equal

304

intrinsic worth and equal natural rights. The latter are necessary means to the development of equally sacred personalities and the attainment of an eternal end to which all are equally destined.

Upon this basis of intrinsic worth and of natural rights, and upon it only, can be erected all the educational, civic and economic opportunities for the individual, and all the specific forms of equality which Professor Smith demands for the "good life."

The ideal of "a happy and efficient society" can readily be rejected on the obvious ground that apart from its constituent individuals society is a mere abstraction, or that society can be so interpreted as to include only the dominant social group. The intrinsic worth of personality rests upon fundamental intuitions which are in some degree perceived by men of all social conditions and which cannot be entirely ignored by any normal mind. To those who are deprived of reasonable equality these intuitions provide the most powerful motives for protest and resistance; to the consciences of those who in practice deny reasonable equality to their fellows, these same intuitions are always a potential source of disquiet.

Professor Smith stresses the fact that many believers in the traditional doctrine were able to reconcile it with the institution of slavery. To this objection there are two replies: first, self-interest and the presumption that is enjoyed by existing social arrangements can always prevent some men from making a logical and complete application of their principles to actual life; second, the welfare of the enslaved persons and of society as a whole may require the temporary continuation of a mitigated form of slavery as a smaller evil than immediate abolition. After all, equality and natural rights (except the right to life) are not ends in themselves. They are merely means to human welfare. In abnormal circumstances this end can sometimes be furthered by temporarily disregarding some of the normal implications of equality and of natural rights. Despite

305

human selfishness and human weakness in the concrete application of equalitarian principles, it was precisely these principles, as traditionally conceived, that mainly brought about the abolition of slavery in the western world. Indeed, an unbiased view of history shows that the equality actually achieved in any social relation must be credited for the most part to the doctrines that all men have spiritual souls, that their persons are sacred and that they possess equal natural rights.

But, objects Professor Smith, these doctrines are no longer serviceable, since they have been overthrown by modern science and modern philosophy. Apparently he concedes to these "authorities" a more unquestioning submission than a Catholic gives to the authority of the Pope. Evolution, they say, shows that man is merely a biological organism, not differing essentially from the lower animals which are his progenitors; hence he is devoid of that additional and independent entity called a spiritual soul. As a matter of fact, studies in evolution are incapable of yielding any such conclusion. Even if biology and kindred sciences had established organic evolution as a fact, and not merely as a more or less plausible hypothesis, they could neither affirm nor deny the existence of the human soul. They might assure us that man's bodily organism has been genetically derived from the lower animals, but they could not tell us whether his mind has thus originated, or whether it is or is not a distinct spiritual entity. This question is necessarily beyond the reach of empirical science, which can deal only with physical facts. The methods of physical science are as incapable of determining the ultimate nature of mind or of establishing the non-existence of the soul as the naked eye is of perceiving the qualities of organisms that can be seen only through the microscope.

Although he nowhere clearly avows it, Professor Smith's basis of equality is simply philosophical materialism. It excludes spiritual values, virtually eliminates belief in God, denies the sacredness of personality, holds that human beings differ only in degree from brutes and deprives the weaker classes of that invaluable protection which is inherent in the doctrine of natural rights. In place of the intrinsic values of Christian ethics, it logically and necessarily enthrones force, physical, political and economic, and superior cunning, as the principles and determinants of social conduct and social welfare. Such is the "pragmatic" substitute for the traditional doctrine of equality. Such is the gift of modern philosophy to the human race. Such are the conceptions of human dignity and of morality to which are exposed the thousands of Catholic young men and women who follow the courses in biology, evolution, sociology, ethics and philosophy in many of our secular colleges and universities.

22. The Commoner

ALMOST one-fourth of this bulky volume is occupied with Bryan's antecedents and youthful formation.[1] His parents and grandparents, his boyhood home and associates, his training, tutelage and formal education, the society and the institutions that conditioned his development,—are all minutely described in the first ninety-six pages and frequently recalled in subsequent pages. The reader is impelled to the conclusion that Bryan the man was never able to overcome the constricting influences of his boyhood environment. He was reared according to a strict moral code; under the constant and dominating guidance of positive-minded women; habituated to rely upon moral emotions rather than rational analysis for the solution of all problems; surrounded by men who counted success—socially and morally approved success—the highest secular aim, and possessed of a deep and simple faith in God and His Providence. "God grant I may use it wisely," he exclaimed, referring to the power that he was able to exert over an audience. "And he knelt down and prayed."

But his religion and his morality were essentially the religion and morality of Puritanism. They were badly balanced, now excessive, now defective, seeing sin where sin there was none and at the same time "neglecting the weightier things of the law." His religious and moral convictions were derived from selected portions of the Bible, privately interpreted; they were not based upon a comprehensive knowledge of Christian teaching nor upon moral fundamentals. In his view, all political questions were also moral questions, a vicious half-truth which misled him more than once. At the St. Louis Convention he

---

[1] Paxton Hibben, *The Peerless Leader: William Jennings Bryan* (New York: Farrar & Rinehart, 1929).

proclaimed that he had "kept the faith," no doubt fully persuaded that he was emulating the Apostle of the Gentiles, although the specific object of his "faith" was not a moral principle but a political measure that had already become antiquated. In his later years he persuaded himself that prohibition was inexorably demanded by the principles of righteousness. Although a prophet of majority rule, he opposed a popular referendum on the ratification of the Eighteenth Amendment in Maryland from fear that the vote of "wet" Baltimore would outweigh the purer suffrages of the rural areas. To him prohibition appeared not as an issue between two great groups of persons possessing equal rights, but as a crusade of all the righteous against a diabolical institution which he called the "liquor power." Surely an amazing simplification of a complex political and social problem! But it was typically Puritan.

Captain Hibben's well documented pages prove that Bryan was never a student nor a thinker. Even in college he was not compelled, perhaps not encouraged, to train himself in these laborious processes. In that part of American society where he was reared, "sentimentality took the place of knowledge and evangelism was the motive force of action. . . . In Salem, Marion County, Illinois, it was the custom to equip a young man with a set of formulas drawn from the Book of Proverbs and MacGuffey's Readers and turn him loose in the world to do or die. . . . Essentially characteristic of America, this confidence that a mere sonorous recital of axioms is the equivalent of thought, was what William Jennings Bryan took with him from Illinois College as the furniture of an adult mind."

In later years his consciousness of and reliance upon his immense oratorical powers together with his activity in politics and on Chautauqua platforms, made him neglect anything like systematic study of even the problems which he discussed, to say nothing of the elements of general culture. Possessing a certain quickness of perception, an exceptional facility of expression and an unequalled power of arousing the emotions, including his own, he never saw the necessity of a more fundamental equipment.

One who had been a faithful follower, Senator R. F. Pettigrew, wrote thus after a week spent in Bryan's home: "I found that he was fairly well versed in the law . . . but that he was utterly ignorant of everything else except the Bible and the evils of intemperance; that his library contained almost no works whatever of value to a man fitting himself to be President of the United States, or even a member of a state legislature. I also found that while his personality was charming, whatever ability nature may have endowed him with had been badly dwarfed and crippled by a narrow education, and that he was not big enough to overcome his training by continuing his investigation of men and affairs after he entered public life." Professor E. A. Ross found that his bookshelves "abounded in crank books, presented by the authors themselves, while the great contemporary authorities on economics were conspicuous by their absence."

His disinclination to hard intellectual labor and his facile reliance upon moral intuitions and emotions were responsible for most of Bryan's major mistakes. He advocated armed intervention in Cuba only two days before the American minister at Madrid had secured from the Spanish government full compliance with the demands of the United States. As he was unaware of this fact, he does not share the infamy which should attach to the name of William McKinley for recommending to Congress a declaration of war against Spain after General Woodford's peaceful message had come into his hands. Nevertheless, Bryan was all his life sincerely devoted to the cause of peace. Had his critical faculty been adequately trained it would have prevented him from being swept off his feet by a jingoistic press following the destruction of the battleship Maine. While his motives were loftier than those of Hearst or McKinley, his intellectual processes were in no way superior to theirs in the Spanish-American business.

310

Enormously more harmful were his efforts on behalf of the treaty which gave Porto Rico and the Philippines to the United States. Had he not "cajoled and dragooned seventeen Democrats and Populists in the Senate into approving the Spanish treaty," our profitless career of colonialism and imperialism would probably never have been begun. Paxton Hibben intimates that Bryan advocated the acquisition of this territory because he needed imperialism as an issue in the Presidential campaign of 1900. At any rate he sadly "misjudged his fellow citizens," for they neither compelled McKinley to set the Filipinos free from American rule nor did they hand the responsibility over to William Jennings Bryan.

One more instance. In the evolution "trial" at Dayton, Tennessee, his intellectual limitations and his excess baggage of emotionalism and pietism were a source of discredit to the cause which he sincerely desired to promote. Had he been a student and a thinker he would not have permitted Clarence Darrow to exploit an assumed conflict between the Bible and science. He would have put this aside as irrelevant, and compelled Darrow to address himself to the question whether the State of Tennessee had the right to prohibit anti-religious teaching in the public schools. This was the constitutional issue and the only issue upon which the case of the defense was based. A textbook or a teacher that "denies the story of the divine creation of man as taught in the Bible and teaches instead that man has descended from a lower order of animals," is undoubtedly sectarian and as violative of the religious neutrality which is required by law in the public schools as would be the teaching of Methodism or Catholicism. Although Bryan had perceived this before the court action began, he failed to govern his course accordingly. The evangelistic urge impelled him to "defend the Christian faith against agnostics" and to submit himself to a damaging cross-examination at the hands of Clarence Darrow.

Had he been a competent student of the theory of evolu-

311

tion he would have seized upon a means which was readily available to bring discomfiture upon the so-called scientists who were badgering him. As Justice Chambliss observed in a supplementary opinion to the decision of the Tennessee supreme court holding the law constitutional, the statute did not prohibit every kind of evolutionary teaching. It did not forbid a teacher to expound to or even to urge upon his pupils the theory that the *body* of the first man was evolved from "a lower order of animals" but that his soul was specially created when God "breathed into his nostrils the breath of life." Several Catholic scientists have so interpreted the "story of the divine creation of man as taught in the Bible." Had Bryan been equipped with the requisite knowledge and the requisite mental habits he could have vindicated not only the constitutional right of the State of Tennessee to prohibit anti-religious sectarianism in the public schools, but the character of the law as neither anti-scientific nor unduly restrictive of academic freedom. He could have put upon the defense the burden of proving that science denies the existence of a spiritual and immortal soul, or asserts that the human soul differs in no essential from the animating principle of the monkey, the snake or the pig, or requires these monstrous doctrines to be presented to public school pupils as equally true with the axioms of geometry. No great effort of the imagination is necessary to visualize the devastating effect of such an argument driven home with all of Bryan's oratorical power. But he was intellectually inadequate. His emotional faith sufficed for his personal needs but not for a public apologist.

Two charges which are occasionally made against Bryan's character receive little or no support in Captain Hibben's volume. He was not anti-Catholic nor did he ever barter his principles for money. In one of the debates at Whipple Academy he upheld the affirmative of the proposition, "Catholicism is more dangerous to the United States than Communism." Whether this side of the question was assigned to him through some rule of the Sigma Pi Society or whether it was his own preference, we are not informed. In the latter hypothesis his choice is sufficiently explained by the anti-Catholic tradition which then dominated as it still dominates many of our rural communities and educational institutions. At any rate, Bryan never afterward indicated adherence to the view which he defended in that debate. In his first campaign for Congress he repudiated the A. P. A., although membership in that organization "would have meant votes for Bryan in Nebraska." In 1928 membership in the Catholic Church meant votes against a presidential candidate in the same state. On the eve of his entrance into President Wilson's Cabinet, Bryan emphasized to Colonel House "the wisdom of including a Catholic and perhaps a Jew in the official family." He also advocated the nomination of John Burke for the Vice-Presidency at the Baltimore convention.

In his later years Bryan's money-making activities gave unholy joy to his enemies and scandal to his more judicious friends, but they are not fairly liable to any more definite ethical criticism than that which is indicated by the canons of good taste; for example, Chautauqua lecturing while in the Cabinet although he did not really need the money. Toward the end of his last term in Congress, when "practically penniless," he became the editor-in-chief of the *Omaha World Herald* at the incredible salary of $30 a week, after having refused an offer of $10,000 a year "to be general counsel for a railroad associated with the Standard Oil Company."

Despite the handicap of his environment and education and the limitations of his mental habits, Bryan was substantially right in almost all the political causes which he espoused in the years when he was an active candidate for office. This statement is true even of his position on the free coinage of silver up to the campaign of 1900. In an era of falling prices the country needed more of the circulating medium. A continuation of the traditional policy of bimetalism would have met that need without substantial

313

injury to any class in the community. While Bryan's knowledge of the money question was never profound and while some of his arguments for free silver were naïve and shallow, both his knowledge and his arguments will compare favorably with those of his most articulate opponents in the campaign of 1896. At any rate he never touched the abysmal depths of irresponsible ignorance and malice sounded by John Hay in his letters written at that time to Henry Adams. Captain Hibben quotes three delectable specimens, one of which is so libelous and malignant that Captain Hibben is constrained to characterize it as "an enduring picture, not of William Jennings Bryan but of John Hay."

In the contest over free silver Bryan's conduct was the essence of rectitude in comparison with that of the principal figures in the opposite camp. Cleveland entered into a conspiracy with the banking interests to put the country on a gold basis, although he had been elected on a platform which pledged him to "attend to the tariff and let the money of the country severely alone." His Secretary of the Treasury consented to the issuance of a circular by the most to the more powerful banks, directing them to take certain steps which would lead straight to a financial panic. The text of this infamous and heartless communication is given on page 151 of the volume that we are reviewing. Those of us who were old enough to be interested in such questions in 1893 have a vivid remembrance of the promptness with which the panic arrived and the enormous and widespread misery that it produced. Some of us do not need to read this circular in order to endorse Captain Hibben's judgment: "Cleveland's course, when all is said and done, was tortuous."

Although McKinley had been "a far more forthright prophet of free silver than Bryan," he completely abjured the doctrine as the price of his nomination for the Presidency. The name of Mark Hanna is identified with the most brazenly materialistic, not to say venal period of

314

American politics that has existed since the days of President Grant. The standards of political morality and the conceptions of national welfare which he helped mightily to create, still cling to our body politic like a modern shirt of Nessus.

Most of the other politico-economic measures advocated by Bryan soon became so respectable that they were taken up by Roosevelt and thus found their way into the Constitution or the statute books. They were, chiefly, income and inheritance taxes, publicity of campaign contributions, direct election of senators, rate fixing by the Interstate Commerce Commission and control of monopolies. "Roosevelt was taking the road along which Bryan had, for twelve years, been trying to guide the Democratic party."

Wrong as he was in his attitude toward intervention in Cuba and the Spanish-American war, Bryan never subscribed to any such program of conquest as Roosevelt had been planning for six months before war was declared. As Secretary of State, he committed or condoned grave blunders in relation to Mexico and Nicaragua, but he steadfastly maintained that American rights should be upheld against England as well as Germany and resigned his office in something near to disgrace rather than participate in an unneutral policy against which he found his protests unavailing. Although he had for many years opposed national prohibition of the liquor traffic, he espoused it finally and inevitably because of his Puritan temper and training. The liquor question is complex, baffling and discouraging to anyone who tries to grasp its essential facts and relations. But it presents a relatively simple aspect to him who is content to solve it in the light only of moral intuitions and emotions.

In his political methods and expedients Bryan was not more disingenuous than many of our political figures who have enjoyed a larger measure of respectability. Perhaps the most damaging record that he made in this respect was in

315

connection with the row over the Ku Klux Klan in the Democratic National Convention. In 1912 he violated the instructions by which the Nebraska delegation was bound to support Champ Clark because the latter was receiving the votes of the New York delegation. In 1924 he found it possible to support McAdoo despite the fact that the latter was receiving the votes of the Ku Klux Klan. Political power wielded by alleged friends of reactionary political policies appeared to him as a greater menace to human welfare than political power wielded by men who would deny their fellow citizens the most fundamental civic rights and who had kindled the fires of religious hatred on ten thousand hillsides. Not only did Bryan condone the support which the Klan gave to McAdoo, with all its ugly implications, but he opposed the resolution which would have brought down upon that detestable organization a well deserved and most effective measure of public discredit and opprobrium. His speech on this occasion was probably the shallowest and most tortuous that he ever delivered. Possibly the fact that the Klan delegates in the 1924 convention paid lip service to prohibition, while the New York delegation to the 1912 convention included several men who had invariably opposed his political ambitions, explains the mutually contradictory courses which he followed in New York and Baltimore.

Whether or not Bryan was the greatest orator that America has produced, he was certainly the most effective and influential. Great as were his achievements, the balance of good over evil in his record would have been greater had he died before the Baltimore convention. In his beliefs and aims he was sincere and as unselfish as the majority of public men. If he sometimes made compromises which seemed inconsistent with sincerity and fine moral principle the explanation will be found in his Puritanism, his emotionalism, his inability to subject complex moral situations to rational analysis. Indeed, most of his offenses, his blunders and his limitations were due to this vital defect in his

316

formation—he had never learned the importance of intellectual processes in contradistinction to moral intuitions and emotional reactions.

Only the first twenty-one chapters of *The Peerless Leader* were written by Paxton Hibben. After his death nine chapters were added by C. Hartley Grattan. The latter seems to have deliberately attempted, and with considerable success, to reproduce Captain Hibben's style. All the chapters of the book make easy reading and in none of them does any important source of information seem to have been overlooked. Not all readers will accept all the interpretations offered by either author, but few will be disposed to doubt that both authors have assiduously sought and noted all the important facts that go to make up the life and deeds of William Jennings Bryan.

23. President Hoover as Statesman

THE remarkable recession of President Hoover's popularity is due primarily to the stock market collapse which occurred in the fall of 1929 and the industrial depression which began about three months earlier. And yet neither of these disasters was set in motion by anything that Mr. Hoover did or left undone. That they occurred in the first year of his administration was simply his bad luck, just as their failure to occur a year earlier was good luck for Mr. Coolidge. Indeed, the over-expansion of business and the orgy of speculation in the fifteen months preceding the middle of November, 1929, are attributable in no small degree to the foolish predictions of continued prosperity uttered by Mr. Hoover's immediate predecessor.

However, these events have been the occasion rather than the cause of the great decline which the President has suffered in popular esteem. It is his actions and omissions subsequent to the crash on the Stock Exchange that have provided the substantial and enduring cause. The things that he has done and the things that he has left undone since November, 1929, have shown that Mr. Hoover does not possess those superior qualities which were attributed to him during the presidential campaign and for some years previously.

In this connection, a curious slip has been made by the able and distinguished journalist who presents "The Gentleman at the Keyhole" to the readers of *Collier's*. In his contribution to the issue for August 9, 1930, he writes: "The country insisted upon overestimating him. It built its idol of huge proportions and now it will see nothing but the feet of clay. No one could be quite the superman it made Mr. Hoover out to be." As it stands, this statement implies that the country had arrived at its exaggerated esti-

318

mate of Mr. Hoover spontaneously—upon its own analysis of his achievements. Now, no one knows better than "The Gentleman at the Keyhole" that the inflated popular estimate was deliberately and systematically created by journalistic and political propagandists.

In any case, there is no doubt that many millions of Americans are now disillusioned on the subject of Mr. Hoover's greatness. They have found that he is neither a great economist nor a courageous and effective leader, nor a master of fundamental principles. Let us examine the facts which have brought about popular disillusionment under these three heads, beginning with the assumption that he is a great economist.

Any trained economist must have realized that this assumption was false after reading Mr. Hoover's speech at Boston in October, 1928. This address contained so much that is superficial, sophistical and evasive, so many fallacies and so many half-truths, that no competent economist could avoid one of two conclusions: either Mr. Hoover was incapable of fundamental economic thinking, or he was trying to throw dust into the eyes of his audience. Inasmuch as the vast majority of the people are not trained economists, it is probable that not many of them put the proper estimate upon the Boston speech. However, a very large proportion of them have been able to evaluate correctly the economic weaknesses in the President's attitude toward unemployment, farm relief and the Smoot-Hawley tariff act.

In December, 1928, Governor Brewster, of Maine, presented to the state governors assembled in New Orleans a comprehensive and fundamental plan for the prevention of unemployment. He more than hinted that his plan had the backing of the President-elect. Many newspaper editors drew the hasty conclusion that the new scheme was Mr. Hoover's own invention. As a matter of fact, it can be found fully set forth in any standard economic text published the last quarter of a century. In essence it proposes

319

an increase of public works during depressions and a decrease in periods of prosperity. Governor Brewster expressed the opinion that through the co-operation of federal, state, county and municipal authorities a fund of three billion dollars could be made available for public works when business showed signs of becoming slack. Given the requisite previous planning and the intelligent expenditure of this huge sum, there is not the slightest doubt that a depression which threatened to be even greater than the one now afflicting us could have been halted before it got thoroughly started.

Unfortunately for the country and for Mr. Hoover, he did nothing toward putting the plan into effect. About four months after it was expounded to the governors at New Orleans, Congress was assembling in extra session to deal with farm relief and the tariff. Here was a golden opportunity to urge the public works plan upon the consideration of the national legislature. Although the report of his Committee on Recent Economic Changes, to mention only one source of information, should have warned the President that the excessive capacity of our industries would soon bring about over-stocked markets, a serious decline in demand and an industrial recession, he did nothing to forestall or minimize these imminent evils. Less than four months later they were unmistakably operative.

To be sure, it is probable that Congress would not have heeded a recommendation to make the necessary provisions for a vast program of public works. This does not exculpate the President. If he had been the able economist and the courageous leader pictured by his propagandists, he would have put the plan before Congress in the hope of returning to it when the need became evident even to the average national legislator. Had he made this recommendation in April, 1929, he would have been in a position to repeat it with much more authority and persuasion at the opening of the regular session the following December. By that time the depression had become so palpable that it could no longer be denied or ignored. Inasmuch as Mr. Hoover failed to urge upon Congress in a practical way the plan that his spokesman had put before the governors in an academic way, he can justly be charged with some responsibility, not indeed for the beginning of the depression, but for its depth and duration.

This responsibility has been considerably increased by the course that he followed since the disaster on the Stock Exchange. Very promptly and very laudably he summoned business leaders and labor leaders to confer on the critical situation. So far as they went, the conclusions and recommendations adopted by these conferences were entirely admirable. To keep up wages and purchasing power, to continue so far as feasible construction work in private industries, and to increase public building,—were all helpful measures. Could they have been carried far enough they would have ended the depression within a month or two. As organized by the conferences, however, they proved utterly inadequate.

The reasons are obvious. An economist who knew human nature would not have expected a general fulfillment of the promise to maintain existing wage rates. An economist who was fully acquainted with the facts would have realized that industries unable to utilize all their present capacity would not undertake to expand their plants. Only the third element in the program of these conferences could have been made adequate to check the industrial decline. That was an increase in public works. To become really effective, this project would have had to assume vast dimensions. An increase of a few million dollars for federal buildings was clearly insufficient to relieve a depression that threatened to be among the greatest of recent times.

Nevertheless, Mr. Hoover seems to have persuaded himself that these puny devices would prove adequate. Toward the end of January, 1930, the steel industry was able to show one week of increased output. Immediately the President announced that the trend of employment had changed

321

in the right direction. His optimism was sadly discredited by all the industrial events and trends of the succeeding five or six weeks. March 8th he again enacted the rôle of hopeful prophet, predicting a business recovery within sixty days. At the end of that period conditions were worse than they had been at the beginning. But Mr. Hoover's faith continued unfaltering. Six days before the close of the disconcerting sixty days he said to the Chamber of Commerce of United States: "I am convinced we have now passed the worst and with continued unity of effort we shall rapidly recover." Referring to his conferences with industrial leaders November, 1929, he made this astonishing assertion: "I believe I can say with assurance that our joint undertaking has succeeded to a remarkable degree." Again events have belied his optimistic prophecy. When he uttered it (May 2) business activity was only 12 per cent lower than it had been twelve months earlier. At the end of January, 1931, it had dropped to 29 per cent below that of October, 1929. Mr. Hoover's assertion that the efforts of the November conferences to check the depression had "succeeded to a remarkable degree," is astonishing and inexplicable in the face of the facts. He must have been aware that the decline in business activity and employment had been continuous from the time of his conferences in autumn to the bright May day when he made this curious claim before the assembled representatives of American business.

A few days after this address he rejected a suggestion by the National Unemployment League that he ask Congress to authorize a very large expenditure for road building. Yet this was the only means whereby employment and purchasing power could have been sufficiently increased to bring the depression to an end within a reasonable time. Undoubtedly the President's refusal to adopt this recommendation was determined by his knowledge that it would involve a very large issue of federal bonds and therefore a considerable increase in federal taxes. His decision may have been good politics, but it was poor economics. If the public

322

works remedy is to be effective at the approach of or during a major industrial depression, it cannot be financed through any current surplus in the treasury. The necessary amount of money can be obtained only through a sale of public bonds. A brief analysis of the economics of the situation will show that there is no good reason for shrinking from this measure.

Certain important industries began to curtail production in mid-summer, 1929, because they could not sell all their current output. Yet there was in existence a social surplus, a reserve of purchasing power, sufficient to take the excess products off the market and to keep these industries in continuous operation. It failed to do so because it was not suitably distributed. Those consumers who would like to buy more had not the money. Those who had the money lacked the desire for more. What was needed then, what is still needed, is a redistribution of this social surplus, this reserve purchasing power. Such a redistribution occurs to some extent through charitable assistance to the unemployed and the low-income classes, and would assume larger proportions through the payment of unemployment insurance. All such expenditures come out of the pockets of those who possess surplus incomes. Some of their purchasing power is transferred to those who desire to buy more goods. If this did not take place during a depression the condition of business would be even worse. Exactly the same principle and the same process are involved in the expenditure of public money for road-building. In this case the social surplus is redistributed through taxation. Instead of investing their savings in industries which are already over-supplied with capital, men buy government bonds; later on they and the other possessors of a surplus are taxed to provide the interest and the sinking fund.

Such is the economics of the matter. We cannot have our cake and eat it. We cannot provide sufficient demand for goods to keep our industries going unless we redistribute the social purchasing power. We cannot go on indefi-

323

nitely increasing our production, saving too much and spending too little. On the other hand, we can create public works in sufficient volume to redistribute purchasing power and to bring about a prompt revival of business only through heavier taxes upon those who are able to pay. Moreover, the latter would gain more through the recovery of industry and the consequent increase of salaries, profits and interest, than they would lose through the increased taxation.

These elementary economic truths seem to have escaped President Hoover. At the moment when he was planning an increase of expenditures for public building, at the end of 1929, he was recommending a reduction of $160,000,-000 in the federal income tax. Obviously the principles underlying these two measures are mutually contradictory. Instead of dissipating the $160,000,000 surplus through tax reduction, Mr. Hoover should have added it to the pitiably insufficient sum that he was devoting to public works for the relief of unemployment. He should have welcomed this opportunity. In advocating lower income taxes he seems to have been following the ridiculous Coolidge-Mellon theory that business men would thereby be enabled and induced to put more money into industry. But industry did not need more money. It was already oversupplied. Not lack of money or credit for productive operations but lack of demand for goods already produced was the cause of the depression. Not more capital but more consumption was the fundamental need. The remitted income taxes became for the most part available to increase the existing superabundant supply of capital. Had the reduction not been made, $160,000,000 would have been available for increased public works, increased employment, increased consumption and increased business activity.

In the summer of 1930, Mr. Hoover repeated this blunder. In order to avoid a threatened deficit in national finances, he urged upon the various departments of the government a reduction in expenditures. At the same time he asserted that this course would not conflict with the program of providing employment through public construction. Well, an inherent contradiction cannot be annihilated by the simple device of denying its existence. It has become notorious that reducing expenditures in the departments means decreasing the number of employees and cutting down the outlay for materials. Part of the good effect of increased public construction is thus neutralized through decreased expenditures by the government departments. The President's purpose was obvious. He shrank from the thought of having to call upon Congress for an increase in federal taxes. As we have seen, however, it is only through increased taxation that the purchasing power of the community can be so redistributed as to bring relief from the industrial depression. Mr. Hoover's course with regard to tax reduction and the decrease of departmental expenses is the authentic recourse of the politician. It exhibits neither the humane statesman nor the competent economist.

In his address at the convention of the American Federation of Labor, October 6, 1930, the President made several statements which show that the increasing months of the depression have not brought him an increase of economic wisdom. I cite two examples. He asserted that most of the 2,000,000 workers who have been displaced in the last ten years through labor-saving devices have "some way, somehow been re-established in new industries and new services." Neither the President nor anyone else knows whether this is a fact. Again, he said that "one key to the solution" of overproduction and excessive labor in the soft-coal industry was to be found in "reduction of this destructive competition." Eliminating destructive competition would indeed make industrial operations and employment more stable in that industry, but it would do nothing toward providing for the surplus workers excluded through the stabilizing process. What is true of soft-coal mining is likewise true of many other industries. It is not merely a question of stabilizing industrial operations, but of finding

325

employment for the excess workers. The President's only
contribution to the solution of this problem seems to be
that "some way, somehow" they will all find employment
in "new industries and new services." No doubt he means
in the long run; but if we make the run long enough we
shall not need to get work for many of them; they will
have died.

The plan of farm relief enacted at the behest of the
President bears striking testimony to his limitations as an
economist. That part of the Federal Farm Act which seeks
to promote co-operative marketing is altogether excellent
in purpose; that part which aims at stabilization of prices
rests upon a palpable economic fallacy. The stabilization
provided for in the law might, indeed, take care of seasonal
crop surpluses, but it is utterly incapable of dealing with
surpluses which recur year after year. Let us assume that
$1.25 per bushel is a profitable price for wheat and that
the supply is small enough to command this price throughout the year, provided that it is brought into the market at
a fairly uniform rate. We will assume, however, that the
quantity marketed during September and October is so
great as to bring the price down to $1.00. A few months
later the very small amount offered for sale may send the
price up to $1.50 per bushel.

Such price variations as these can be prevented through
stabilization. The Federal Farm Board, or any other
agency with the requisite amount of money, could take
sufficient wheat off the market in September and October
to maintain the price at $1.25, and then it could sell its
holdings without loss the following spring. Thus it would
have stabilized the price at about $1.25 for the entire year.
The same thing is possible when the surplus arises from an
exceptionally good yield which is followed the next year
by an exceptionally poor yield.

Suppose, however, that the surplus is not seasonal nor
confined to a single year. Suppose that year after year the
supply is so great as to keep the average price down to

326

$1.00. A stabilization agency might purchase sufficient wheat in the fall or any other time of the year to force the price up to $1.25 per bushel for the time being, but it would be compelled eventually to sell its purchases at a loss, owing to the excessive continuous supply. Exactly this has been the experience of the Federal Farm Board. In 1929 it bought 70,000,000 bushels of wheat at a figure considerably above the market price. A few months later it sold one-seventh of its holdings at a loss of more than thirty cents per bushel. Its loss on the remaining 60,000,000 bushels will probably be at least as great. Hence it wisely refused to go further along this way of disaster, rejecting the purely political suggestion of Senator Capper that it add 100,000,000 bushels to its unprofitable store. Indeed, the Chairman of the Board declared that "stabilization cannot be made to work for continuous, cumulative and permanent surpluses." It is too bad that Mr. Legge did not see this great light a year earlier; too bad that his vision had to be sharpened through the expensive method of experience. Happily for him, the huge cost of his enlightenment will be borne by the Treasury of the United States.

The McNary-Haugen bill proposed to meet the situation in a different way. Like the Farm Board Act, it authorized purchasing the surplus at a profitable price to the farmers. Unlike the Hoover law, it did not fatuously assume that the purchased surplus could be thrown upon the domestic market later without depressing the price and causing a grave loss to the United States Treasury. The McNary-Haugen bill would have taken the surplus off the market permanently, selling it abroad at whatever price it would fetch, and recouping the loss through the equalization fee collected from the farmers themselves. While this plan probably would have broken down within two or three years, it had at least the merit of dealing with the problem squarely, honestly and realistically. The Farm Board Act either misconceived the problem or made it the subject of futile and costly experimentation. Its ill-considered scheme

327

of stabilization is now denounced by both friend and foe as a complete and disastrous failure.

Was not Mr. Hoover aware that the surpluses in several of our agricultural staples are continuous? If he was, he should have seen that the failure of this stabilization scheme was as certain as an axiom in geometry. In that case he must have adopted it as a temporary expedient, in the hope that somehow something would turn up to prevent the exposure of its insufficiency. On the other hand, if he thought that the surplus was temporary he lacked elementary knowledge of a practical economic situation.

As a final example of his economic limitations I would cite his statement on signing the Smoot-Hawley tariff bill. More than one thousand economists in our leading colleges and universities had condemned the bill as the worst measure of its kind ever framed in the United States. That they were right in this judgment is not seriously doubted by any intelligent person who is at once adequately acquainted with the bill and mindful of the welfare of the American people. President Hoover not only gave it his official approval but apologized for it in a statement that abounded in half-truths and misleading statistics.

So much for the assumption that he is a great economist. Of his lack of courageous and effective leadership many illustrations might be given. I shall mention only two. There is no doubt that he was dissatisfied with the kind of tariff measure that he knew was taking shape long before it was finally adopted by Congress. Had he desired to exemplify the qualities of courageous and effective leadership, he would have exposed and denounced the bill months before it was passed, thereby arousing public opinion against it and rendering impossible the inclusion of some of its worst provisions. A Roosevelt or a Wilson would not have hesitated to speak out. Mr. Hoover remained silent.

The other example is provided by his attitude toward the Veterans' Pension bills. One of these he vetoed, the other he signed. Yet the latter will prove the less defensible of the two in the long run, for it is susceptible of much wider extension. The bill which the President signed makes a smaller raid on the treasury for the present, but it renders more easy a larger levy in the future. In these circumstances the great courage attributed by partisan journals to Mr. Hoover's veto of the first bill seems to be somewhat doubtful.

President Hoover has not shown himself to be a master of fundamental principles. Some of the principles that underlie right political action are intuitive, as that all men are endowed with natural rights. Others are inductive, are generalizations from experience, as that governments cannot wisely undertake to provide for all human wants. The statesman should have a clear grasp of the former kind of principles and a considerable facility in deriving the latter from experience. In neither of these fields has Mr. Hoover exhibited a high degree of insight or skill.

Who's Hoover?, the campaign biography written by William Hard, includes these sentences: "His mind turns every theoretical principle into an instant application. The principle becomes overlaid at once with practice. It becomes a silent assumption" (Page 240). Now, the great defect in Mr. Hoover's method seems to be that his application of principles is too "instant," too hasty; that in his hands the principle becomes not only "overlaid" but obscured and forgotten. He attempts to fit a principle to practical issues before he has taken the trouble to understand the principle. As a consequence his practical decisions are not infrequently erroneous and socially injurious.

Illustrations of this defective method are seen in his treatment of unemployment, farm relief, and the tariff. Other and perhaps more conspicuous illustrations emerge from some of his remarks on prohibition in his Inaugural Address, from his opposition to government operation of industry, and from his nomination of Judge Parker to a seat on the Supreme Bench. Let us consider briefly these three instances.

329

In his Inaugural Address the President laid upon "honest men and women" the "duty" of discouraging violations of the prohibition laws. Since neither the Eighteenth Amendment nor the Volstead Act enjoins any such obligation upon the citizen, Mr. Hoover could not have been thinking of *legal* duty. He must have meant *moral* duty. Now, the business of interpreting the moral law for the benefit of the people is not mentioned among the functions or prerogatives of the President described in the Constitution. The solemn pronouncement cited above exemplifies usurpation, sheer abuse of power and position. It represents a disregard of fundamental principles.

Moreover, it was inexact and incorrect. What the Schoolmen called "legal justice" does, indeed, bind the citizen not only to obey the civil law himself but to promote, so far as he can without undue inconvenience, its observance by his fellow citizens. But this obligation refers to civil law in general, not to every statute that proceeds from every legislature. The obligation does not extend to laws that are unjust, ineffective or unreasonably burdensome. Now, millions of Americans put the prohibition laws in one or more of these categories. Mr. Hoover seems to have assumed that they are morally binding simply because they are legislative enactments. He committed himself to the false and tyrannical principle that the state can do no wrong.

The statement by Mr. Hoover that we are now discussing undoubtedly lowered his authority in the popular mind and brought more harm than good to the cause of prohibition. The people realized that he was not only mistaken about a fundamental principle but that he was willing to abuse his great office for the sake of administrative expediency.

In this same address the President showed his misconception of an important empirical principle. He asserted that the surest way to get a bad law repealed is through rigorous enforcement. This is an assertion of fact, a sup-

330

posed induction from political experience. Its correctness cannot be assumed merely because it has become a familiar slogan. In all probability it is false. Very few obnoxious laws have been repealed as the direct and immediate result of strict enforcement, or even of ensuing popular resentment. Even in those cases where enforcement had been consistently carried on for a long time the laws were generally repealed only after a subsequent period of lax enforcement and general violation. It seems probable that this will be the fate of prohibition.[1] Moreover, a large proportion of unpopular laws have neither been consistently enforced nor formally repealed. They have fallen into "desuetude," become inoperative through universal dislike and disobedience. Examples: The Blue Laws of our older commonwealths.

Apart from the question of fact underlying Mr. Hoover's belief in repeal through rigid enforcement, there is the question of justice. Continued effort to enforce a law which imposes upon the people unreasonable burdens is a species of tyranny.

Apparently Mr. Hoover thinks that he is enunciating a demonstrated political principle when he declares that the government should enter business only "as the by-product to some great major purpose, such as improvement in navigation, flood control, irrigation, scientific research and national defense." Hence he opposes government operation of the power plant at Muscle Shoals and of barges on our navigable rivers. Of course, there is no such principle. The true principle is that government should not undertake any economic activity unless by so doing it can serve the public better than private enterprise. Whether the government could fulfill this condition in the generation, say, of electric power or in the operation of boats on our rivers, or in any other field, is a question of fact and experience. Mr. Hoover has never attempted to provide a respectable amount of factual support for his *a priori* generalization.

[1] See the Wickersham Report, *passim.*

His nomination of Judge Parker shows that he either did not know or deliberately ignored a fundamental principle in the realm of judicial law-making. Even if he had previously been unaware of the issue, he should have learned all about it when he encountered senatorial opposition to the nomination of Charles Evans Hughes. For upwards of fifteen years a majority of the Supreme Court has consistently upheld property rights at the expense of human rights. It has done so for the most part in its construction of the Fifth and Fourteenth amendments to the Constitution. It has thereby increased considerably the power of the economically strong to oppress the economically weak. As conspicuous examples, I would cite the decisions in the Coppage case, the Hitchman case, and the District of Columbia minimum wage case.

Fearing that Mr. Hughes would align himself with the conservative majority in the interpretation of the "due process" clauses in the Fifth and Fourteenth amendments, his opponents in the Senate made the issue and the situation abundantly clear. No intelligent man who followed the discussions could doubt the enormous power possessed by the Court to promote or to hinder economic justice. Now, the decisions rendered by the Court in the application of the "due process" clauses to economic conditions are determined mainly by the social, economic and ethical views of the individual justices. Therefore an intelligent lover of justice who is charged with the tremendous responsibility of nominating members of the Court should welcome the opportunity of selecting jurists who place reasonable opportunity for the masses above excessive solicitude for the interests of property. Nevertheless, Mr. Hoover sent to the Senate the name of Judge Parker, whose decision in the Red Jacket case manifested complete agreement with those members of the Supreme Court who produced the unjust decisions in the Coppage and Hitchman cases. The President was either unable to grasp or was indifferent to a great principle of human rights.

332

PRESIDENT HOOVER AS STATESMAN

Mr. Hoover's deficiencies and decline have caused little surprise to discriminating Americans. Neither a great engineer nor a great administrator, nor one who possesses the qualities of both, will necessarily make a great President. The technical equipment of the engineer is at best irrelevant, while administrative competency has value for only one part of the presidential office. More important than his administrative or executive tasks is the President's function of conceiving, recommending, fighting for and approving great legislative policies, policies that profoundly affect public welfare or the welfare of important classes. Such are the policies involved in legislation to meet the problems of unemployment, the agricultural depression and tariff revision. In this great province Mr. Hoover had no previous experience, and his campaign speeches showed that he had given this class of subjects no profound study.